SMALL BUSINESS RESEARCH

In memory of Joe Leveson

Published in association with the National Small Business Management
Teachers' Association.

This book is to be returned on
or before the date stamped below

UNIVERSITY OF PLYMOUTH

ACADEMIC SERVICES
PLYMOUTH LIBRARY
Tel: (0752) 232323
This book is subject to recall if required by another reader
Books may be renewed by phone
CHARGES WILL BE MADE FOR OVERDUE BOOKS

Small Business Research

The Development of Entrepreneurs

edited by
TERRY WEBB,
THELMA QUINCE
Durham University Business School
and
DAVID WATKINS
Manchester Business School

Gower

Published by
Gower Publishing Company Limited,
Gower House, Croft Road, Aldershot, Hampshire, England.

Printed and bound in Great Britain by
Robert Hartnoll Limited Bodmin Cornwall

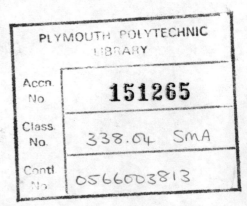

British Library Cataloguing in Publication Data

Education and assistance for the entrepreneur.
  1. Small businesses - Management
  2. Small businesses - Professional education
  I. Webb, Terry   II. Quince, Thelma
  III. Watkins, David
  658.3'03'07   HD2341

  ISBN 0-566-00381-3

Contents

Preface

This book arose out of a research conference held at Ashridge Management College (Hertfordshire, England) in October, 1979, convened under the auspices of the UK National Small Business Teachers' Association. It focusses on the process of identifying and educating business founders and subsequently providing them with effective and relevant assistance as their firms develop.

The book forms part of a series emerging from these annual research conferences. That it has taken considerable time to produce reflects the fact that a decision was made by the editors to extract a partial theme from the conference, that of education and assistance, and to commission a number of additional papers to complement those of the original contributors. Thanks are due to those authors who have waited with understanding and patience for their papers to be published.

There is one gap in the book, however, that cannot be filled.

The untimely death of Joe Leveson in late 1979 robbed the editors of a stimulating paper on his pioneering work at Dundee College of Technology in educating young people about entrepreneurship. Joe had kindly agreed to enlarge his Ashridge contribution into a report on the results of his initial experiments on small firms education for undergraduates to be included in this book.

The NSBTA would like, therefore, to dedicate this book to Joe; a pioneer in every sense of the word. He was not only a member of the first National Teachers' Programme, but had the vision and commitment to implement the ideas he generated in 1976. His gentle but persuasive manner will be sadly missed by many.

Thanks are also due to Philip Sadler, the Principal of Ashridge, and to his Management Committee for hosting the Conference and subsequently allowing us to make generous use of the College's Word Processor. We would like to thank two other members of the Ashridge staff in particular; Ken Walker for the illustrations and figures, and Christine Baldwin who has patiently translated the manuscripts into the format you are now reading.

The editors are grateful to the Small Firms Division of the Department of Industry for its permission to publish the final paper in this Volume by David Watkins.

Finally the editors would like to thank the authors of the individual papers for their cooperation in rewriting their papers in an attempt to produce a book which reflects some continuity of comment and thought upon this subject.

Terry Webb
Durham University Business School.
December, 1981

1 Introduction

The latter half of the 1970s has seen the growth of many education, training, counselling and advisory services aimed at the would be entrepreneur and the existing small firm. Underpinning these initiatives have been a range of assumptions about the way that entrepreneurship and small firm development can be influenced including:

- the way that training and assistance for small businesses and would-be starters should be organised

- the type of people that will come forward to start their own business and the knowledge they need

- the motivation of such people and the methods by which this can be channelled into entrepreneurship

- the form that training should take

- the stage in the formation process when a training intervention will be most effective

- the criteria that can be used to judge those who should be helped

- the way in which these initiatives can be evaluated.

The papers in this book provide a timely exploration of many of these assumptions.

The papers presented are not necessarily the result of methodologically sophisticated or rigorous pieces of research work. Nor can they be considered definitive in their area. They have been chosen, either because they have something new to contribute in terms of thinking about some of the issues raised above, or because they provide interesting empirical evidence. The purpose of bringing them together in book form is to stimulate discussion and to maintain a dialogue, for unless policy makers exchange views in particular with researchers and practitioners, then there is a real danger of either supporting ineffective schemes at a time when resources are scarce or of abandoning initiatives because inappropriate criteria have been used to assess their effectiveness.

The book can be divided into three main sections. The first comprises three papers which describe basic, student programmes at under and post graduate level aimed at developing interest in entrepreneurship both in the United Kingdom and United States of America. The second, and major section, includes six papers which take up the story a stage further on. The fist two papers in this section deal with the question of who starts a business while the remaining four examine ways in which would-be business founders can be helped. The third section has three contributions on how to continue to help small businesses once they have been established.

The opening paper by Allan Gibb describes how in the USA, an attempt has been made within the Small Business Institute Programme (sponsored by the Federal Small Business Agency) to link the process of learning about founding a small firm into the American formal education system by encouraging business students to become actively involved in providing assistance to such firms. The paper describes how the SBI Programme is structured, how it works, its aims and objectives, the relevance of these to, and the possible problems of, establishing a similar programme in the United Kingdom.

The second and third papers take up one of the themes developed by Allan Gibb, namely that apart from pedagogical arguments in favour of teaching small business, there is much to be gained by developing a wider understanding by the population at large of small business. The first of these two contributions by Sue Birley and Peter Wilson, argues, that a cultural step is necessary at the student level if the independent business is to be seen as a legitimate career option on graduation. Their paper describes their decision to develop a course for existing students at the London Business School, aimed at improving their understanding of the small firms' sector and comments on its initial success.

The approach to teaching masters' degree students discussed in this paper is based on the belief that the management problems and needs of small business are different to those of large firms and that, while most students will find employment in large firms, an understanding of these problems and needs is necessary in their everyday contact with small firms, whether as customers, suppliers, advisers or investors.

The third paper by John Hornaday and Karl Vesper complements that of Birley and Wilson by reporting on the results of a piece of evaluation research aimed at discovering the views of alumni several years after taking a course in entrepreneurship at undergraduate level. This paper not only attempts to trace whether the entrepreneurship programme has been successful in stimulating people to join or start up their own business, but what in hindsight were the strengths and weaknesses of the entrepreneurship course undertaken.

Hornaday and Vesper highlight how important evaluation studies of this kind, particularly on a cooperative basis, between institutions, can be to the sound development of small business education and practice in the 1980s. In this sense, therefore, these authors underline the whole purpose of this kind of research conference in attempting to identify fruitful areas for future study while simultaneously ensuring that existing research is effectively utilised at a variety of levels.

Having begun by considering how the seed bed of business founders might be enlarged the fourth paper by John Eversley, Allan Gibb and John Ritchie seeks to clarify -

-   who wants to start up a business?
-   what sorts of people are they?
-   what aspirations and motives do they have?

Unlike many studies on these issues this one is not retrospective. It draws upon evidence from the first 'Build your own Business Competition' sponsored by Shell UK and organised by Durham University Business School. John Ritchie and his colleagues have therefore had the opportunity to study at first hand a sample of people who were sufficiently committed to the idea of starting a business to expose their aspirations, motives and plans to rigorous analysis within the structure and processes of the Shell Competition.

The next paper by Tom Milne and John Lewis continues and extends this theme by focussing on the following issues:

- is it possible to spot winners among aspiring business founders?
- what kinds of education do they need along the way?
- is there a particular need to move the owner/ manager from being self-employed to being manageri- ally orientated?
- how can this be achieved?

This paper sets the scene for the next four contributions by David Watkins and John Morris, Jerry Dyson, Ronnie Lessem and Grenville Jackson all of which focus on the issue of how far the process of educating and supporting prospective business founders can be accommodated within 'conventional' teaching/training frameworks or should be abandoned in favour of a more explicit 'action learning' orientation which aims to develop the individual as much as his or her business.

In addition to expanding on the theme of 'spotting winners' and 'getting them into business', each of these papers reflects a different form of co-operation between national and local government agencies, privately financed small firm promotion bodies (like URBED) and educational institutions. The papers by Watkins and Morris and Dyson, for example, examine some aspects of New Enterprise Programmes which are the product of cooperation between the Training Services Division of the Manpower Services Commission and four business schools (Durham, London, Manchester and Glasgow). Lessem, on the other hand points to the initial experiences gained by URBED in working with local government and other groups (with some additional financial support from the TSD) in attempting to facilitate business founding in London. Finally, Jackson describes yet another form of regional aid to the potential business founder by reporting on the work of the Development Board for Rural Wales.

The paper by Watkins and Morris describes the origins, aims, objectives and methods of the NEP. It shows how Joint Development Activities which have been successfully applied to other areas of management development and education with large companies were adapted to meet the requirements of the small firms sector. This paper, therefore, provides an important historical record of the factors which led up to the first experimental New Enterprise Programme.

The three subsequent papers in this quartet of four devoted to enterprise development, emphasise how quickly development and practice have progressed, following the initial experience at Manchester Business School, and in particular the need to match courses to different stages of business founding and development.

Drawing on the experience of Durham University Business School in running six NEP's, Jerry Dyson identifies six stages of preparation required for founding a business and eight categories of individuals who form potential business founders. He utilises these 14 elements to build a model for examining the hypothesis that different kinds of 'support programmes' will be required for different kinds of potential business founders at different stages of preparation. He not only examines how this model can be used to identify the sort of people who will benefit from a particular kind of programme, but how winners' can be selected to participate in the 'results' orientated NEP which is sponsored by the government with the primary objective of generating businesses and jobs.

Although Dyson points to the supportive nature of the NEP which enables potential founders to 'learn free of risk' Lessem argues that overall the NEP's are inflexible, focus too strongly on the acquisition of techniques and too little on the development of the person. His view is that educating potential business founders is as much about the development of the person as about the acquisition of business tech-niques. The detailed description given in his paper of the 'self development' experiences of one group of potential founders as they passed through the URBED programme nicely complements the categories of starters and stages of preparation outlined by Dyson. In doing so however, Lessem strongly advocates action learning as a method capable of accomplishing the need to relate the person, the business idea and the environment in the education of the business founder.

Grenville Jackson by

- touching on the need to start education earlier and the notion of 'business = self development' raised by Lessem,
- introducing the need to consider local conditions and the sorts of activities that can feasibly be encouraged in an area, and
- introducing the topics of assistance

provides a useful link between the preceding issues of how and when to educate and the papers that follow which are primarily devoted to a discussion of ways in which assistance and advice can be got to the established small firm. The main content of this paper is an account of the promotional activities carried out by the Development Board for Rural Wales combined with a review of their experiences with a Start Your Own Business Programme (1).

Continuing the regional assistance theme the second individual contribution from Allan Gibb reports on the American Small Business Development Centre Programme which aims at the comprehensive development of management and technical assistance for the small firm in a region. Unlike the SBI programme whose aims are primarily (although not exclusively) 'educational' the SBDC programme is more concerned with setting up a centre (which may well be in a university business school or college) capable of co-ordinating and controlling specialist sources of advice for small firms. The paper describes the programme and highlights its key components and once again tackles the all important question of the relevance of the programme to the UK.

In contrast to the American experience outlined by Gibb, John Howdle describes the outcome of his study of the Department of Industry's Small Firms Counselling Service in the South West of England. He evaluates the usefulness and influence of this governments sponsored source of specialist advice and assistance for small firms in the UK.

Although there have been a number of developments in the Counselling service since this study took place, the basic findings raised by this paper remain important issues for debate amongst those interested in, and responsible for, developing networks of advice and assistance for small businesses.

The final paper by David Watkins continues the theme of how to provide help to existing small businesses by returning to the subject of education. This time, however, the context is not one of helping to develop a 'seed bed' of potential business founders or helping to establish new enterprises, but of developing owner/managers of small firms to ensure the long term effectiveness and endurance of their businesses.

In the middle of 1977, the Small Firms' Division of the Department of Industry commissioned a study of the management and training needs of small firm owner/managers and the extent to which these needs were being met. This paper describes something of the context of this research and reports on some of the main findings.

Among the topics discussed, are the educational and work experiences of owner/managers and the relevance of these to the tasks undertaken within the firm and more significantly in the context of this book, the extent to which management education is seen, or not seen, as a solution to the problems of the firm 'viz a viz' other potential sources of advice and assistance.

NOTES

(1) Start Your Own Business Programmes are aimed at self-employment rather than the founding of businesses which may generate more jobs.

2 The Small Business Institute Programme in the USA and its relevance to the UK

ALLAN GIBB
Small Business Centre,
Durham University Business School

INTRODUCTION

Education for entrepreneurship is likely to be a central issue in the 1980's. As yet, there are but few guidelines as to how this might be attempted within the broad spectrum of the UK educational system. The issue has, however, been faced, at least in part, in other countries. In the USA in particular, the government has attempted to foster a special relationship between American Business Schools and Colleges and small business, by means of a Small Business Institute Programme. The Programme is financed by the Small Business Administration of the US Federal Government. Its objective is to promote links between the education institution, its students and the small business community.

This paper is based on a field study carried out in the US in January/February, 1979. It provides a detailed review of the Programme's operation and considers its effectiveness and relevance to the UK. A study was made of eight business schools operating the Programme. Time was also spent with the Small Business Administration in Washington and at various regional and district offices of the S.B.A. located throughout the USA. In each location interviews were conducted with S.B.A. officers, the staff and students of the university and small businessmen. In addition relevant written material was obtained.

THE S.B.I. PROGRAMME - A BRIEF DESCRIPTION

The Programme dates from 1972 when it was started by the US Small Business Administration with the students and faculty of 36 universities. It has gradually gained momentum; until today some 470 schools participate, and in 1978, 7950 small business clients were dealt with. Thus business students from colleges and universities across the country work directly with the owners of small businesses in the surrounding community in an effort to solve management problems. In Kansas State University for example, students travelled up to 100 miles to assist a small repairer of agricultural implements improve his book-keeping system. In Chico in Northern California students were helping the local sports goods dealer move into the market for ski equipment. A small engineering company in Arizona was being helped to improve its factory layout and in Washington D.C. students were helping a 'Mamma and Pappa' store threatened with re-development, to find a new location. Very often the small businessman will be the recipient of a loan from the S.B.A. The agricultural engineer, referred to above, was running into difficulty on repayments and was referred by the S.B.A. District Office, to the Director of the S.B.I. Programme at Kansas State University, who then visited the company to acquaint himself more fully with the problem. There are thus always four parties involved in the Programme: the small firms; the university or college; the students; and the S.B.A. (as the source of funds and ultimate control).

THE SMALL BUSINESS

As the above examples indicate the Programme concentrates on the very small business: the majority of firms dealt with are in the retail or service sector. They are usually located within easy distance of the S.B.I. Programme centre and are frequently companies in the early years of their existence. The company may seek assistance by enquiring directly of the local office of the S.B.A. or may go through the university centre. In some cases the company may have been 'passed on' through the counselling service known as SCORE(1) as suitable for more in-depth work. Alternatively, the company may have been approached by the S.B.A., particularly if it is known to be having difficulty in repaying loans covered by the S.B.A. Loan Guarantee Scheme. In these instances there may, therefore, be some pressure for the company to submit to student counselling.

The university obtains most of its cases by way of the SBA Regional or District Offices. Cases are selected either from the S.B.A. Loan Guarantee Portfolio or from general enquiries for management assistance. The initial selection is done by either the resident S.B.A. Management Assistance Officer (MAO) in the District Office or the Small Business Co-ordinator, who may be appointed to deal with all the cases awarded to the colleges in that district. The former is a full time employee of the S.B.A.; the latter may be employed part time and will possibly be recruited from local academic staff. Where the Programme is well established the cases may be obtained by the college itself (subject to S.B.A. approval). Overall, however, there seems to be no shortage of cases.

Irrespective of whether the company has asked for counselling or been approached, it must formally agree to be involved in the S.B.I. Programme by signing a form. This form absolves the S.B.A. from any legal claim in respect of outcomes of the assistance offered. The firm is also asked to give reasonable access to information and to co-operate with students sufficiently for them to have a reasonable chance of success. Co-operation is of course, enforceable where the small firm has a loan guarantee: in other cases it depends on goodwill. This obligation on the part if the small business owner does not mean that he must be heavily involved in the project. Nor is he obliged to accept the final report although non-acceptance is rare. If the report is accepted, the owner will be asked to sign a form to this effect: not as an indication of satisfaction with quality but merely as a receipt. His signature is nevertheless important to the institution as it cannot be paid the S.B.A. fee unless the company has accepted the report.

The type of problems dealt with by the scheme can vary greatly: they include problems of layout in retailing or manufacturing; advertising; promotion; market research; record keeping; raising finance; book-keeping; and problems of recruiting personnel. The projects are always with existing companies - start-ups are regarded as too risky, in that they can easily fold before the students have time to properly undertake the work. The reports to the companies average from 12 to 20 pages and are kept to a reasonable level of simplicity concentrating on one issue that might be dealt with in a relatively short time.

THE UNIVERSITY OR COLLEGE

The obvious motivation for the college to be involved in the S.B.I. Programme is to link directly with the local community while at the same time providing a means for students to undertake practical work in the environment. From the limited evidence collected during the research it appeared that the strength of this motivation varied considerably depending on the degree to which the college was seen by the President and Dean of the Faculty as having a community as opposed to pure academic orientation. One major motivational element was that the Programme was now being run in such a variety of institutions that a college increasingly could not afford to be left out.

The S.B.A. for its part prefers colleges operating the Programme to be running a four-year course. The majority of S.B.I. work therefore is undertaken at universities. There is, however, a tendency for universities with higher academic status in a region to avoid participation in the Programme, or to have, when they have participated, experienced some difficulty. At the other end of the scale, community colleges have joined the Programme more recently, although great care has reportedly been taken in selecting these. The S.B.I.'s criteria for selection include: catchment area; quality of staff; and overall competence and capability to undertake project work. The aim, nevertheless, has been to extend the Programme as widely as possible so as to provide the greatest catchment area for small business. This has almost certainly meant some decline in standards.

The college must enter into a formal agreement with the S.B.A. to undertake the work. The contract is awarded from Washington (on regional recommendation) and will specify the number of counsellings to take place, the time period, the price and the obligations of the school and the S.B.A. It also makes provision for the setting up of a local steering committee comprising S.B.A. Management Assistance Officers, University Co-ordinators and other S.B.A. or SCORE personnel, and sets out the reporting and payment procedures. On presentation of the report and after acceptance by the client, the school, in return is paid $250 a case. Two copies of the report must go to the S.B.A. District Office within 30 days of the end of the semester, together with a form which summarises the type of case and problem. This form is the basis for computer analysis undertaken in Washington which is subsequently fed back to the region. The S.B.A. Regional Office will then recommend approval for payment from S.B.A. headquarters.

The sum paid to the college has not changed for several years. The money was obviously an important factor initially in encouraging the widespread development of the S.B.I. Programme. It is still regarded as extremely useful in that it allows an element of departmental flexibility to the Programme Director and can provide a small perk to the Department as a whole, and to those members of staff involved.

The S.B.I. Director has a number of important responsibilities. He must liaise with the local office of the S.B.A. over contracts and number of cases; he is responsible for the development of a suitable background course and/or identification of other programmes into which S.B.I. work can be fed; he must negotiate S.B.I. work with other members of staff and ensure satisfactory conclusions; he has responsibility for handling the budget and for supervising the students, including intro- ducing them to the company and monitoring their progress, and the final acceptance of their report. Finally he must be concerned with evalua- ting the Programme and reporting on it for internal and external control purposes.

STUDENTS

The S.B.I. Programme is open only to post graduate or final year students. Students are therefore 21 years and over. As many American universities operate part-time degree courses many students are considerably older.

Even the younger students will take part-time jobs in order to supplement their income for some period during their degree course. Students therefore probably have more work experience than typical undergraduates in this country. Apart from the age criteria it is felt that the student ought to have a minimum level of business education before tackling the work in the company: for this reason the S.B.I. Programme is concentrated in higher level institutions, although not exclusively so.

Students typically undertake the S.B.I. Programme as part of a course. It is felt by the S.B.A. that a course context is essential. Not all students seem to be aware that the course they had opted for used the S.B.I. Programme at the time they elect for the course. There are broadly four types of course providing an umbrella for the Programme:

      (i)   The integrative business policy type course

     (ii)   The small business management course

   (iii)   The specialist course built around the project
             e.g. "counselling in small business"

    (iv)   The independent specialist course e.g.
             accounting, market research, etc.

Such courses may last up to 40-50 hours over 8 to 12 weeks. The majority of the time is spent on work in the company or in feedback sessions to the class. In the places visited the course was open to undergraduates and post graduates alike. On completion it would count for so many credits towards a degree.

The students who opted for the Programme were brought together into groups of two or three to provide a balance of skills. It is felt however that all students should have basic accounting skills before going into a company, and in order to match students with projects before the course starts, the tutor may collect background data on each student including information on previous courses taken.

Only in one of the schools visited was there a special introductory programme on counselling and this was not given to all students who undertook the S.B.I. Programme. In others the amount of specialist preparation varied. Students were normally given a briefing paper which described the general parameters of the Programme and the tutor's expectation of them. In addition students were introduced to the particular characteristics of a small business likely to confront them when they went into their project companies.

On the first visit to the company the students may be accompanied by the tutor. Generally they make between four and eight company visits over the 12 weeks semester or quarter, report back to the class at regular intervals and complete weekly, fortnightly or monthly report forms. These forms provide the basis for the Director's report to the S.B.A. which has to be made in mid term. When completed, the Director will, if necessary, edit the final report, and ensure that it is likely to be acceptable to the client.

THE S.B.A.

The Programme involves the S.B.A. in a number of activities at head office, and at regional and district levels. Head office takes responsibility for the contract, overall evaluation of the projects and the production of publicity and literature for the Programme. In addition the head office sponsors a national competition for the best Small Business Institute case each year. A number of useful guides on how to go about setting up an Institute Programme, have been produced.

At the regional office the S.B.A. is involved in selecting schools allocating programmes in their district, obtaining, distributing and monitoring cases, drawing up agreements, recommending payments, and finally checking on the implementation of findings.

HOW THE PROGRAMME OBJECTIVES WERE MET

Officially the aims of the S.B.I. Programme are:

- To provide free, meaningful 'management assistance' to small business, particularly very small business, by the use of business students in universities and colleges throughout the country.

- To encourage students to be involved with the small company, to learn about its methods of operation and give them an opportunity to evaluate the experience in the context of their own future careers.

- To provide an incentive to the university or college to link more closely with the needs of the local small business community.

Broadly these aims seem to be met. While it was difficult, from the

11

small number of companies interviewed to evaluate the objective of 'providing meaningful management assistance' the S.B.A.'s own national evaluation undertaken in 1975 indicated strongly that this objective was met. Certainly all the companies spoken to during the visit were positive in their assessment (although the sample was obviously biased). It was clear, however, that the results of the project were not always of great value to the company and were infrequently implemented. There was general agreement among students and staff interviewed that this was the case. Lack of implementation is scarcely surprising: very few professional consultants reports are fully implemented. It would moreover be unrealistic to expect a team of students, paying half a dozen visits to any small company to have a significant impact. It was agreed, however, that very careful selection, so that not only 'problem' companies were involved, could lead to better results.

The key factor in the success of the programme from the college or university viewpoint was the degree to which it was supported by the President or Dean of the Faculty, which in turn was related to the degree to which the institution had a track record of work for the local community. Without the support of the hierarchy it was difficult for the Programme Director to make an impact on the Department. In this respect the status of the person in charge of the Programme was very important, thus in one institution which had a track record of high community orientation the Programme was run by a full professor of some standing and tenure who knew the hierarchy of the university and the department well and was a close ally of the Dean. When interviewed the Dean showed considerable enthusiasm for and involvement in the Programme.

In contrast in another insititution the Dean and Deputy Dean, while expressing considerable interest in the Programme, obviously knew very little about it. It was not surprising therefore to find that the person responsible for the Programme had considerable difficulties. In another institution, however, the Director, very much an entrepreneur, operated in virtual isolation but had gained the respect of his colleagues and the Dean largely because of his drive, personality and obvious ability.

A key factor in the integration of the Programme into the institution is the academic status of small business work. Although the Programme is now extensive throughout the United States it does not appear to have associated with its substantial academic credibility. As in the U.K. such credibility is normally built up by specialist subject expertise and the publication of papers within the area of expertise. Unless therefore the college and organisation was prepared to reward community effort then the Directorship of the S.B.I. Programme could be dysfunctional to the career of the academic involved.

Where the Director has academic status in the institution this enhanced the opportunity for the Institute Programme to be integrated with a wider range of teaching programmes. The monetary incentive was not a major factor in this for the reward is not very great compared with what might be obtained by outside consultancy. There were also problems in the limited understanding of many of the staff of the small firm and the resultant risks in terms of quality and acceptability of the final report involved in putting out project work to them. It was pointed out on more than one occasion that academics are accustomed to evaluating reports in terms of their academic acceptability with little concern for their acceptability to companies. Despite these difficulties it was clear in the institutions visited that the scope for extending the Programme into a variety of departments was great and the general view was that the work constituted a practical and valuable exercise for the student and made a substantial contribution to the department.

The only other major problem encountered by the university or college was the relationship of the Programme to other sources of assistance for the small businessman. It was unusual in institutions visited for the Programme to have close links with other forms of counselling, except when the Programme was conducted under the umbrella of the Small Business Development Centre (see the later paper in this book by the same author). To facilitate collaboration between the S.B.I. Programme and the other principle source of counselling: the SCORE, one university had virtually established its own SCORE Chapter on the campus. This facilitated the discussion of cases with the students and the joint undertaking of project work.

The Programme was universally popular with students. All of the students interviewed found it worthwhile largely because of its practical value. Not always, however, did the project work smoothly, occasionally, as might be expected, there were difficulties in working with the owner manager in the company: in some cases the owner was wildly supportive, in others rather hostile. There was always difficulty in getting the owner to implement the report and the majority of students doubted whether recommendations would be implemented. There did not, however, seem to be difficulty in approaching the company although sometimes information, particularly financial information was difficult to obtain. It was also evident that although all students had undertaken accountancy options on their programmes before the S.B.I. counselling visit they were often at a loss when endeavouring to set up simple book keeping systems. Adequacy of knowledge, seemed to be less a problem than the fact that in each institution visited a small minority of cases were of companies in dire difficulty and with little hope of survival. It was felt that there were too many of these on offer (perhaps reflecting the selection criteria used by the S.B.A.). For students the value of the Programme seemed to be maximised when a number of conditions were met including: support from the tutor in the introduction to the company; a positive attitude from the owner; the incorporation into background courses of some training in approaches to small businesses and counselling; and close control by the tutor of the progress of work.

S.B.A. staff of the centres visited recognised the problems involved in choosing companies from the Loan Guarantees file; at one time all companies chosen were Loan clients. At the time of the visit this proportion varied from half to three quarters. The reason for the change was that colleges or universities had complained about the number of poor quality cases. Obtaining new cases from elsewhere was, however, an onerous task involving a constant search of the files.

Smooth administration of the Programme also depended on finding the right staff within the S.B.A. to liaise with the university and on finding an enthusiastic Programme Director within the college. Even where there was enthusiasm and commitment there could still be

difficulties in allocating cases between other forms of management
assistance, particularly SCORE, and the S.B.I. The administration was
exacerbated by the amount of form filling to be done and by S.B.A.'s
responsibility for following up of all cases, in order to complete a
report. There was little evidence to suggest that this follow-up was
done systematically in terms of helping the company implement findings
of the project.

Despite the difficulties of implementation, it was clear that the
Programme was meeting, broadly, the objectives set out above. All the
S.B.A. offices visited were enthusiastic. The courses associated with
the Programme were very popular in all the institutions visited and
students rated the Programme highly, and the Programme seemed to
stimulate the community orientation of the university and college.

RELEVANCE OF THE S.B.I. PROGRAMME TO THE U.K.

How relevant is the S.B.I. Programme to the U.K.? It can be argued that
this depends upon:

      (i)   Whether there is a similar gap in the assis-
               tance framework in the U.K. for the very small
               firms for which the S.B.I. type programme is
               most relevant. Is there a need?

      (ii)   Whether there is a need for greater student
               orientation towards small busines and towards
               the community as part of their education. Is
               there a gap in business education?

      (iii)   Whether there is a need to influence educa-
               tional institutions to recognise gaps. Are
               our educational institutions responding inade-
               quately to small business needs?

(i) The assistance framework for very small businesses in the U.K.

The gap which the S.B.I. Programme in the U.S.A. aims to fill is the one
to which the efforts of the U.K. Department of Industry Counselling
Service are substantially directed, namely assisting the very small
firm. In the U.K. this type of firm lies outside of the influence of
the Industrial Training Boards, and is too small to have much appeal to
consultants. In the rural areas the services of the Council for Small
Firms in Rural Areas (CoSIRA) are available but there is no urban
equivalent. The very small firm's resources are scarce and often not
even substantial enough for it to make greater use of any management
accounting services offered by the accounting profession. A need would
therefore appear to exist in the U.K. Whether there is a 'gap',
however, is still the subject of debate. On the one hand there are
those who question whether assistance should seek to do more than remove
particular discriminations against the small firm in the 'free' market.
On the other there are those who would argue for a comprehensive
institutional support system for small business to remedy a 'bias' in
the environment towards the larger organisation.

The arguments can become complex and it is not intended to dwell on them here. Two points can, however, be made. First it can be suggested that the very small firm is discriminated against in the provision of training assistance when compared with its larger counterpart. This is because one major source of management training assistance in the U.K., the Industrial Training Boards, are financed largely by the tax payer: and evidence suggests that in the main their efforts are concentrated on the larger company. Even if this point is conceded the question remains as to whether any gap in assistance is wide enough to merit additional and complementary assistance over and above the existing Department of Industry Counselling system.

Second, there may be fundamental differences in philosophy between the U.S. and the U.K. with regard to small business which may well condition whether such programmes as the S.B.I. or S.B.D.C. could be implemented here. One such difference centres on whether it is regarded as legitimate to structure the supportive environment for small business. Thus, for example, while there is a great deal of open criticism in the U.S.A. of the operation of the Small Business Administration, this tends to focus on the efficiency of the organisation and the effectiveness of particular programmes rather than on questionning the very principle on which the S.B.A.'s existence is based. The impression gained by the author during his investigation, was that the institutionalisation of the small business support system in the U.S.A. is not in itself an issue: what is debated strongly are the ways of best doing this. In the U.K. the former still seems to be an open area for debate.

(ii) Student orientation towards small business in the U.K.

The case for greater student orientation rests fundamentally on whether there is a need in education to do more to prepare students for setting up their own business. It can be argued that hitherto, business management education as taught in British Management schools, poly-technics and colleges has been built on the model of the student as an eventual employee rather than as a potential employer, i.e. there has been a gap in business management training of students (2).

While in line with the current fashion, entrepreneurial and small business options on degree and professional courses are increasing, there is still a very long way to go. Evidence collected by recent research underlines that there is some interest and involvement with small firms in a large number of educational establishments but generally no major systematic commitment. Thus there is a need for guidance in the approaches adopted.

(iii) Institutional orientation towards small business in the U.K.

Those who attend the U.K. Small Business Management Teachers' Programme find many difficulties in integrating small business work in the college or university which stem from the traditional behaviour of the institu-tions themselves. Mainly this is manifested in their remoteness, from the small business client. Here it is possible to draw an analogy between the classical sub-contracting small firm and the education institution in terms of 'supply and production' rather than 'demand and marketing' orientation. Pursuing the analogy further, it can be argued that a great deal of the energy of the institution is devoted to pro-ducing product 'excellence' (frequently academic excellence). Arguably at the root of this product orientation is the appointment of staff of the institutions as 'subject experts' who can gain rewards mainly by pursuing their excellence within the subject discipline.

Traditionally it has been possible for educational institutions to maintain this particular philosophy while continuing to meet the needs of professional management from large companies, because such managers frequently welcome the intellectual challenge from subject specialisation and will accept its possibly limited relevance to their present job situation on the grounds that it is part of their personal development. Attendance at business development programmes is likely to further the career possibilities of the professional manager - for him there are clear rewards to education.

These factors have probably served to underwrite the education supply rather than the training demand role of many institutions and also to reinforce the 'expert' role of the members of the teaching staff. They help to explain why many institutions have difficulty in making specific provision for the training of the small firm owner/manager or the development of entrepreneurial education. Evidence suggests that the owner/manager is concerned primarily with the immediate relevance of education to the development of his business. He is impatient of expertise when it is not relevant and has little to gain personally by 'passing out' from courses. Even in teaching small business to students there are difficulties. For example, in certain institutions problems arise in presenting 'small business' as a 'subject' and in convincing colleagues, immersed in subject expertise, that is has any intellectual content.

There may, therefore, be a case for challenging much of the 'employee' and 'supply' orientation of management training and education, if it is admitted that this makes for practical difficulties in encouraging education institutions to deal more adequately with the needs of the small firm in the U.K. The experience of any national programme aimed at overcoming these problems is obviously of interest: such is the case with the S.B.I. Programme in the United States.

POSSIBLE PROBLEMS IN SETTING UP AN S.B.I. TYPE PROGRAMME IN THE U.K.

If the case for an S.B.I. type initiative in the U.K. is accepted then there is much to be said for following certain American guidelines, given the excellent documentation. It is, however, clear that in all attempts at 'transfer of technology' there will be some major problems resulting from differences in organisation and philosophy here between the U.S.A. and the U.K. These can be broadly grouped under: problems of small firm selection and acceptance differences of the scheme; problems of administration; and problems of selecting institutions and appropriate staff.

POSSIBLE SMALL FIRM SELECTION AND ACCEPTABILITY PROBLEMS

The most immediate problem is that of finding the cases. There is no loan guarantee portfolio (3) in the U.K. Cases would therefore have to be found through the existing Small Firm Information Centres (S.F.I.C.'s) and/or through the Department of Industry's Counselling Service. The latter would demand co-operation between counsellors, the

S.F.I.C.'s and the college and there may be difficulties as in the American situation. Alternatively, or in conjunction, a programme could be marketed directly by the college itself and through other media such as relevant trade associations, training boards, etc.

This still leaves the problem of the acceptability of the programme to the smaller business. It is likely that there would be some difficulty in the early stages in this respect. Overcoming this would necessitate the Programme Director having close control of the setting up of the case and the 'selling' of the service to the company. Ultimately the scheme could only be sold on the basis of previous 'success' stories. Any initial trial of the programme should therefore be well resourced to ensure success.

POSSIBLE ADMINISTRATIVE PROBLEMS

The 'official' administration could presumably be undertaken by the Small Firm Information Centres: they would obviously need additional manning in the long run if the operation was to reach any scale. There would have to be very careful demarcation between the Department's Counselling Service and a student service. This might not be too difficult. Counsellors could indeed produce cases meriting more intensive and extensive attention. They could also be organised to help with implementation.

It is probable that if the programme was to be disseminated widely some financial incentive would be needed. This was regarded as an important means by which the S.B.A. in Washington had increased the coverage of the Programme. Since finance was still an important ingredient to the continuation of the Programme in the institutions visited.

PROBLEMS OF SELECTING THE ESTABLISHMENT AND ITS PROGRAMME DIRECTOR

The importance of this to the success of any programme cannot be emphasised enough, particularly if the programme in turn is to influence the institution. There are undoubtedly many institutions within the U.K. which could operate this type of programme. The programme could be inserted into a number of courses at polytechnics and university business schools, including M.Sc., M.B.A. final undergraduate business programmes, D.M.S., I.W.M., and H.N.D. type courses. Care would have to be taken, however, to ensure that an adequate course was built round the programme. With funding, there should be little difficulty in interesting colleges and universities in the idea. Quality control would, be a major problem.

One particular barrier in this respect is the absence of small business orientation in many colleges. Small business management teaching is much more developed in the U.S.A. than in the U.K.; hence there are more staff available with the relevant experience. This difficulty would be exacerbated by the academic and subject orientation among staff of U.K. institutions. This underlines the importance of ensuring suitable course development to provide the framework and the selection of a committed Director, with a suitable track record. In the U.K., teaching staff may need assistance in developing suitable

17

'context' courses.

Any difficulties in matching cases with the educational institution's needs could be overcome by ensuring that there are academic advisors associated with the scheme and its initial evaluation.

CONCLUSION

The barriers to undertaking a pilot scheme in the U.K. along the lines of the S.B.I. Programme in the United States do not seem to be insurmountable. The programme could have a ready base in much of the project work already undertaken at university business schools and polytechnics. It would undoubtedly provide an impetus to colleges to be involved for them to do so. It would also provide a focal point for support for small business activity in the institution and if care was taken with selection of programme centres and programme directors this could be an important lever to institutional involvement with the small firm. There would also undoubtedly be a need to develop suitable context courses, the existence of which would be important to the success of the programme: and there would be associated training needs of members of staff. Thus the costs would not be insignificant. But the benefits might be considerable, not only in providing a vehicle for helping to fill a 'gap' in assistance to the very small firm, but also in providing a major influence in business education.

NOTES

(1) The Small Business Counselling Service of Retired Executives

(2) The U.K. Small Business Management Teachers Association believes this to be the case and for the last five years, supported by the Foundation for Management Education, has been running programmes for teachers from U.K. higher education institutes.

(3) Since the writing of this paper the Government has of course announced an experimental loan guarantee scheme in its March, 1981 Budget.

3 Students and small business

SUE BIRLEY AND PETER WILSON
Small Business Institute,
London Business School

INTRODUCTION

Interest in small business has not only increased amongst politicians and businessmen in recent years, but also in the academic world. Five years ago, the number of small business teaching activities in any part of the Further or Higher Education sectors in the UK could be counted on one hand. In 1981, there are more than 100 institutions offering some form of small firm education.

The development of small business teaching has not been without its problems. As in any 'new' area, the type of course offered will be very much a function of the interests of faculty and their entrepreneurial efforts. There are, however, though not mutually exclusive, two distinct options - whether to service the practitioner, in this case the small businessman himself, or the existing internal student body. In making this choice faculty must consider the needs of their institution as well as their own particular skills and motivations. However, in looking at the small business area it is important to recognise that, unlike some other fields, the experience, methods and material needed to develop small firm managers are vastly different from those needed to help students understand how to make strategic choices as well as to prepare and interpret cash flows. In the small firm class the student needs to understand the particular significance of cash flow amongst all the other issues facing the small firm manager.

Thus, to cover both fields, the teacher has to be both a generalist and a technician at the same time. The only other area where this problem could be deemed to be similar is in the field of Business Policy. But here the technical teaching is the responsibility of faculty in the various functional subjects. In the emerging small business area, the teacher may feel that this support is not appropriate or available when dealing with the small businessman. Indeed, with only a few exceptions, the experience, material and contacts of most faculty tends to be in the large firm sector.

It is with this background in mind that individuals in institutions have made differing choices about their first small business initiative.

At the London Business School we decided to develop a course for our existing students to improve their understanding of the small firm sector. Interest is now so high that most students take at least one, and many take two or three electives on the two year Masters Programme. The first, and by far the highest subscribed (a steady 80 per cent of the available student body(1)) is called 'Small Business Management' which is a core course using the Small Business Case Book (Birley, 1980) as a text book. Further elective choices are available to students who wish to investigate the operational and start-up issues facing the owner-manager and entrepreneur. The objectives of the core small business course, as outlined to the students, are to satisfy the following needs:

(i) Most students will, at least initially, work for larger firms. Many will, however, deal with small firms either as customers, suppliers, bankers or advisors. Since small firms have different values, goals, and systems from larger firms, it is important for the large firm manager to understand these if he is to deal efficiently with the small firm.

(ii) Some students come from small firm backgrounds themselves. This is an opportunity to discuss the particular pressures they face in making the choice between 'breaking-away' or staying within the family firm.

(iii) A number of students feel that they would like to work in a small firm and, indeed, have a very romantic and sometimes over-stated view of their potential value in creating order out of apparent chaos. The course is an opportunity for them to explore this idea without doing any damage - to themselves or to the firm.

(iv) Some students would like to start their own businesses and this is a first chance to examine the start-up process.

There are other benefits to the course, such as the opportunity to explore a total business more easily than is perhaps encountered elsewhere, or the chance to meet some different people from those usually encountered in the business school environment. Over-riding all this is a perception that small business is different and fun.

In order to test the effectiveness and appropriateness of these objectives, the following surveys were conducted in the class of Masters students graduating in 1981:

Stage 1: In the first week of their two year programme at the London Business School. (100 students)

Stage 2: At the start of the Small Business Course (2). (80 students)

Stage 3: At the end of the Small Business Course.

We were able to compare the findings of these surveys with two earlier studies. The first was a survey of 57 students graduating between 1968 and 1978 who were currently working in a small firm; the second was a survey of students completing the Small Business Course in 1979 (72 students). The findings reported below refer to the 1981 class.

Where appropriate, comparisons will be drawn with the two earlier surveys.

SURVEY RESULTS AND COMMENT

(i) Experience

The number of students with small business experience was surprisingly large. Some 70 per cent had worked in either small business, family business or had been self-employed. It is doubtful, however, whether this constitutes genuine experience of the management and related economic and social issues in small business even though the students' combined experience of 97 years in these categories represents a large proportion (32 per cent) of total experience. Indeed, Table 1 shows that only 15 students had more than one year's experience.

Table 1

Students' employment experience*

Years	Small Business	Family Business	Self-Employed	All Employment
0.1-1	20	9	3	11
1.1-2	6	2	2	10
2.1-5	7	1	3	29
>5	2	1	1	30
Total	35	12	9	80

*All figures are numbers of students

In only a few cases had students spent a large proportion of their working lives in small business with only four having more than five year's experience whilst 59 had more than 2 years experience working in other, larger, organisations. It is therefore likely that such limited exposure provided little more than a superficial understanding of the problems of setting up and managing a small enterprise.

Exposure to the small firm is not necessarily limited to direct work experience, and indeed, almost all students had gained some under-standing, particularly of family related problems, either indirectly through friends or more directly through a family firm. Indeed, the number of 'sons of fathers' in the class was a surprise to the authors (see Table 2). It did, however, underline the need felt by a number of

21

second generation potential owners not only to learn professional
management methods, but also to explore the peculiar family problems
which they faced.

Table 2

Small business contact

Contact*	Number of Students	Percentage of Group
None	26	32
Family business	30	38
Friends in business	32	40
Started own business	17	21

*Some students had more than one type of contact

These figures are consistent with those for the 1979 class where 31
per cent came direct from a family-owned business (38 per cent in 1981
class) and a further 38 per cent had had direct experience in a small
firm (44 per cent in 1981 class).

The second surprising finding was the large number of students who had
already started and run some form of business. Although many of these
were part-time activities, often set up to supplement university grants,
they nevertheless indicated the basis of an entrepreneurial spirit.
Indeed, it is worth considering whether, as in the USA, the possible
lack of grants in the future could be a spur to more self-employed
activity.

(ii) Defining the small business

Students were asked to define small business at the three stages during
the two year programme. The answers have been classified in Table 3.
The 'size classification' denotes a specific statistic, such as less
than 100 employees or £2m turnover. The most significant observation is
the dramatic shift from a concentration on a numerical measure of size
at the start of the programme to structural measures at the end of the
Small Business Course.

Moreover, many of the numerical sizes quoted at Stage 1 were well
outside any accepted definitions. For example, one student considered a
company with sales of around £20m to be representative of the small
sector and another one with up to 500 employees. (In manufacturing, a
size of 200 employees is normally taken as the upper limit of the small
firm sector.)

Since a number of students gave more than one definition, the results
were re-classified as in Table 4.

Table 3

Small business defined: number of students

Definition	Stage 1	Stage 2	Stage 3
Size of turnover, employees, assets	37	81	26
Limited management/few directors	2	11	-
Limited products/markets	3	-	-
Limited resources	-	-	-
Non-public	-	8	-
Owner managed/controlled	6	19	30
Family involvement	1	19	14
Manager knows all employees	2	8	-
Few people (not qualified)	-	-	22
No structure	1	11	-
Company lasting more than 2 years	-	-	2

Table 4

Definitions of size

Definition	Stage 1 %	Stage 2 %	Stage 3 %
Quantitative	59	26	8
Qualitative	8	28	60
Quantitative and Qualitative	33	46	32
Total	100	100	100

This table demonstrates clearly the shift in thinking amongst the student group and highlights one of the major threads running through the Small Business Course. Although we spend a short amount of time midway through the course discussing the structure and size of the small firm sector, the majority of the discussion centres around the managerial issues associated with starting and growing a company through to the creation of a first line management structure.

(iii) Expectations regarding the small business course

Prior to the start of the Small Business Course, students were asked to describe in their own words, what they expected to gain from the course. Table 5 summarises their answers.

Table 5

Learning expectations

Content	%
Problems and opportunities at the start-up stage	33
Internal:	
Problems and opportunities in small business	27
External:	
Evaluating problems in small business	37
Don't know	3
Total	100

These results were particularly satisfying since they reflected the view that we had previously taken about the varied needs of the group. A large proportion of the students were interested in the issues because they might start a business or manage one (internal) while the remainder had an external or 'adviser's' interest in the small business. Furthermore, there was no clear concentration of interest, and whilst it is difficult to satisfy such varied expectations, our experience in the past has shown that the diversity of backgrounds and motivations enriches classroom discussion and helps to re-orientate the perspective of many students. To illustrate this, students in the class of 1979 were asked to indicate their attitude to small businesses before and after the course. Answers prior to the course included the following:

Corner shop
Limited scope
Boring
Low salaries
Stressful

whilst after the course -

            Attractive life-style
            High rewards
            Interesting
            Owner motivated
            Hard work

Whilst there is an element of truth in both of these lists, over two thirds of the class had moved from an essentially negative attitude towards small firms to one which was decidedly positive.

(iv) Gains from the small business course

As expected, it was impossible to classify the lessons learned from the Small Business Course. However, all students listed a variety of lessons which clould be loosely grouped into technical, conceptual and people. The technical answers concerned the issues relating to starting up in business, the different legal structures, financing problems and the taxation implications of running a small business. Conceptual answers varied from the general issue of the 'problems of managing a small firm' to answers like:

            succession problems
            'more like a marriage than employment'
            the relationship between ownership and control
            the problems of creating structure

However, by far the most fundamental lesson to the students appeared to be the importance of the human element in the small firm. This was seen in two ways. First, there were the characteristics of the entrepreneur and the understanding that this was a generic term rather than one which tightly defined people who started their own business, whether or not in the end it proved to be successful. Second, there was the view that 'people are vital' or that, unlike in a large firm, it is not possible to identify the people and the firm as separate elements until a certain critical mass, and thus structure, has been attained.

(v) Expectations regarding employment

Research data elsewhere have suggested that new graduates tend to look towards the larger firms for employment, at least initially, in the expectation of gaining the all important industrial training and experience. We were interested to learn whether this behaviour applied to our potential business graduates and, further, whether their view changed during the course. Accordingly, they were asked to indicate what size of firm they expected to join on leaving the Business School. The results at Stage 1 are shown in Table 6. As expected, about a third of the group still had an open mind with regard to the size of company they would join. What was surprising, however was the distribution of the rest.

Table 6

Employment expectations at Stage 1

Type of Firm	%
Open mind	35
Small	16
Medium	30
Large	-
Start own	19
Total	100

No student was attracted by large organisations, the majority feeling that a medium sized company would have sufficient structure to absorb their particular talents in an interesting way. The rest were attracted by growing something which was much more their own.

The question was again put to the students at Stage 2, at the start of the Small Business Course one year later. The results showed a more realistic picture. Nevertheless, over half the group still preferred to look towards the small to medium end of the sector for initial employment.

Table 7

Employment expectations at Stage 2

Type of Firm	%
Large company or public sector	41
Small to medium sized business	34
Own family business	12
Self employed	6
Don't know	7
Total	100

It is important to note that this shift or hardening of option took place over the first year, the technical part of the Masters Programme. In this period of study, with the exception of project work or functional exercises, students had no real exposure to the particular opportunities in the smaller business, and it is likely that they were influenced accordingly.

(vi) Desire for employment in small business

All of the students attending the Small Business Course (Stage 2) indicated a desire to work in a small firm at some time in their careers, if not immediately on completing the Masters Programme, but the majority (67 per cent) felt that this would be in the long term, after gaining experience in either medium-sized or larger organisations. Nevertheless, the number who wished to join a small firm immediately on graduating was much higher than expected and does reflect the general disenchantment amongst students with the perceived rewards of working in large firms.

However, many of these students tended to view the small firm with undue optimism, perceiving themselves as having many of the skills required to 'save' struggling small companies. Nevertheless, on completing the course (Stage 3) motivation remained high although a number had changed their minds, either about their own motivations and abilities or about the initial rewards of managing a small, unstructured enterprise. The findings differed only slightly from Stage 2 (Table 7), 77 per cent wishing to work within a small firm 'possibly in the long term' and the remaining 23 per cent wishing to go into a small business immediately on graduation. But many will not realise this dream as there is still the need to match company and graduate, and many owners remain very suspicious of the advantages of 'professional' management, fearing a loss of control. Nevertheless, in a separate survey we were able to identify 57 students graduating between 1968 and 1978 currently working in small firms (approximately five per cent of all graduates) of which 24 had started immediately on graduating. This number includes 12 graduates who had come from, and subsequently returned to, family firms, a fate which is common amongst the second or third generation students at some stage in their careers. Although we could identify that only about five per cent of all graduates were working in small firms, the difficulties of conducting such a census probably account for such a low share. On the other hand, given the problems of placing graduates in small firms, the aspirations of the members of the class who wished to work in a small firm immediately on graduation, seem somewhat unrealistic.

(vii) Plans to run own business

At the start of the course (Stage 2) a significant number of students retained the desire to start a business of their own. Thirteen students intended to put this into action immediately on graduation and a further 52 indicated a wish to pursue it in the long term. By the end of the course (Stage 3), a number had revised their view about the timing and many had abandoned what was in reality no more than a faint dream. Nevertheless, 29 of the students still retained a strong motivation to start up a new business and indeed, 18 of them were already actively pursuing a specific business idea, albeit on a part-time basis for the immediate period.

CONCLUSION

The impact of small business teaching on students extends beyond merely
legitimising employment in small business as an appropriate career
option.   Although the teacher's role is to inform as well as to
instruct, by raising the students' awareness of the problems of managing
a small business, there is the attendant danger that too much classroom
knowledge without the excitement of active small business management may
discourage as many as it may attract to the 'small is beautiful'
movement. But we have shown that very few students have much more than
a superficial knowledge of the management issues of small business.
Indeed, most students thought of 'small' only in quantitative terms
before the course started; many had unrealistic perceptions of the
opportunities offered by the small firm and how their own abilities
might be used in managing them more efficiently.

Teaching about small business can correct these misperceptions. The
students' general understanding of how a business works in toto - something that can more easily be assimilated with the small business model
- is improved, as well as their understanding of the people who run
them, and the unpredictable nature of the environment in which decisions
must be taken. To some students, the management task appeared to be
either insurmountable or unattractive, but to nearly a quarter of the
group surveyed, the Small Business Course either changed or reinforced
the desire to work in a small business on graduation. In either case,
teaching students about small business satisfies two objectives. First
it opens up new career options and provides the information necessary
for rational choices. Second, it better equips the large firm manager
and adviser to communicate with, and thus deal with, the owner-manager.

NOTES

(1) That is, exluding students away on Exchange Programmes at the time.
(2) This takes place in the first term of the second year.

REFERENCES

Birley, S. Small Business Case Book. Macmillan. 1980.

4 Alumni perceptions of entrepreneurship courses after six to ten years

JOHN HORNADAY
Babson College
and
KARL VESPER
University of Washington,
and Babson College (Visiting)

INTRODUCTION

In a study by Vesper, reported to the 1980 Conference on Entrepreneurial Education at Baylor University, responding professors cited several criteria for judging the quality of courses. "Alumni comments years later" was rated as the most significant--higher than formal course ratings by current students, informal feedback from students, class size, examination results, businesses started by students, and other criteria.

This paper presents the results of an evaluation of an entrepreneurship course as viewed by alumni several years after taking that course. The authors intend this to be the beginning of an evaluation effort which will continue over time, will involve additional colleges, and will use methodology which is further refined by experience. Thus, in presenting this paper, the authors hope both to recruit other colleges into a collaborative effort of entrepreneurship course evaluation aimed at improving course effectiveness and to elicit ideas regarding how the evaluation process itself can be made more effective.

At many colleges, course evaluation forms are used each term in every course. The forms are usually administered just before the end of the term when students are facing a final examination, while they are still too close to the content of the course to stand back and evaluate it objectively, and when even a temporary "up or down" relating to a specific experience with the instructor or with the course may affect their analytic comments. Waiting until six to ten years after completion of the course may allow development of greater objectivity as well as acquisition of more experience on which to base judgments. One disadvantage is that the alumnus may not remember the details of the course as clearly.

PLAN OF THE STUDY

The date for this study consist of responses to a questionnaire mailed both to alumni who had taken one of the courses in "Entrepreneurship" at Babson College between 1971 and 1975, inclusive, and to alumni who had not. The questionnaire was developed to reveal:

    (i)   the participant's perceptions of the strengths and weaknesses of the course taken some years earlier,

   (ii)   the participant's business history, and

  (iii)   the degree of satisfaction of the alumnus with his or her job.

There were also questions to ascertain whether the alumnus had taken the course as a graduate or as an undergraduate, the present business address, and other such information. (See copies of survey form in Appendix.)

Two matched groups of business graduates were established, made up of former students in one of the Entrepreneurship courses (Group E) at Babson College, and the other group (Group C, control) was matched in regard to degree obtained, year of graduation, six, and, roughly, the home country. The questionnaire for the control group was modified by the elimination of questions about the perceived value of the entrepreneurship course, but the portion relative to the individual's career history was the same.

The upper limit, 10 years since taking the course, was selected because the course was first introduced at Babson ten years ago. The other limit, six years, was set in order to allow at least that much time to have passed to allow for career development. We hope to continue tracking as further time elapses in the future.

SELECTION OF THE SAMPLES

Since an entrepreneurial course has been offered at both the undergraduate and graduate levels since 1971, class rolls for both levels and for all instructors were obtained for that period through to 1975. It was decided, in order to avoid the complexities of getting clearance for release of personal data, that course grades would not be obtained or studied (although the relationship of grades to other selected variables would be interesting in itself). Mailing addresses were obtained from the alumni office for each of the names on the class rosters so that subjects could be contacted by means of a mailed questionnaire.

Attrition occurred at several points in the process of developing the list. Originally, there were 520 names supplied of former students registered for the course. No names were eliminated by the investigators for any reasons other than: the alumni office file indicated no address for the individual (contact with the alumnus had been lost), the address used resulted in the return of the mailed questionnaire by the post office as being undeliverable, it developed that the student had not taken the course although registration for it had occurred (the later withdrawal, indicated in the grade column, would not have been seen on the roster because the grade column was not reported to the investigators), or the alumnus elected not to fill out the questionnaire and return it. Table 1 reveals the number of cases in the original list and the final number of returned questionnaires.

The matched control group (C) differed from Group E in that none was supposed to have had a course in entrepreneurship. This would allow comparisons between the two groups on those items that were similar in the two questionnaires. In the control group, no evaluation questions about the entrepreneur courses could be asked, but some general questions about their college courses were substituted. Questions about the entrepreneurial endeavors and experiences in business were comparable. The attrition rate in the control group was somewhat higher; 318 usable questionnaires were received. (See Table 1.) Analysis was not limited to those cases in which both the control and experimental matched pair returned usable forms; it was considered that the groups were large enough and similar enough to allow overall comparison of response percentages.

Table 1

The Samples

	Took the Course			Matched-No Ent. Course		
	Under-grads	Grads	Total	Under-grads	Grads	Total
In original lists	193	327	520	193	327	520
Inappropriate addresses	8	23	31	4	1	5
Had dropped course	18	3	21	-	-	-
Took course elsewhere	-	-	-	3	28	31
Attrition for above	26	26	52	7	29	36
Eligible alumni	167	301	468	186	269	484
Did not respond	40	76	116			164
Uninterpretable forms	3	0	3			2
Usable surveys	124	225	349			318
Percent usable returns	74%	75%	75%			66%

Estimated percentage of those who finally responded:

Response to 1st mailing	Approx.	60%		Approx.	65%
Response to 2nd mailing	Approx.	12%		Approx.	10%
Response to 3rd mailing	Approx.	8%		Approx.	25%
Response to 4th mailing	Approx.	20%			

(Only three mailings were sent to the Control group.)

PROCEDURE

After the first mailing, follow-up reminders were sent to those from whom no response was received. For those who did not respond, there were, for the E Group, three follow-up letters, sent at ten day intervals after the original. There were two follow-up letters for the Control group. For both groups a second copy of the questionnaire as sent with the last mailing.

RESULTS AND DISCUSSION

Are students who take entrepreneurship courses more likely to end up with their own companies than those who do not take the course? The answer, according to responses from this survey, appears clearly to be 'yes', as can be seen from the figures in Table 2. Slightly over twice as many of those who took an entrepreneurship course are now in businesses of their own. The 2:1 ratio is striking considering the similarities of their backgrounds.

Table 2

Percent of Alumni Who Started Businesses

	Took Course %	Did Not Take Course %
Solely in a business of their own (Full time self-employed)	21.3	14.2
'Moonlighting' in a business of their own (part time self-employed)	12.4	2.5
Total	33.7	16.7

Many respondents apparently lower the risk in the early years by 'moonlighting' in their entrepreneurial efforts; that is, working for someone else while the new, independent business gets underway. The results in Table 2, therefore, are divided into the categories, Full Time Self Employed (FTSE), and Part Time Self Employed (PTSE). Table 2 indicates that those students who took the course are about twice as likely to have started a business in this length of time since the course.

All students in both the Experimental and the Control groups majored in business, so that their educational backgrounds were similar except for the Entrepreneurship course. Actually, 48.5 per cent of those who took the course did so with the intention of starting their own business. Of those who took the course intending to become entrepreneurs, 46 per cent did; of those who did not so intend, 20 percent did start a business. Table 3 summarizes those data.

Of the 101 alumni who took the course only as undergraduates, 28 per

Table 3

Frequencies of starting business by alumni who did and did not intend to do so when taking the entrepreneurial course

	FTSE		PTSE		Total in Business		Works for Others		Total
	N	%	N	%	N	%	N	%	N
Intended to start business	51	31	24	15	75	46	87	54	162
Took course without intention of starting business	16	12	10	8	26	20	104	80	130
Total									294*

*This does not total 349 because 42 answered "Possibly" and 13 did not reply.

33

cent have their own business (of which 7 per cent are on a moonlighting basis); of those 225 who took it only as graduates, 34 percent have their own business (of which 14 percent are moonlighting); and of the 23 students who took entrepreneurial courses at both levels, 52 percent have their own business (35 per cent are solely in their own business; 17 percent work for others and moonlight in their own business). These data (see Figure 1) indicate that, in fact, the more courses taken the more likely it is that the student will later start a business.(1)

Studies have indicated that the average age for beginning ventures is 32-35 years which would be, in the typical case, about 10 years after completion of undergraduate courses. Because relatively few years have passed since many of these alumni were students, it is of particular interest to know their future plans and expectations. For that purpose, a six-point scale on both the E group and the C group questionnaires elicited an indication of the respondent's expectation for going into business at a future time. Of those not now in business for themselves, 50 per cent of those who took the course think it 'Probable' or 'Highly Probable' that they will start a business at a later time. The corresponding percent for those who did not take the course is 30. Later studies will reveal the extent to which these expectations worked out in fact.

In Table 4 it should be noted that the FTSE usually avoid manufacturing and that may be because it is the most difficult to get started. For the moonlighting (PTSE), the figures are service 40 percent, sales 10 per cent, and manufacturing 50 per cent essentially the same as those working for others. When they do go into manufacturing, they appear to protect themselves by having a job in another organization. Other than that, the percentages follow essentially the same patterns (except the very small sample in the PTSE in the Control group).

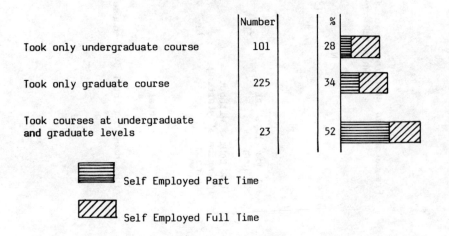

Figure 1.   Relationship of level and frequency of taking entrepreneurship to self-employment.

Table 4

Types of business started by various groups of alumni

Kind of Business	FTSE				Work for Others				PTSE				Total Respondents			
	Took Course N	%	No Course N	%	Took Course N	%	No Course N	%	Took Course N	%	No Course N	%	Took Course N	%	No Course N	%
Service	41	56	31	69	96	43	133	51	17	40	6	75	154	45	170	54
Sales	22	30	9	20	31	14	28	11	4	10	0	0	57	17	37	12
Manufacturing	10	14	5	11	98	43	98	37	21	50	2	25	129	38	105	34
Unemployed*	0		0		0		0		0		2		2		3	
N/A	1		5		5		3		1		7		7		3	
Total Working	73		45		230		262		42		8		340		312	

Of those who work in their own business full time, slightly more go into service business (69% vs. 56%) if they have not had the course.

*Students or 'Housewives'

35

For those students who were in the Control group, a question was included to reflect their reason for not taking Entrepreneurship while in college. The range of answers is presented in Table 5 and is broken down by those who started a business (either as their sole occupation or in combination with working for others) and those who work full time for others. It is of interest to note that the most frequent answer was that it was 'Not Offered,' but it should be pointed out that the course did, in fact, overlap with the time that they were enrolled. Those figures may indicate a failure on the part of the administration to make known to students that a new course had been introduced. Aside from that answer, the most frequent response was that they were 'Not Interested.' Note however, that nine of the 'Not Interested' students have since started a business on a full time basis.

Another question of interest to educators was (for those who did not take the entrepreneurial course): 'What areas needed more emphasis in your education?' The range of answers is given in Table 6, in which it can be seen that Management was seen as most important by alumni who worked for others whereas Finance was regarded as most important by those who were in the FTSE group.

A similar question was asked of those students who did take the entrepreneurship course: 'Are there areas essential to entrepreneurial success that you feel should have received more emphasis in the entrepreneurial course(s) you took?' The range of answers is presented in Table 7, and it can be seen that Finance was the most frequent answer. Management also ranked high, as it did for those students who had not taken the course but who had later started their own business.

Earlier studies by Hornaday and Kuder on job dissatisfaction, found that about 40 per cent of respondents who work for others often preferred a different kind of work entirely. The identical question was included in the present study with a number of interesting results. Of the total students (349) who took the course, 95.5 per cent answered relative to their degree of satisfaction with their work. Of these, 31.5 per cent wanted a different kind of work entirely. Those included, of course, those who work for themselves and for others as well. Of the 73 in their own full time business who responded, only 8 per cent wanted a different kind of work; of those who work in others' businesses, 38 per cent wanted a different kind of work entirely, fairly close to the 40 per cent found in other studies.

Thus it appears that there is a much higher degree of job satisfaction among alumni who are in business for themselves than by alumni who work in others' organizations. Recognizing that the early years are often the most challenging, it will be interesting to learn in follow-up studies whether the degree of satisfaction for these individuals increases in the future. In later studies, of course, provision will be made for indicating business failures, and the relationship of that factor to dissatisfaction will also be studied.

Table 5

Percentages of those who did not take the course responding with answers
to a question: 'Why Not Study Entrepreneurship?'

	FTSE 45	Work for Others 264	PTSE 8
1. Not offered*	40	26	50
2. Didn't know of it	7	3	
3. Not interested	9	15	13
4. Not top priority	4	14	
5. Didn't consider	2	3	
6. Didn't consider: wish I had	11	4	
7. Scheduling	7	10	13
8. Didn't know what I wanted	2	3	13
9. Wanted large company	4	2	
10. Thought it was useless		3	
11. Too new		1	
12. Can't learn entrepreneurship		1	
13. Took it elsewhere	2	1	
14. No space	4	1	
15. Thought took it		1	
16. Don't know		1	
17. Other	2	5	
18. No answer	4	7	13

*The course was offered while these students were still enrolled;
however, it may have come in too late to be included in their schedule.

Table 6

Percentage answers for students who had not taken the course, the
question was asked: 'What Area(s) Need More Emphasis In Your
Education?'

	Full Time Self-employed 45	Not Self-employed 264	Part Time Self-employed 8
Nothing	9	9	0
Accounting	9	5	13
Economics	2	2	13
Field Studies	13	2	0
Finance	22	9	25
Human Relations	13	20	25
Legal Government	7	5	0
Management	18	23	38
Marketing	16	5	13
Quantitative Methods	2	12	13
Liberal Arts (writing)	11	16	0
Entrepreneurial Studies	9	3	25
Careers	2	3	0
Research	0	1	0
International	2	2	0
Personal Development	7	5	0
Other	2	2	0

Table 7

Areas of study seen as particularly important to alumni who had taken the entrepreneurial course and had started a business.

	Number	Percent
Accounting	7	2
Field Studies	13	4
Finance	89	24
Human Relations	18	5
Legal/Government	14	4
Marketing	23	6
Management	45	12
Quantitatives	6	2
Other	55	15
Nothing Needed	94	26
		*364

*As many as three areas might be cited by a single respondent.

CONCLUSIONS

The tables presented in this paper are a sample of those that might be obtained from the present data, but equally or more interesting will be similar studies at other colleges offering entrepreneurial courses as well as longitudinal studies over periods of five to ten years apart in order to reflect the career development of students in entrepreneurship courses. As emphasis in these areas of education and of practice continues to increase during the 1980's, course evaluation studies become particularly important, and it would be most beneficial if co-operative efforts can be made among colleges so that a greater variety of areas for investigation will be opened. It is the authors' hope that such a cooperative effort will develop out of this study.

NOTES

(1) At the time these subjects were in college, one graduate course and one undergraduate course were offered; Babson College now has four entrepreneurial courses at the undergraduate level and two at the graduate level (with the expectation of adding a third graduate course next year). Later follow-up studies can make a more refined investigation of the effect of number and level of courses taken.

Babson College--Center for Entrepreneurial Studies

A FOLLOW-UP STUDY OF THE BABSON COLLEGE ENTREPRENEURSHIP COURSES

Name:_____

Address:_____

_____

Company Name_____
and Address:

_____

Type of Business:_____

If you had your choice, which of the following would you choose? (Check one)

_____ The job you have now

_____ The same kind of work but with some changes in working conditions or people you work with

_____ A different kind of work entirely--in an enterprise that you start yourself

_____ A different kind of work entirely--but not in an enterprise of your own

Definition (for this questionnaire): An entrepreneur is one who starts a business and assumes his or her own financial risk: or one who takes over an existing business and significantly redirects it, assuming financial risk for the venture.

PART I.   ENTREPRENEURIAL COURSES:

1.   Did you take: an undergraduate course in entrepreneurship? Yes No
                   a graduate course in entrepreneurship?   Yes No
                   a seminar in entrepreneurship after
                   graduation?   Yes No

2.   If you answered No to all three parts of 1., please indicate why you did not take a course in entrepreneurship.

     _____

     If you answered Yes to any of the questions in 1., please answer 3. through to 6.

3.   How many courses in entrepreneurship have you taken?_____

4.   Did you take the course(s) with the intention of becoming an entrepreneur? _____

5.   Did the entrepreneurial course(s) have an effect on the direction your career has taken? Yes   No   Comment, if you wish:

     _____

6. Are there areas essential to entrepreneurial success that you feel should have received more emphasis in the entrepreneurial course(s) you took?

_____

_____

(Please turn over this sheet and answer appropriate sections of Part II).

PART II. BUSINESS EXPERIENCE

A. If you started your own business since college (or took over an existing business), please answer questions 1-5 immediately below. (If you are not now and have not been an entrepreneur, skip to Section 'B' below.)

1. What is (or was) your job title in the enterprise you started or took over? _____

2. Did you start the business alone? _____. If not, what was the role you played in relation to others? _____

3. How many employees (average) during the year? _____
    At peak period? _____

4. Number of years you have been in this business: _____

5. Your product or service: _____

6. Please list the factors you feel are (or were) most important in determining the success and/or difficulties in this enterprise.

    _____

    _____

    _____

7. Why did you become an entrepreneur? _____

B. If you work for someone else, please answer the following:

8. What is your title and very brief job description? _____

    _____

9. Are you employed in your family's business? _____

10. Do you think it probable that you will have your own business some day?

Circle 1:   Highly Probable   Probable   Some Possibility

               Wish so; Likely not   Probably Not   Almost No Chance

Comment on the reason(s) for you answer if you wish: _____

_____

_____

42

YOUR RESPONSES WILL BE TREATED AS CONFIDENTIAL.   THANK YOU FOR YOUR CO-OPERATION.

If you would like to have a statistical summary of the survey results, please check _____.

A FOLLOW-UP STUDY OF BABSON COLLEGE COURSES

Name:_____

Address:_____

_____

Company Name _____
and Address:

_____

Type of Business:_____

If you had your choice, which of the following would you choose? (Check one)

_____ The job you have now
_____ The same kind of work but with some changes in working conditions or people you work with
_____ A different kind of work entirely

A.   If you started your own business since college (or took over an existing business), please answer question 1-7 immediately below. If you are not now and have not been in your own business, skip to Sections 'B' and 'C' on the back of this sheet.

   1.   What is (or was) your job title in the enterprise you

        started or took over?_____

   2.   Did you start the business alone? _____. If not, what was

        the role you played in relation to others?_____

   3.   How many employees (average) during the year?_____

        At peak periods?_____

   4.   Number of years you have been in this business:_____

   5.   Your product or service:_____

   6.   Please list the factors that you feel are (or were) most important in determining the success and/or difficulties in this interprise.

        _____

        _____

   7.   Why did you start or take over that business?_____

        _____

(If you do not work for someone else, please go directly to section C).

B.   If you <u>work for someone else</u>, please answer the following:

    8.   What is your title and very brief job description?_____

          _____

    9.   Are you employed in your family's business?_____

    10.   Do you think it probable that you will have your own business some day?

Circle 1:   Highly Probable   Probable   Some Possibility
            Wish so; Likely Not Probably Not Almost No Chance

Comment on the reason(s) for your answer if you wish: _____

_____

C.   From your perspective of having taken Babson College courses and having been in the business world several years, please help us by answering the following particularly important questions.

    11.   Did youy courses at Babson produce a change in the direction your career has taken?   YES   NO
    12.   The course(s) most valuable to you in your career?_____

          _____

    13.   Are there areas essential to success in business that you believe should have been given more emphasis in your college courses? If so, please indicate those:

          _____

          _____

    14.   Did you take a course in entrepreneurship while you were a student at Babson College? YES   NO   If yes,   GRAD   or UNDERGRAD?

    15.   If you answered No to 14., please indicate why you did not take a course in entrepreneurship.

          _____

YOUR RESPONSES WILL BE TREATED AS CONFIDENTIAL.   THANK YOU FOR YOUR CO-OPERATION.

If you would like to have a statistical summary of the survey results, please check: _____

5 Aspirations and motivations of would-be entrepreneurs

JOHN RITCHIE, JOHN EVERSLEY AND ALLAN GIBB
Small Business Centre,
Durham University Business School

INTRODUCTION

Improving the rate of new small firm formation has become an important goal towards which industrial and economic policy has been increasingly directed. This reflects the recognition of the vital role of the small business sector in future economic prosperity, not least through the provision of jobs, together with the awareness that one means of re-generating the small business sector as a whole is through an increased level of formation. (Economists Advisory Group, 1978).

So far measures have been aimed primarily at removing the constraints and difficulties thought to face existing small businesses, hence measures have included changes in personal and corporate taxation, financial incentives through regional and industrial support schemes, changes in employment law, and the provision of advice and information through Small Firms Information Centres and Counselling Service. Changes have been proposed in rating, and planning and building regulations in the New Enterprise Zones.

In enacting these measures policy makers are expressing not only the belief that a more favourable climate for existing entrepreneurs will be created but also, by implication, the belief that factors such as personal taxation, and the availability of finance, premises and advice, are capable of stimulating the aspiring entrepreneur to put his or her ideas into effect.

Any review of existing work on entrepreneurship reveals that despite the diversity of disparate disciplines under which the subject has been studied pitifully little is known about that dynamic complex of personal, social, cultural economic and geographical factors which mould the aspiring entrepreneur, nor about his or her aspirations and motivations. An understanding of both would seem of vital importance to policy makers: the former to describe and identify the would be entre-preneur and to provide answers to such questions as 'Which social strata is likely to provide most would be entrepreneurs?' 'What factors encourage them, which inhibit?' 'What will their backgrounds have equipped them for?' 'Where might training needs lie?' and the latter to pinpoint the stimulae which transform ideas into actions.

This paper sheds new light on the aspirations and motivations of the would be entrepreneur. In describing the motivation of those persons striving to put their ideas into effect the evidence reported here, differs significantly from the majority of existing studies of entrepreneurial motivation. Most of the latter are based on studies of those who have translated their ideas into action and, as such, their recall of their desire to go into business will be highly selective. By inference the paper also provides information about the factors capable of influencing the initial aspiration towards entrepreneurship.

THE COMPETITION AND ITS BACKGROUND

The goal of improved national new small firm formation has particular practical significance for economically less prosperous regions like the North. Here the combination of contraction of older, heavier industries and subsequent infusion of newer industry, often in the form of externally owned and directed subsidiaries and branch plants, has been insufficient to absorb and fully utilise the region's productive and employment resources.

In response to this problem Enterprise North was formed in the early 1970's as a grass roots organisation, with the objective of improving the process of new small firm formation in the region. As a system of voluntary panels - which freely advise and counsel the intending starter - Enterprise North aimed to harness the skills of practising managers and other relevant business and professional specialists toward developing new entrepreneurial capability within the region.

Enterprise North, as a grass roots response to the region's problems, naturally attracted considerable outside interest such that further opportunities to develop the intending entrepreneur's start up environment became apparent. As an independent voluntary association Enterprise North alone was not equipped to exploit all these opportunities. Its record was, nevertheless, already such that it helped attract funds and resources sufficient to mount the complementary New Enterprise Development Project at Durham University Business School.

Funds and resources for this subsequent project have come from major industrial sources such as ICI, the Joseph Rowntree Trust, and Shell as well as the Department of Industry. They have enabled the NEDP team to operate full time in dealing with an increasing number of aspiring entrepreneurs and outside agencies and institutions by means of a consultative network which links together many different industrial, governmental, and educational interests alongside the existing Enterprise North system. This remains complementary to the services already provided by an active regional Small Firms Centre.

This whole system was given further impetus by the Shell Small Business Start Up Programme launched in November, 1978. Shell had previously conducted their own research into the problems and prospects for national industrial regeneration in the light of changing economic circumstances and concluded that small firms could make an exceptional contribution to future employment generation. To back this up they sponsored a Build Your Own Business Competition in conjunction with Enterprise North and NEDP, for those seeking to locate and establish new manufacturing and industrial service businesses in the North as part of a general package of measures to help the smaller business. In total the Shell Small Business Start Up Programme comprises the competition together with various specially mounted counselling, support, and education and training events. The competition itself ran from

November, 1978 until final prizes were awarded in June, 1979 and attracted 374 entries. It is the findings from the analyses of these entries which form the basis of this paper.

EXISTING EVIDENCE

It is useful to set the findings from the competition against those of other work upon entrepreneurship. Because entrepreneurship and small business in general have been investigated by researchers from a variety of specialist disciplines, ranging from history, geography, economics to sociology and psychology, it is more meaningful to consider the findings of other work under three headings which seek answers to the following questions:

- the people	- What are their personalities, their educational, social and cultural backgrounds, their skills and occupational experiences and what motivates them?
- the businesses	- What types of businesses are most commonly established and how footloose are they?
- the problems of actually setting up	- How prepared are those who start, what are the major areas of weakness and what determines success or failure?

The people

Research into the backgrounds and identity of entrepreneurs shows that the majority are men, who, through parental, family or friendship connections have some acquaintance with small business practice (Deeks, 1972). Much remains to be discovered about the most potent age group and stage of career development (if any), although several studies identify the 30-40 age group as being the most important. It is suggested that at about this age the individual approaches or enters an unsettling mid-career stage(Schein, 1978).

Early work revealed that entrepreneurs tended to have performed erratically during their school years but more recent evidence from studies in Scotland (Scott, 1975), Japan (Watanabe, 1970) and the USA (Cooper, 1973) all point to an increasing level of educational attainment among entrepreneurs. In particular graduates, especially in applied subjects, are becoming more important.

As regards employment immediately prior to starting a business, a wide variety of occupations are cited. Many entrepreneurs whose route was via managerial roles often began employment as apprentices and stress the importance of their acquisition of practical skills (Scott, 1975). There is, however, increasing evidence that employment in smaller companies provides the most conducive 'incubator' environment for potential entrepreneurs (Johnson, 1978) as such individuals often feel unable to express themselves fully and to use their most valued skills and abilities in larger organisations (Bruce, 1976).

Evidence on the social origins and psychological traits of entrepreneurs, points to possible reasons as to why such individuals may feel 'blocked' and 'frustrated' in employment, particularly in large companies. Entrepreneurs tend to experience feelings of what is termed 'social marginality', that is a lack of affinity to the established major class or cultural groups in society (Stanworth and Curran, 1973). This feeling is often linked with their affiliation to minority religious, political or racial groups. Psychological research suggests that entrepreneurs have strong drives towards individual achievement and independence (McClelland, 1961).

Finally the personality and background of entrepreneurs usually means that the act of starting a business is an iterative one, in which attempts are repeatedly made and the experiences learned from (Mayer and Goldstein, 1961).

The business

Few, new small businesses are really innovative in the technical sense and the exceptions of high technology projects based on research and development spin offs tend only to be common in technologically advanced and highly specialised environments, as for example found in Silicon Valley and other science parks in the USA (Rothwell and Zegveld, 1979).

The majority of new small businesses are formed in those sectors of the economy where costs of entry are low and in which small firms are numerous (Firn and Swales, 1978). The tertiary or service sectors are currently attractive in these respects, since entry into these areas requires less complex technical, human, managerial and financial resources (Gershuny, 1978).

In general terms, therefore, research suggests that the majority of start ups take place with limited resources, in rudimentary and unsophisticated premises and in locations familiar to the entrepreneur. The last mentioned is further supported by evidence that new entrepreneurs, and small businessmen in general, show limited social and geographical mobility and the former are often actively committed to remaining in certain localities (Scott, 1975).

The problems of setting up

Whilst there is little information about the length of time over which potential entrepreneurs develop their ideas, i.e. "the gestation period", research suggests that initial planning is very selective, lacks real rigour and displays limited anticipation of critical marketing and financial problems. Furthermore, until recently many new entrepreneurs appeared to make little use of, or contact with, agencies which could highlight these deficiencies. The result of the lack of prior market research or advertising is often an initial high dependence on few customers. Whilst the limited resources of personal and family savings and inputs from friends are relied on to provide finance, with banks and funding agencies regarded either as unco-operative or capable of imposing terms threatening the entrepreneur's control and independence (Economists Advisory Group, 1978).

In general the financial, administrative and managerial resources required to run a new business are not appreciated to the full. Hence it is hardly surprising that many new entrepreneurs feel fully stretched in meeting only their existing customers' demands and feel particularly constrained by lack of time, resources, and money (Mayer and Goldstein, 1961). Such pressures occur at a time when entry into the role of proprietor has usually shattered previous life patterns.

It is hardly surprising, therefore, that most studies show that very few new small firms survive more than five years. No single determinant of success or failure has so far been identified; however a study by Hoad and Rosko (1964) suggests that variations in managerial ability are highly significant, with failures often lacking in marketing ability and knowledge, and successful entrepreneurs able to combine education and experience and to diversify their skills through the acquisition of partners or teams.

THE FINDINGS FROM THE COMPETITION

At the time of writing this paper only the general findings from all of the competition entrants can be discussed. Fuller details about personal backgrounds, occupational origins and motivations are currently being obtained from a follow up investigation of 61 of the entrants. The findings from the competition will be discussed under the same headings as used to describe existing evidence about entrepreneurs.

The people

The view that the aspiration towards entrepreneurship is still predominantly masculine was supported by the analysis of the competition entrants. The overwhelming majority (90 per cent) were men, 76 per cent were married men with single women comprising only 4 per cent of the entrants. As Table 1 indicates over a third of the contestants were in the age group most commonly associated with the unsettled mid-career stage i.e. 31 to 40 age group.

Table 1
Age distribution of the entrants

Age Groups	Percentage of Entrants
Up to 18	1
19 to 30	26
31 to 40	36
41 to 55	28
Over 55	6
Unspecified	3

Other studies have suggested that the educational attainment of entrepreneurs may be increasing. This study confirmed that notion: 71 per cent of the contestants had received some higher education beyond secondary school and 47 per cent claimed graduate or professional qualifications. The educational attainment of the entrants were to some degree reflected in their occupational backgrounds. Table 2 demonstrates the predominance of contestants with managerial and professional and technical backgrounds. These two categories accounted for more than 55 per cent of the contestants.

Table 2
Occupational Backgrounds of the Entrants

Occupational Groups	Percentage of Entrants
Student/Trainee	5
Manual	15
Nursing	1
Clerical/Secretarial	5
Sales Representative	6
Professional and Technical	37
Supervisory and Administrative	11
Managerial	18
Other	2

Given the manner in which the competition was publicised and the need to complete a comprehensive proposal form it might have been expected that most interest in the competition would have come from the more literate and better informed managerial, professional or technical person. Nevertheless the very large number of entries from this group was not expected. The working class element, traditionally very important in the social structure of the Northern Region, was not much in evidence among the contestants. On the basis of work by others, two reasons can be suggested for the occupational and social class bias among competition entrants: firstly, it may be that manual workers have difficulty in abstracting and articulating on paper their aspirations, and secondly, the level of education and literacy may in itself be an important factor influencing the motive to organise. The entry form did not, however, provide any information as to whether those in managerial and professional and technical occupations had progressed from manual or craft occupations. This aspect is being studied in the follow up investigation.

Although it was not always possible to classify categorically the employment status of all contestants, it appeared that just over two-thirds were in employment and a further 20 per cent stated that they were self employed. The small number of entries received from those who were unemployed supports the view that few move into entrepreneurship in this way.

The level of previous experience of either starting or running a business appeared to be particularly high among the contestants. In addition to those who were self employed a further 42 per cent claimed such experience, thus supporting the iterative nature of entrepreneurship.

Given their backgrounds what was the personal attraction of small business to those who entered the competition? The most prominent reasons stated related to independence, self-development and work satisfaction (56 per cent). It was clear that for many these needs were not being fulfilled in their existing employment situations. Indeed, many appeared to have reached a stage in their life where they had become increasingly concerned with the 'quality' of their working life. For some (19 per cent) the new business was seen as a natural extension or progression from their past experience. A very small proportion, only 6 per cent, mentioned the desire to make money or generate income as the attraction. Thus for the vast majority of contestants starting a small business was seen as providing an opportunity, not so much to make money, but more to realise greater personal independence, self development and work satisfaction.

The business

As anticipated, the number of highly innovative proposals was low: only 14 per cent claimed to have progressed into the patenting of their idea. Neither was the concentration of proposals in the service sectors, as indicated in Table 3, entirely unexpected.

Table 3
Target Industries of the Entrants

Industrial Sector	Percentage of Entrants	
Primary Sector		
Mining and Extractive	2	
Food	4	} 6
Manufacturing and Construction Sector		
Mechanical Engineering	5	
Electrical Engineering	6	
General Plastics and Containers	5	
Furniture/Timber	4	
Clothing	2	
Safety Equipment	2	} 36
Equipment for the Disabled	1	
General (unspecified) Manufacturing	6	
Civil Engineering	1	
Building	4	
Tertiary and Service Sector		
Fashion Design	4	
Design and provision of Crafts, Toys and Sports	8	
Photography, Printing, Publishing	5	
Motor Vehicle Servicing	4	
Hotel/Catering	3	} 58
Tourism	2	
Consultancy	3	
General and Unspecified Services	29	

What the competition did reveal, however, was that the boundary between manufacturing and service sector activities appeared to be much more fluid and flexible than has hitherto been suggested. Many of the contestants wishing initially to provide a service, had as their ultimate goal manufacturing. This was particularly true for those planning to undertake design activities. In many respects service activities could be seen as providing a valuable training ground before launching into manufacturing.

The competition unearthed few footloose entrepreneurs, i.e. those located in other regions who were prepared to relocate in the Northern Region. Over 80 per cent of the 374 contestants came from Northern England, that is the Northern Region together with Yorkshire and Lancashire, with 60 per cent coming from the North East. These findings would appear to support views mentioned earlier concerning the limited geographical mobility of entrepreneurs; however no information about length of residence in the North was collected.

The problems of setting up

How well equipped through past experience and training were the contestants and what appeared to be the major problems that they would be most likely to encounter in starting up? As indicated earlier nearly two-thirds of the entrants claimed previous experience of starting or running a business or were self employed. Comparatively few contestants however, had received any formal management training: two-thirds had received no management training and only 14 per cent had studied management to some formal qualification level and this was often as part of another course.

The business plans and proposals put forward by many of the contestants suggested that there may have been considerable gaps between what they believed they had gained from previous experience and their actual abilities to face the problems of start up. It was suggested earlier that the initial planning undertaken by many entrepreneurs is highly selective and lacks rigour. This certainly appeared to be the case with a large proportion of the contestants. Many proposals (44 per cent) did not include any explicit statment of cash flow; others lacked precision, despite the fact that 89 per cent of the contestants believed that they were able to understand balance sheets.

In general there appeared to be considerable discrepancies between projected capital requirements and availability, and whilst the majority of the contestants claimed that making money was not the primary attraction of starting a new business their lack of awareness of financial requirements could have proved crucial to the realisation of their ambitions.

The competition did not yield any explicit information on how far the contestants had undertaken any systematic market research. Many contestants however, had thought about the aspects upon which they could compete. Nonprice factors such as quality, availability and service were quoted by two-thirds of the entrants as being the predominant incentive for customers to buy their products or services, whilst half of the remainder quoted other factors as being equally as important as price.

The failure of many contestants to undertake adequate financial planning could not be wholly attributed to the length of time they had spent developing their ideas. As Table 4 indicates only 17 per cent had spent less than 12 months and more than 40 per cent had spent more than two years developing their projects.

Table 4
Development time of entrants' projects

Time Period	Percentage of Entrants
Less than 6 months	17
7 months to 1 year	20
1 to 2 years	21
2 to 5 years	17
5 years plus	13
Unspecified	12

The results of the competition suggest that the gestation period of many new business ideas is considerable. Undoubtedly the competition attracted a cross section of projects at widely different stages of development, (although there were surprisingly few proposals which exhibited a completely raw idea). The length of the gestation period appeared to be a function of a number of factors including the degree of innovation of the idea, the scale of the project, the entrant's resources, his motivation and his level of knowledge of factors likely to affect the viability of the project.

Entrants were asked to comment on what they thought would be the major problems which they would encounter in setting up. Marketing and financial aspects were the two most frequently mentioned specific problems (Table 5). The relatively low proportion who envisaged that they would encounter capital or cash flow problems may have been a reflection of the failure to undertake adequate financial planning.

Table 5
Problems anticipated by entrants

Type of Problem	Percentage of Entrants
None	10
Marketing	23
Capital/Cash Flow	20
Equipping and setting up	8
Premises	6
Staff	7
General	22
Other	4

The inadequacy of financial planning together with the perception of future marketing problems suggest that many contestants needed to develop the business and commercial sides of their projects. This may have been particularly true for those who claimed to have progressed their ideas to the design stage (46 per cent) or to have developed prototypes (42 per cent). Against this however, the large number of respondents willing to take partners (83 per cent) may have been some indication of their awareness of their own limitations in these areas.

THE IMPLICATIONS FOR POLICY FROM THE RESEARCH

This study has a number of important implications for policy which stem from the awareness of three characteristics of the start up process:

- it is part of the process of personal development

- it is a developmental process often taking a considerable length of time

- it is a social process in which whilst economic motivations and influences may not be of prime importance, economic constraints can be crucial.

A process of personal development

(a) Whilst the majority of contestants were motivated by desires for self fulfilment, for many, their background experience and training had not equipped them with the abilities needed for starting and running a business. The gaps in this respect point quite clearly to policy implications for training. These training needs are in part being met by, for example, the Manpower Services Commission's entrepreneur development programmes and to a lesser extent by the counselling services provided by the Small Firms Counselling Service and in the Northern Region by Enterprise North and the New Enterprise Development Project.

(b) Because the aspiration towards entrepreneurship appears to be more personally than business or commercially orientated there is a need to bring the would be entrepreneur to the point of acknowledging his own shortcomings and identifying his training needs. In some respects this would argue for an intermediary mechanism to interact between the would be entrepreneur and the training agencies and institutions.

The need for such interaction may be even greater between the aspiring entrepreneur and the funding and assisting institutions. The latter are quite obviously interested in the degree of fit between the person and the project. However, such institutions need to be able to disentangle the project which is being presented to them from the personality of the presenter and any deficiencies in abilities which he or she might have.

The importance of this lies in the fact that clear distinctions can be made between a good business idea, a good financial projection and a good business proposal. The last should incorporate the previous two. However, whilst the first mentioned is a necessary requirement for a sound business a good financial proposal alone, is not. It is important that the would be entrepreneur is not deterred by lack of technical abilities which can probably be remedied by appropriate training.

(c) The extremely personal nature of entrepreneurial aspirations and the resultant close relationship between the idea and the ego has implications for the design of policies aimed at 'teasing out' the entrepreneur. The competition itself demonstrated one successful strategy in offering: first, circumstances designed to encourage the would be starter, without pressure, to think out his proposal; second, building on this by a process of support from peers (Enterprise North and the Counselling Service) in a friendly atmosphere; widening the relevant horizon by the introduction of the entrepreneur to a variety of relevant assisting institutions in circumstances where he could make personal contact; and the encouragement of the setting of targets which represent small commitments within his capability.

It can be argued that given the employment situation in regions like the North where large enterprises are running down their manpower that such approaches may be successfully mounted internally for those facing redundancy.

(d) The occupational and social class bias of the contestants in a region in which manual workers predominate raises important questions about basic education. In the long run the health of the small firm sector may depend on the direction of, and emphasis placed in, the general education system.

A developmental process

(a) The findings on the length of time that individuals may nurse and develop their ideas indicates that there may be considerable scope for creating artificial incubator environ-ments in which this process, may be speeded up. Again, the Manpower Services Commission sponsored New Enterprise Programmes provide but one example of how this may be achieved.

(b) Of wider interest is the finding that many of those intending to set up in a service activity had as an ultimate goal manufacturing and that this movement was part of a long term strategy. This emphasises the potential danger of official policy concentrating too strongly on manufacturing and ignoring the fact that the service sector may provide a useful training ground for individuals with limited experience and resources, who may later move into manufacturing.

A social process

As suggested at the outset of this paper much offical industrial policy has focused on creating the right climate for entrepreneurs largely through the provision of financial inducements. The findings from the competition indicate that only a minority of would be entrepreneurs are attracted primarily by the desire to make money, rather it is the desire to achieve personal fulfilment which is paramount.

And yet financial aspects cannot be entirely ignored; money is undoubtedly important in assisting the would be entrepreneur to overcome constraints and to ease his transition into entrepreneurship. Whilst financial inducements have been assumed to exert influence, financial support may have been ignored. In as much as many aspiring entrepreneurs enjoy secure and reasonably well paid employment the 'opportunity costs' to the individual and the risks incurred when moving to entrepreneurship are great and have probably increased significantly in recent years. If, for economic reasons would be entrepreneurs are to be encouraged to make the transition then there is an argument for taking steps to reduce this opportunity cost to the individual. One possible means of help could come by launching new companies with existing company support during the start up stage. In addition existing security arrangements could become better adapted to help would be entrepreneurs maintain their families alongside the needs of the business.

CONCLUSIONS

The findings from the competition tended to confirm the findings of other studies: the majority of the contestants were male, who were entering an unsettled mid career stage between the ages of 31 and 40; few projects were innovatory and most were in the services sector; and the planning, particularly in respect of finance, undertaken by a large proportion of contestants was selective and inadequate. Important implications for policy are seen to arise out of the findings in that the overwhelming attraction of entrepreneurship was to achieve personal fulfilment, that this attraction was expressed largely by employed persons who came from occupations associated with higher levels of educational qualifications, that for a significant number the desire to undertake service activities was a stepping stone in a longer term strategy which led to manufacturing, that the gestation period for business ideas is often very long and that for many there were considerable gaps between their experience and training and the abilities and skills needed to run a business.

Several areas have been identified as requiring policy initiatives; helping the would be entrepreneur identify his training needs, helping assisting agencies disentangle the project from the personality and possible deficiencies of the person presenting it, other approaches for teasing out would be entrepreneurs, and the question of incubator environments. However the questions, the answers to which remain crucial, as reflections of the degree to which this society values the entrepreneur, are those of the values incalcated through the general education system and the provision of financial support during the transition stage.

REFERENCES

Bruce, R., The Entrepreneurs: Strategies, Motivation, Successes and Failures. Liberation Books, Bedford. 1976
Cooper A. C., 'Technological Entrepreneurship: What do we know?' R/D Management. vol.3, no.2, 1973, pp. 59-64.
Deeks, J., 'The Educational and Occupational Histories of Owner Managers and Managers.' Journal of Management Studies vol. IX, 1972, pp. 123-149.
Economists Advisory Group, Evidence to the Committee to Review the Functioning of the Financial Institutions E.A.G. London. 1978.
Firn, J. R. and Swales, J. K., 'The Formation of New Manufacturing Enterprises in the Central Clydeside and West Midlands Connurbations 1963-1972: A comparative Analysis' Regional Studies vol.12, no.1, 1978, pp. 199-213.
Gershuny, J. After Industrial Society: The Emerging Self Service Economy. MacDonald, London. 1978.

Hoad, W. H. and Rosko, P., Success and Failure of New Small Manufacturers. University of Michigan. 1964.

Johnson, P. S., 'New Firms and Regional Development: Some Issues and Evidence Centre for Urban and Regional Development, Newcastle University,' Discussion Paper no.11. 1978.

McClelland, D. C., The Achieving Society Van Nostrand, Princeton. 1961.

Mayer, H. and Goldstein S., The First Two Years: Problems of Small Firm Survival and Growth. SBA Washington. 1961.

Rothwell, R. and Zegveld, W., 'The Role of Small Manufacturing, Enterprises in Innovation: An Overview of Recent Research Planned Innovation. no.1, 1979, pp. 3-5.

Schein, E., Career Dynamics, Addison - Wesley, New York. 1978.

Scott, M. Entrepreneurs and Entrepreneurship: A Study of Enterprise Founding. Unpublished Ph.D. Thesis, University of Edinburgh. 1975.

Stanworth, M.J.H., and Curran, J., Management Motivation in the Smaller Business. Gower Press, London. 1973.

Watanabe, S., 'Entrepreneurship in Small Enterprises in Japanese Manufacturing.' International Labour Review. vol. 102, no.6, 1970, pp. 531-576.

6 Models and approaches to teaching entrepreneurship

TOM MILNE AND JOHN LEWIS
Department of Management Studies,
University of Glasgow

INTRODUCTION

Enterprise is a quality possessed by everyone. The extent to which it will find expression in the creation of successful businesses is related to the values of society, which may or may not encourage or reward such activity. The application of the quality of enterprise to the creation of a business is the phenomenon which we call entrepreneurship. Entrepreneurial activity can be seen to vary substantially from society to society and from time to time within a society. There are, assuming the human remains fairly constant, three possible explanations for this:

> First, social and economic rewards and penalties for the activity may vary from place to place.

> Second, cultural factors may enhance or inhibit the desire to express enterprise in a business context.

> Third, the tasks of developing a business may become more or less complex, demanding greater or lesser skill and commitment. Arguably the tasks have become more complex in the developed world over the past century or two.

The first of these explanations implies that the economy is being run in such a way that two effects are manifest. First the economy should be providing a steady stream of commercial opportunities: the larger the stream, the higher the probability of successful entrepreneurship. This effect will arise from a steady growth state, which has been relatively lacking in Britain as a whole and has been seriously deficient in the more northerly regions. Second, the economy should provide rewards commensurate with the skills, the complexity of the task, and the importance of the achievement implied by successful entrepreneurship. In this respect we would argue that Britain offers adequate incentives and the economic rewards for successful entrepreneurship are very high indeed.

Entry of talented people into entrepreneurship appears to be culturally influenced and certainly in Scotland there is a strong middle-class antipathy towards manufacturing entrepreneurship. Professional, financial or agricultural entrepreneurship - setting up in private practice as an estate agent or insurance broker, or becoming a farmer appear to be socially sanctioned, and shopkeeping is an 'approved' occupation at sub-professional levels: but there undoubtedly exists a curious and totally irrational social denigration of the status of the manufacturer. To be 'in trade' is to be at the bottom of the social pile.

Since education and training are one influence upon our culture, the question we are interested in becomes one of whether the education system is capable of doing two jobs - first, overcoming the cultural disincentives to entrepreneurship implicit in an inhibitively settled society, and second providing a grounding in the skills necessary to translate the entrepreneurial drive into successful and effective businesses.

The concern which underlies this paper arises from the entrepreneurial decline in Scotland witnessed during the 20th century and especially the post-war period, coupled with the question as to whether some set of educational activities, relevant to the business schools, have a role in helping arrest or even reversing this declining trend.

To explore the possibilities of training for entrepreneurship we need to recognise that the particular strength of formal education is in the transmission of didactic knowledge, skills and techniques to people who have recognised that for some purpose they require this knowledge and these skills. What universities and higher education colleges are good at is the training of doctors, engineers, teachers and the like. They have only recently begun to become involved with managers, in which their success is far from being beyond question. Entrepreneurship represents even more particular problems to the teacher. The question of this paper is, are we yet in a position to identify skills, knowledge and techniques which entrepreneurs can learn from teachers so as to make them more effective entrepreneurs? In other words, is there anything worthwhile which can be done in the classroom?

THE SCOTTISH ENVIRONMENT FOR ENTREPRENEURSHIP

There are a number of features in the Scottish business environment and in its economic development which effectively differentiate it from the remainder of the United Kingdom. Of paramount importance, perhaps, is the distance of the region from the main centres of consumption in England and Europe, and from the main centres of policy making in Brussels, Luxembourg, Strasbourg and London. The region has, however, enjoyed semi-autonomous government for several generations, with particularly strong powers in local economic development led by the Scottish Economic Development Division of the Scottish Office. Since the Second World War, business has sponsored the Scottish Council (Development and Industry) as an economic development pressure group, which has worked in close alliance with the Scottish Trades Union Congress to influence Government industrial location policy. In the 1950's and 1960's the combined efforts of these agencies led to the region being the most successful in Europe in attracting immigrant industry. Scotland, and especially West Central Scotland, has been extremely heavily discriminated in favour of. As a result, regional economic catastrophe has been stayed off, but by no means totally obviated. In the 70's the Scottish Development Agency was created with a specific role for industrial development as well as for environmental

rehabilitation.   One division of the Agency is the Small Business
Division.

In addition to the needs of the Region generally, the specific
development needs of the Highlands and Islands have been recognised by
the creation of a Highlands and Islands Development Board, which has
been conspicuously successful in supporting appropriate small business
development.

A further distinctive aspect of the Region's development potential has
been the existence of a separate and highly developed banking system and
capital market.   There are three major joint stock banks with head
offices in Scotland and Edinburgh, and to a lesser extent Glasgow, have
for long been major autonomous financial centres.   An important expression of this has been the existence of regionally based financial,
investment and unit trusts, created with capital accumulated from 19th
century business ventures, many of them overseas, for which alternative
business investment possibilities could not be found.   In the last two
decades, some of this capital has been used to create indigenous
merchant banks.

As a result there has been a long-standing phenonemon of a surplus of
supply of capital in relation to indigenous business development
opportunities.   It would be extremely difficult to assert that within
Scotland at any time in this century that business development has been
hampered by non-availability in the Region of the appropriate level or
form of institutional investment funds. On the other hand, the case has
been made that there has been a shortage of the small amounts of
privately owned 'seedcorn' capital required to launch small new ventures.   Here the argument is that in Scotland there is a very much
higher proportion of public authority housing than elsewhere, with the
result that the prospective small entrepreneur is less likely to have
the security of a house to back his initial capital requirement. To the
extent that one accepts the view that one of the most fruitful sources
of small enterprise is likely to be the disoatioficd working class
striver, this could conceivably be a significant inhibitor.

The picture of regional business development with which we are
dealing, then, is one in which, either because of lack of economic and
market opportunity, or because of a social and cultural/historical
interaction, leading to poor management and disaffected workers, the
pre-existent indigenous enterprises have had a very long history of
failure to survive, while the economic balance has been redressed at a
policy level by encouraging immigration of large manufacturing
establishments controlled from England or abroad. Meanwhile the surplus
of capital available in the region has been employed in world wide
portfolio investment rather than in regional business development.

The foregoing description is consistent with one of the findings of
Michael Scott (1976), that business formation in Scotland appears to be
below the U.K. average.   It also fits with the studies by David Storey
(1979) which indicate that a 'Branch Factory' economy can inhibit the
creation of indigenous entrepreneurial ones.

Scott (1976) and Michael Cross (1979)(1) also appear to be suggesting
that in Scotland it is harder to distinguish the "special breed" aspect
of entrepreneurs than has been asserted by a number of the more evan-

gelical authors, or has been uncovered by some of the well established findings of, for example, Smith (1967) or Stanworth and Curran (1973). The evidence we have been able to gather generally appears to support the Scott and Cross view, leaving aside only the obvious case of immigrant entrepreneurs. It is not necessary to develop highly discriminating psycho-sociological models to identify this phenonemon, although from a world-wide point of view, other scholars might be interested in those dimensions as an explanatory factor in the decision to emigrate.

Here again, of course, Scotland provides an interesting case, as a net exporter of population for over a century and more, many of whom deployed enormous entrepreneurial energy in the lands of their reception.

If, in Scotland, there have been relatively few entreprenuers, there have been, arguably, even fewer who have achieved full scale success for their businesses. There are numerous possible ways of defining success: one is that the firm should be capable of autonomous development and existence in the absence of the entrepreneur: in other words that in his or her lifetime a business should have been created which is capable of capitalising itself and continuing to develop under professional management. We have been able to identify only very few businesses in Scotland which have achieved this standard from a starting position of nothing in the post World War Two era.

With the growth of official interest in new and small business support systems, various local authorities, particularly in West Central Scotland, have endeavoured to make themselves more attractive to small businesses. The building of small units for short lets has been one successful development, initially started by British Steel Industries and since followed by Clydebank District. The introduction of venture workshops, where a potential entrepreneur can try out his idea at little cost, and receive technical or development assistance, in the Strathclyde Region and Glasgow Districts has encouraged entrepreneurs to come forward. The availability of managerial assistance at the various stages of development, from start-up onwards has also been a consistent feature of these schemes.

At the Clyde Workshops; a complex of 60 small companies, the combination of short lease, management assistance and common secretarial services has uncovered a large demand for this low risk start type of facility (over 300 serious applications have been rejected).

The Scottish Development Agency provides three main services to small companies, premises, loan finance for buildngs and other fixed assets, and a limited consultancy service. These services are largely complementary to the other initiatives being more suitable often for existing companies. An Industrial Development Division is further prepared to invest in small companies with good growth prospects and hence encourage the transition towards success in our terms, of long term viability.

For several of the local authority initiatives the managerial or consultancy input has been provided by the Scottish Business School, based on Glasgow, Edinburgh and Strathclyde Universities. The School is, however, particularly suited to the higher growth opportunities rather than operational assistance with accounts or factory organisa-

tion. This does not imply high technology, we have seen from Scott
(1976) that this is not a likely road to success, but does involve high
commercial innovation. Previous attempts at technological development,
such as the Strathclyde Centre for Industrial Innovation have been less
successful at meeting commercial needs with academic input. We have,
therefore, concentrated. The recent efforts of the school have therefore
been concentrated on training those entrepreneurs capable of
development.

Innovation on the grand scale is increasingly a big business peroga-
tive and the scope for entrepreneurial activity lies in commercial
rather than technological innovation. The number of Scottish high
technology, successful innovators is minimal: the best known example,
Nuclear Enterprises of Edinburgh, seems unlikely to meet our criterion
of lasting success defined above. National cases might best be
exemplified by Sinclair Electronics. We are prepared to leave this
topic with the assertion that high-technology based enterprise is the
business of big business or Government, and therefore the province of
scholars other than ourselves. We accept that just very occasionally a
genius will show that, like all generalisations, the foregoing one is
deficient.

From this analysis we would expect to find that the majority of
innovations upon which commercially successful new enterprises were
founded were based upon service or commercial innovations. As we shall
shortly see, this is very strongly borne out by the companies which we
have so far identified.

Our experience is that successful small company formations and
developments are unlikely to be associated with technological innovation
or invention. This must be contrasted with two phenomena: first, the
cultural belief that production is to be preferred to other forms of
economic activity, most recent manifestation of which was the Wilson
Administration's deeply harmful Selective Employment Tax. And second,
the situation in which Local and National Government Authorities in
their policy instruments, through provision of investment incentives and
factory and workshop provision, are pursuing ends which may be running
against a real tide. The deepseated culture favouring manufacturing is
not well reflected in the realities of contemporary Scottish business
development. The successes we can identify are predominantly in
services, although not exclusively.

motivation
INCENTIVES TO ENTREPRENEURSHIP

Entrepreneurship is one avenue open to the individual who is
dissatisfied with, or alienated from, the combination of security,
frustration and mediocre economic performance implicit in working for
others. Generally it can be pursued independently of, or in conjunction
with, other strategies designed to provide greater self-fulfilment such
as emigration or adoption of ecologically-based lifestyles. Successful
entrepreneurship offers a unique combination of psychological and
economic rewards, combining individual growth and fulfilment with high
net income and the creation of substantial personal capital for the
benefit of heirs. The incentives, indeed, are so overwhelming, that the
question to be explored should be, not why do people become entrepreneurs, but, why do they not do so?

65

It might be hypothesised that fear of penalty for failure is a sufficient disincentive. If this is so, then people's perceptions are out of line with the realities of small business failure. Even serious bankruptcies may provide only a limited economic setback to the owners provided that they have secured limited liability.

One of the things we should be able to educate for is how entrepreneurs can protect themselves and their families properly against the potentially severely damaging consequences of failure. A harder job might be to convince potential but frightened entrepreneurs that such protection can be obtained and can be effective.

Perhaps a more fundamental inhibitor is lack of economic opportunity. The evangelist for entrepreneurship, who is inclined to fall back on act of faith, asserts that there is always an opportunity if you have the ability to see it, and that the slackness of large organisations will always leave gaps in the marketplace. We have already argued that there is very limited scope for individual technological entrepreneurship in Britain because existing manufacturers are already substantially satisfying the marketplace (many of them from abroad), and that Government mismanagement of our economy and labour relations over the best part of half a century have produced conditions inimical to high achievement in manufacturing. The majority of economic opportunities involving a scale of capital available to the individual or small team starting out will be in the service industries. The cause of entrepreneurship cannot be helped by the policy emphasis upon manufacturing incentives.

After discounting the possible economic inhibitors, it is difficult to avoid the conclusion that there is a more deep-seated set of inhibitors to entrepreneurship at work in the region: we take into account a feeling that young people are conditioned not to develop their lives on a basis of the model of self employment, unless they already come from self employed homes. It would be difficult to overestimate the importance of a set of inhibitors of this sort, backed up by early parental conditioning, a puritan/Marxist basis for moral values, and reinforced throughout childhood by formal education patterns.

The salience of such factors in inhibiting entrepreneurial drive is central to the model needed to establish the kind of education appropriate to entrepreneurship, and in this our argument depends heavily upon the idea put forward by Leveson (1979) at the Ashridge Conference and the conclusions of Gibb in the papers presented elsewhere in this book. This is an area in which we must seek in order to see how to generate a larger population of entrepreneurs.

One possible argument is that the regional culture is one which fails to produce a high-acheivement motivation, following McClelland's (1961) model. Some unpublished work by Carruthers in the University of Glasgow suggests that such a view of early cultural influence would be an oversimplification, at least as far as the present generation of middle managers is concerned. In interviewing managers on courses in the University of Glasgow, Carruthers found that they had exceptionally high achievement motivations, and also exhibited high levels of frustration. The problem, it seems, is not to create the achievement motivation, but to channel it into entrepreneurship. Our own concern, however, is not primarily with the antecedents of entrepreneurship so much as with the effectiveness of the entrepreneur in creating a viable business as a significant contributor to economic activity. In this, we share a similar set of concerns to those described by Ritchie, Eversley and Gibb elsewhere in this book.

MODELS OF ENTREPRENEURIAL SUCCESS

Our studies have adopted as a central focus the problems of measuring and predicting entrepreneurial success, and we have concentrated upon examining successful entrepreneurs and their companies. We started from two points of view: the first was a tentative adoption of the Smith model of craftsmen and opportunist people, combined with rigid or flexible organisations.

For readers unfamiliar with Smith's (1967) findings, these may be summarised by saying that he was able to partition the entrepreneurial population into "opportunist" type people who founded "flexible" organisations and "craftsman" type people who founded "rigid" organisa- tions. In the words of his own conclusion,

"A startling contrast between the growth of these two groups" is observed. The craftsman rigid achieves sales after an average life of 9.5 years (implying higher mortality) of $535,551, while the opportunist - flexible achieves sales of $5,896,437 after 11.9 years average (implying lower mortality). The groupings on which this is based are shown in Figure 1.

The second starting point was a very pragmatic view that the best people to tell us how to be a successful entrepreneur were successful entrepreneurs, and that since we knew so little about entrepreneurship, and had such poor models to test, we had better not structure what they would tell us too much. As a result we are left rather more with impressions than with reportable data. It should be stressed that we were at the hypothesis formulation stage, and a long way short of testing.

Altogether we have recorded interviews with 36 entrepreneurs, conducted by four interviewers, and unrecorded interviews with many more. Before going into detail, it is better to outline our conclu- sions. Most importantly, we can find no evidence that entrepreneurs are a "special breed" except insofar as their situation has put them in a position of social marginality - a phenomenon already adequately analysed in the literature (see for example Stanworth and Curran 1973). Hence to fulfil themselves they have had to display a little more resourcefulness, energy and initiative than most of us have sufficient incentive to do. They started out as perfectly ordinary people. By the time we have interviewed our entrepreneurs we can see that they are special and different, for example, by being more energetic, more resourceful and decisive, better informed, more fulfilled and richer. They became that way, however, by being entrepreneurs. They all assert that they have changed as people as a result of successful entrepren- eurship. We therefore reject the Messianic models of entrepreneurship.

The second major finding which emerges from interviewing our success- ful entrepreneurs is that, knowing all too little about what they were

Figure 1
The Entrepreneurial Types and the Firm Types Plotted on a Rectangular Coordinate System

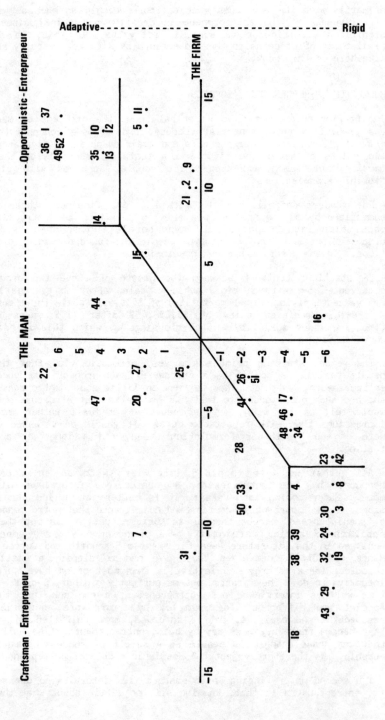

doing as they set out, and making a wide range of mistakes, they very rapidly developed a portfolio of knowledge in two fields: first, the product or service techniques and technologies appropriate to their business, and second the business of being a businessman. We have no evidence that deficiencies in either side were greater or lesser than the other.

We are also prepared to make certain other assertions with reasonable confidence, although we have not tested them in detail. Entrepreneurs do not take risks: in fact, they are risk avoiders. Entrepreneurship is not a gamble. Entrepreneurs are idealistic, gaining more satisfaction from their contributions to the economy, society and technology than from the economic rewards they obtain for themselves. The individual reward appears to be the challenge successfully overcome.

The foregoing assertions are based upon the findings of four approaches to the study: first, the findings in the nature of entrepreneurship reported in the literature, second, informal or semi-structured interviews or meetings by the authors with 12 entrepreneurs of proven success, third, semi-structured interviews by two of our graduate students, R. A. Scott and M. Gilroy, the former attempting to isolate entrepreneurs in Smith's (1967) opportunist category and the latter investigating impediments to growth in essentially craftsman-based organisations. Both successfully completed twelve cases, using the open-ended unstructured interview technique. Respondents were selected by ourselves, Scott and Gilroy on a basis of personal and local knowledge of successful entrepreneurial companies and their owners.

In conducting the initial set of interviews, our concern was to try to learn what was the "magic ingredient" which made successful the entrepreneurs who were manifestly successful. We were most conscious of Smith's opportunist/ flexible-craftsman/rigid dichotomy, and we began by finding the most successful entrepreneurs we could, in the expectation that their interview responses would be easily plotted as high on the opportuniot/flexible quadrant.

This process immediately began to produce two results. It quickly became clear that the psycho- and socio-metric variables used by Smith to describe his entrepreneurs and their organisations appeared to bear only a limited relationship to the phenomena which were emerging from our results. Secondly, although we could identify craftsmen and opportunist starters, the word opportunist seemed to have little relationship with the phenomena we were observing. The opportunist, in Smith's terms, was emerging in our discussions as no more than a commercially orientated, probably well trained and experienced, businessman. We continue to have difficulty in ascribing real meaning to Smith's opportunist concept. We were forced to conclude, in the end, that the concept was less meaningful than we had originally supposed or else our population consisted of non-opportunist individuals. Nevertheless, we could still distinguish different degrees of success amongst the entrepreneurs we were meeting, and this certainly reflected the evolution of phenomena within the organisation such as delegation, readiness and ability to employ professionals, to diversify, and to control finance. Perhaps it would not be insignificant to record in passing a view expressed by certain successful entrepreneurs that the difference between the able entrepreneur who succeeded and the able entrepreneur who failed was an ability to cope with a sudden access of wealth and avoid over indulgence in the elementary temptations of alcohol and gambling.

The impression with which our interviews left us is that if there is one factor differentiating the very successful from the less successful it is flexibility; an ability and willingness to learn, adapt and evolve in response to the success which the individual's business is achieving. All successful entrepreneurs appear to agree that they are changed people as a result of the success of their business. Given that we have difficulty in identifying an opportunist category, we have to fall back substantially on craftsmen but we can perhaps discriminate along the dimensions of ambition and adaptability of the individual leading to growth and adaptability of the organisation.

In particular, it is quite clear that an attribute which the successful entrepreneurs themselves stress is the importance of being able to learn quickly, learn from mistakes, and adapt to changing circumstances.

Robert Scott (1979), himself an entrepreneur, set out in his interview programme to test various models of entrepreneurs against 12 successful entrepreneurs known to him, some as a client relationship. (The general format of Scott's responses is shown in Table 1.) In particular he examined the fit of his entrepreneurs and their organisations against Smith's (1967) model (Table 2) as well as those of Mancuso (1973) (Table 3) Watkins (1978) Bolton (1971) and Stanworth and Curran (1973) (Table 4) and M. Scott (1978) (Table 5). Scott found that in two cases he could not relate the entrepreneurs to Smith's categorisation - one a second generation Polish immigrant, the other a second generation descendant of a Russian Jewish immigrant. These two were Scott's most successful entrepreneurs. It would not be surprising to discover that immigration and being a Jew were particularly important spurs to entrepreneurship in the West of Scotland but would be a less significant discriminator in the American mid west. Scott points out that neither of these were tradesmen or skilled in any formal fashion, and Smith's classification does not allow for this. Otherwise Scott finds a fair degree of consistency in identifying Smith's entrepreneurial types, but where the model breaks down completely is in attempting to relate these to a rigid or flexible type of organisation. The distribution of responses reveals a very poor fit (Table 2), with craftsman, opportunist and unclassifiable types alike exhibiting a high incidence of flexible organisation responses. It should be borne in mind that Scott had set out to interview entrepreneurs in successful companies, expecting them to exhibit opportunist/flexible characteristics. In finding that the flexible organisation type was dominant, and that this could not be related to entrepreneurial characteristics, Scott crystalised our own intuitive interpretation of our pilot interviews.

One sidelight on Scott's findings is the extraordinarily high incidence of deceased fathers of successful entrepreneurs, which has led us to question the whole basis of the "special breed" school of entrepreneurship. If the incidence of childhood parental loss is higher amongst entrepreneurs than in the population generally, then this may be a significant indicator of potential entrepreneurship. It is not, however, sufficient merely to say that the incidence of a trait is high: the "special breed" school requires to demonstrate that the incidence of the special characteristic was significantly greater than in the population as a whole at the time the entrepreneur embarked upon his career. To say, then, that most successful entrepreneurs are ambitious middle class risk avoiders with supportive wives and families may not carry us very far forward. Most of us would at least tell an interviewer that that is how we are. In this case, however, the high incidence of migration and parental death does appear to lend support to the social marginality hypothesis.

Martin Gilroy's interest was in testing the validity of an Engineering Employers Federation (E.E.F.) survey into the effects on growth of the the employment legislation of the last few years. He had a good deal of reason to suspect that the survey was heavily biased to produce an overwhelming answer that growth had been inhibited by employment legislation and other Government activity.

He surveyed 12 entrepreneurial companies of which 11 were in engineering subcontracting and one in electronic engineering. All had participated in the E.E.F. survey. Before ascertaining their responses to the E.E.F. survey he partitioned his respondents using the Smith methodology. Of his 12 respondents, five were **very** strongly 'craftsmen-rigids', three were strongly 'craftsmen rigid', two were borderline 'craftsmen/opportunist', but strongly rigid, and two were 'opportunist/adaptive'.

Gilroy found that the eight strongly 'craftsmen rigid' entrepreneurs had all claimed in the E.E.F. survey that growth had been restricted by high taxation, difficult trading conditions or employment legislation, the three environmental factors being assessed. Three companies instanced one factor, three two factors, and two three factors in restricting their growth. The two borderline companies reported that their growth was restricted only by the owners' managerial ambition. Of the two 'opportunist-adaptive' entrepreneurs, the one less strongly so cited difficult trading conditions as a deterrent to growth, but the one strongly 'opportunist-adaptive' company reported that growth had not been hampered by any of the factors instanced, and was, indeed being actively pursued.

We can draw two tentative conclusions from Gilroy's study: first, that the population of engineering entrepreneurs in West Central Scotland is unlikely to generate growth companies, and second that we should not take too seriously the claims of those who assert that Government policy is hampering small business success. The companies which report the inhibitions are those that the theory suggests are least likely to become viable successes.

When we bring together the set of very successful companies identified by ourselves, the set of successful companies interviewed by Scott, and the set of engineering companies interviewed by Gilroy, 36 entrepreneurial businesses in all, perhaps seven had their start in a clearly identifiable 'opportunist-flexible' mode. In evaluating that number it should be borne in mind that two of the studies were explicitly seeking proven successes, which by Smith's token should have given us a large number of 'opportunist-flexibles'. Instead, six of the 24 are in this category, the seventh having cropped up in the engineering study.

This then has led us to re-evaluate Smith's model in the Scottish context, and the Scottish context in the light of Smith's model.

Table 1
General Format of R.A. Scott's Interviews*

Companies

Characteristic	A	B	C	D	E	F	G	H	I	J	K	L
Name												
Age when started	24	21	23	24	22	22	22	37	41	33	22	32
Own family	3	3	2	2	2	4	2	3	3	2	3	3
Parents:-												
Father dead?	no	yes	no	yes	yes	yes	yes	yes	yes	yes	no	yes
Mother dead?	no	no	no	no	yes	yes	no	no	yes	yes	no	yes
Position in Family	1st	1st	1st	1st	1st	1st	1st	1st	1st	2nd	1st	2nd
Father self-employed	no	yes	no	no	yes	yes	no	yes	no	no	yes	no
Particular management skills	several	several	none	none	none	none	none	good	good	good	good	good
Personal energy	high	high	high	fair	high	fair	high	high	fair	high	high	fair
Family/Wife supportive	total	total	total	fair	fair	poor	fair	fair	total	total	total	total
How long in business - (years)	15 yrs	50 yrs	8 yrs	15 yrs	12 yrs	22 yrs	15 yrs	12 yrs	12 yrs	16 yrs	25 yrs	21 yrs
What goals/ prospects	public	none	public	public	unsure	unsure	unsure	family	family	public	public	family
Views of risk	low	low	low	high	low	low	low	low	low	low	low	low
Rewards - (eventual)	cash	cash	cash	cash	cash security	cash security	cash	cash	cash	cash	cash	cash
Why not work for an employer												

* see case studies in original paper by R.A. Scott

Characteristic

Companies

Characteristic	A	B	C	D	E	F	G	H	I	J	K	L
Commitment to business	total	medium	total	total	total	poor	total	good	good	good	total	total
Finance control	strict	strict	fair	good	strict	fair	fair	strict	strict	fair	strict	strict
Education background	poor	fair	poor	poor	fair	high	poor	high	high	medium	medium	poor
Marketing knowledge:-												
(a) At start	none	none	none	none	none	none	none	none	good	none	good	good
(b) Now	good	good	good	good	good	good	good	good	good	good	good	good
Outside Finance Support	yes	no	no	yes					no	no	yes	no
Administration Skills:-												
(a) At start	fair	none	poor	none	none	fair	none	none	good	good	fair	good
(b) Now	good	good	good	good	good	fair	fair	good	good	good	good	good
Knowledge of Laws and Statutes concerning Business, Employment, etc.:-												
(a) At start	fair	none	none	none	none	none	none	fair				
(b) Now	good	good	fair	gooc	good	good	poor					

*Note: This table shows the relationship between the 12 successful entrepreneurs interviewed by Scott and a number of characteristics suggested in the literature as indicative of success in entrepreneurship.

Table 2

Smith's Criteria in Relation to R.A. Scott's Respondents*

	A	B	C	D	E	F	G	H	I	J	K	L
Craftsman Entrepreneur												
1. Poor at school, educated at evening classes	yes	-	yes	yes	-	-	yes	-	-	yes	-	yes
2. Success at work	yes	-	yes	yes	-	-	yes	-	-	yes	-	yes
3. Skilled tradesman	yes	-	yes	no	-	-	yes	-	-	yes	-	yes
4. Blue-collar background	yes	-	yes	yes	-	-	yes	-	-	yes	-	yes
5. Does not wholly identify with movement or unions	yes	-	yes	yes	-	-	yes	-	-	yes	-	yes
6. Entrepreneurship neccessary for self-idenfication	yes	-	yes	no	-	-	yes	-	-	no	-	no
Opportunistic Entrepreneur												
1. Well educated	-	yes	-	-	no	yes	-	yes	yes	-	no	-
2. Could be manager before becoming entrepreneur	-	yes	-	-	no	no	-	yes	yes	-	yes	-
3. Well connected to top management	-	yes	-	-	no	yes	-	yes	yes	-	no	-
4. Middle class	-	yes	-	-	no	yes	-	yes	no	-	no	-
5. Identifies with top management	-	yes	-	-	no	yes	-	yes	yes	-	yes	-

Types of Organisation Craftsman

	A	B	C	D	E	F	G	H	I	J	K	L
1. Paternalistic	yes	yes	yes	no	yes	yes	no	yes	yes	yes	yes	yes
2. Prefers other marginal people	no	no	don't know	no	yes	no	no	no	no	no	no	no
3. Expects and gives loyalty	yes	yes	yes	no	yes	yes	yes	yes	yes	yes	yes	yes
4. Usually has partners for finance	yes	no	no	yes	no	no	no	yes	no	yes	yes	no
5. Sells through personal contact	no	no	no	no	no	no	no	no	no	yes	no	no
6. Doesn't travel and has limited social life	no	no	no	no	no	no	yes	no	yes	no	no	no
7. Restricted and closed universe	no	yes	no	no	no	no	no	no	no	no	no	no

Opportunistic

	A	B	C	D	E	F	G	H	I	J	K	L
1. Psychologically removed from employees	no	no	no	yes	no	yes	yes	no	no	no	no	no
2. Impersonal objectivity to emotional situation	no	no	no	yes	yes	yes	yes	yes	no	no	no	no
3. Delegates authority quickly and in many ways	yes	no	yes	no	no	yes	no	yes	yes	yes	yes	yes
4. Borrows from outside sources	yes	no	yes	yes	yes	yes	no	yes	no	yes	yes	yes
5. Very active in marketing his company	yes	yes	yes	yes	yes	yes	yes	no	yes	yes	yes	yes
6. Good at communications	yes	yes	no	yes	yes	yes	no	yes	yes	yes	yes	yes
7. Travels widely	yes	no	yes	yes	yes	yes	no	yes	no	yes	yes	yes
8. Meets competition head-on	yes	yes	yes	yes	yes	yes	yes	yes	yes	yes	yes	yes
9. Sees open-ended growths	yes	no	yes	yes	yes	yes	yes	yes	yes	yes	yes	yes
10. Wishes his Company to grow	yes	no	yes	yes	yes	yes	yes	yes	yes	yes	yes	yes
11. Lots of personal involvement	yes	yes	yes	yes	yes	yes	yes	yes	yes	yes	yes	yes

*Note: This table shows the relationship between the 12 successful entrepreneurs interviewed by R.A. Scott and the criteria set up by Norman Smith in his 1967 publication entitled "The Entrepreneur and his Firm".

Table 3

Mancuso's Criteria in Relation to R.A. Scott's Respondents

	A	B	C	D	E	F	G	H	I	J	K	L
1. First or only child	yes	yes	yes	yes	yes	yes	yes	yes	yes	no	yes	no
2. Early 30's (when starting)	24	21	23	24	22	22	22	37	41	33	22	32
3. Father – self employed	no	yes	no	no	yes	yes	no	yes	no	no	yes	no
4. Middle Class	no	yes	no	no	no	yes	no	yes	no	no	no	no
5. Individualist	yes	yes	yes	yes	yes	yes	yes	yes	yes	yes	yes	yes
6. Opportunist	yes	yes	yes	yes	yes	no	yes	yes	yes	yes	yes	yes
7. Views of risk	low	low	low	mod/high	low	low	low	low	low	low	low	low
8. Motivated by idea – not money	yes	yes	yes	no	yes	yes	no	yes	yes	yes	yes	yes
9. Married with supportive wife	yes	yes	yes	no	yes	yes	no	yes	yes	yes	yes	yes
10. Suffer from cognitave dissonance	yes	no	yes	no	yes	no	yes	no	no	no	yes	yes
11. Survive failure	yes	yes	yes	yes	yes	yes	yes	yes	yes	yes	yes	yes

*Note: This table shows the relationship between the 12 successful entrepreneurs interviewed by R.A. Scott and the criteria chosen by J. Mancuso in his publication entitled "The Entrepreneur's Philosophy" (1973 Addison/Wesley).

76

Table 4

Citeria of Watkins*, Bolton, Stanworth and Curran in Relation to R.A. Scott's Respondents

	A	B	C	D	E	F	G	H	I	J	K	L
1. David S. Watkins, Manchester Business School, paper presented at Copen Hagen, May, 1976:-												
(a) Un-successful self-employed father	no	no	no	no	no	no	no	no	no	no	no	no
(b) Interrupted or incomplete education (as perceived by entrepreneur)	yes	yes	yes	yes	no	yes	no	no	yes	no	no	no
(c) Independence	yes	yes	yes	yes	yes	yes	yes	yes	yes	yes	yes	yes
(d) Finance - self	no	yes	yes	yes	yes	yes	yes	yes	yes	yes	yes	yes
2. Bolton Report - H.M.S.O. 1971:-												
Formal Management Training	none	none	none	none	none	none	yes	yes	yes	none	none	none
3. Stanworth and Curran, Management Motivation in the Smaller Business Gower Press 1973:-												
(a) Artisan	yes	yes	yes	-	-	yes	yes	-	yes	yes	-	yes
(b) Classical	-	-	-	yes	yes	-	-	yes	-	-	-	-
(c) Manager	-	-	-	-	-	-	-	-	-	-	yes	-

*Note: This table shows the relationship between the 12 successful entrepreneurs interviewed by R.A. Scott and the criteria which appeared in the following publications Watkins, D.S. May, 1976. Paper presented in Copenhagen; Bolton Report - H.M.S.O. 1971 and Stanworth and Curran 1973, Management Motivation in the Smaller Business. Gower.

Table 5

Michael G. Scott's Criteria in Relation to R.A. Scott's Respondents

	A	B	C	D	E	F	G	H	I	J	K	L	M.G. Scott Finding
1. Innovative	no	no	no	no	yes	yes	no	no	no	no	no	no	no
2. Technological	yes	no	no	no	no	yes	no	no	yes	yes	no	no	yes
3. Family tradition of ownership	no	yes	no	yes	yes	yes	no	yes	no	no	yes	no	yes
4. Apprentice training	yes	yes	no	no	no	no	yes	no	yes	no	no	yes	yes
5. Graduates	no	no	no	no	no	yes	no	yes	yes	no	no	no	30%
6. Applied training	yes	yes	yes	no	no	no	no	yes	yes	no	no	yes	yes
7. Change of address	no	no	no	no	no	no	no	no	yes	no	no	no	no
8. More than 20 employees after years	yes	yes	yes	yes	yes	yes	yes	no	yes	yes	yes	yes	yes
9. Part-time foundings	no	no	no	no	no	no	no	no	no	no	yes	no	no
10. Partners own capital	no	yes	yes	no	no	yes	yes	no	yes	no	yes	yes	yes
11. Commercial Banks													
(a) Supportive	no	yes	no	no	no	yes	no	yes	no	no	no	no	no
(b) Unsupportive	yes	no	yes	yes	yes	no	yes	no	yes	yes	yes	yes	yes
12. Government etc. assistance	yes	no	no	no	no	no	no	no	no	no	no	no	no
13. Perceived market gap	yes	yes	no	no	no	no	no	yes	yes	yes	no	no	some
14. Need for independence													
(a) Blocked promotion	yes	-	yes	-	-	-	-	-	yes	-	-	yes	yes
(b) Desire to remain in Scotland	-	-	yes	-	-	-	-	-	yes	-	-	yes	yes
15. Antagonism towards large organisations	no	no	no	no	no	no	no	no	no	no	no	-	yes
16. Desire to 'get on'	no	yes	yes	yes	yes	no	no	no	yes	no	no	yes	yes
17. Product/image to be of high quality	yes	yes	yes	yes	yes	yes	yes	yes	yes	yes	yes	yes	yes

*Note: This table shows the relationship between the 12 successful entrepreneurs interviewed by R.A. Scott and the criteria used by Michael G. Scott in his PhD Thesis (Edinburgh 1976).

78

From this we conclude that the Smith taxonomy retains its general validity, and it is from the 'opportunist flexible' segment that real growth and development will be generated with minimum effort by Government and community.

Secondly, we have encountered difficulties in applying Smith's taxonomy directly, and it may be that the American cultural origin biases our results so as to produce particularly negative scores especially on the craftsman dimension. We certainly appear to encounter a substantial number of entrepreneurs of craftsman origin who adopt adaptable business strategies and flexible organisation designs, so as ultimately to be able to grow substantial businesses.

Thirdly, the engineering industry may be biased towards craftsman-rigidity.

Fourthly, a very large number of entrepreneurs appear to be dedicated to essentially social ideals - better quality and service at lower cost, with business seen as a means to the end of achieving these. This appears to generate a conflict in some entrepreneurs between these, and the commercial disciplines, especially in marketing but also in finance which are necessary for rapid business growth. A characteristic of the most successful entrepreneurs appears to be an ability readily to resolve these conflicts.

Finally, we are uneasy about the label opportunist. The characteristic which appears to us to typify the ultimately very successful entrepreneur is not some inborn opportunism, but his ability to acquire and practice the general set of managerial skills exhibited by chief executives of all successful organisations - awareness of market requirements, understanding of finance, and ability to recruit, train and delegate to a team of subordinates. As Bob Scott's work clearly shows, many entrepreneurs start out deficient in these skills, and the successful ones acquire them very quickly.

The real constraints on entrepreneurial growth are three:-

    (a)   ambition
    (b)   attitude towards the commercial and managerial aspects of the business.
    (c)   ability to acquire the key commercial and managerial skills.

THE CRAFTSMAN-FLEXIBLE ENTREPRENEUR

The 'craftsman-flexible' entrepreneur enters entrepreneurship with most of Smith's craftsman attributes - technically trained rather than academically educated, a career progression to supervisory or junior managerial roles only, looking to fellow workers as a reference group, and having a self-employment motivation through the production of a better product or service. They are also, however, ambitious and socially mobile, keen to learn, open-minded and adaptable, and have a vision of something grand behind their immediate company development.

It is the latter set of characteristics that appears to give these men an ability to learn rapidly from experience, and a keenness to seek advice from professional sources. Part of our experience in dealing with potential entrepreneurs has been in recruiting students for a New Enterprise Programme. A characteristic which came through very strongly in the candidates selected, was a willingness to listen to ideas and consider alternatives generated by the interviewing panels, which invariably included a successful entrepreneur. Many of the rejects were characterised by a closed-minded defence of the configuration they had presented of their business idea, even when challenged by an entrepreneur whose success standing demanded that his views were treated with respect.

THE ROLE OF TRAINING

Our analysis suggests that the open-minded craftsman entering entrepreneurship for the first time is likely to bring with him some attitudes which will inhibit the achievement of the full potential for the development of the business, and is likely to be deficient in certain business skills, as well as concerned about his own perceived deficiencies. These may be relatively trivial compared with his deficiencies in the strategic areas.

The 'craftsman-flexible' type will seek help, learn quickly from it and develop in response to the developing situation in which he finds himself. They are willing to modify their attitudes, learn from experience, teachers and consultants, and to adapt their strategies as a result of their learning. Advice, education and training will be of particular value to them in the areas of commercial and managerial practice. The real differentiation of the "opportunist" category, we suspect, is that in this category the business and commercial training has come along as part of earlier education and training. While still likely to be a user of the whole range of business support systems, an entrepreneur in this category is not likely to benefit from a basic business training course of the sort that institutions are good at. A remaining question is how to influence the culturally or mentally rigid craftsman type? Can we make him more flexible, more ambitious, more responsive to change? Frankly we do not know. Our experience, however, over ten years of trial and error in mounting small business courses suggests that the progress which can be made with a rigid and defensive type of man is limited.

The effort, then, should be concentrated upon those who are ambitious, open minded, but lacking in basic skills or knowledge relevant to the strategic manager. The objective is to produce a healthy balance between the commitment to craftsmanship - the quality of the product or service, and the commercial well being and dynamism of the business.

We have employed a number of very ineffective models on "run your own business" and other courses. Simply to advertise for owners will normally produce a dozen men and occasionally a woman, who are dickering with the idea of going into business or have been in business for a short time. In enrolling on a 20 evening or two weekend course, their primary expectation seems to be that the teachers will clarify for them all the rather frightening aspects of legislation, and will imbue them with the techniques of sales and marketing, finance and accounting, personnel and labour relations, production management and (nowadays) micro computing. We have no evidence that that process makes any difference to anyone, although on our own courses the participants have normally been kind enough to say that it was a good course.

We have some evidence from courses run on this model on other topics in Glasgow University that the extent of knowledge and skill transfer into the organisation is negligible, unless very favourable conditions for this transfer to occur exist (Huczynski and Lewis 1980). In the case of small business courses, conditions for this transfer are really unfavourable. In a specific technique course which enabled the participants to identify an immediate need for the technique and also to experiment with its implementation, only about 10 per cent subsequently made use of it. All agreed that their knowledge was adequate and most agreed that the organisation was not hostile. In addition many had specifically requested to come on the course.

The 'craftsman flexible' entrepreneurs we have uncovered are, however, great thirsters for advice, skill or knowledge which will enable them to improve the performance of their businesses. Since they are so busy, they are unlikely to come on courses, and must seek advice on a 'catch as catch can' basis. They are at a peculiar disadvantage in seeking consultancy, for what they often need is for someone to spend a short time looking at a particular aspect of a problem and advise them in a ten minute chat what to do about it. Consultants are not geared to do this, and entrepreneurs almost certainly go without advice on marketing, finance or strategy because the sources of it are not known. The bank and accountant, unless the entrepreneur is very lucky, are likely to be concentrating on the nuts and bolts of the money and accounts and advice will not normally embrace the issues of financial strategy.

We would argue that the most promising source of consultancy advice along the above lines should come from business school and higher education establishments which are capable of handling strategic level problems on a basis of limited input. A little well-directed advice when it is sought is perhaps the most cost-effective way of changing what happens in a small company. Almost by definition, the entrepreneur who seeks such advice will be adaptive in outlook, hence more likely to operate a flexible organisation. The business schools, then, have to develop the specific small firm expertise, and package and market the service.

The other point at which real pressure can be brought to bear is at the point of business creation. Elsewhere in this book Lessem discusses the action learning concept, which we whole-heartedly endorse as significantly the most effective way of developing the high level business skills. It is a particularly appropriate vehicle for the craftsman-adaptive type of entrepreneur. When the two can be brought together as is done in the New Enterprise Programmes, discussed elsewhere by Dyson, then there is a real opportunity to help the adaptive entrepreneur to a sounder start, not merely by providing him with reassurance and some technical information, but also by imbuing him with a sense of commercial and managerial values and disciplines previously associated with the opportunist, and the strategic planning, marketing and financial analysis and practice that are the hallmark of the effective chief executive.

This is consistent with the hypothesis which we are now proposing to test, that making available highly relevant advice and training to acceptant craftsmen will accelerate the process of their development, and reassure them as they develop increasingly flexible and growing organisations.

CONCLUSION

The most appropriate education for entrepreneurship model we have so far been able to devise therefore is one containing three components:-

> First, the selection of people already in business who are ambitious, able and open minded.

> Second, a systematic programme of action learning.

> Third, consistent, low-involvement advisory follow-up.

These criteria can be met through the vehicle of the New Enterprise Programmes, but the shortcoming of these is that they only catch the entrepreneur precisely at the point of start up. The next task must be to devise a model embodying the same three essential features which will be accessible to the entrepreneur who is already running his company.

NOTES

(1) This paper forms part of a wider study by Michael Cross which has recently been published by Gower under the title "New Firm Formation and Regional Development".

REFERENCES

Bolton, J.E., Report of a Committee of Inquiry into Small Firms, Cmnd. 4811. HMSO 1971.
Cross, M., "New Firm Formation and the Local Labour Market." Paper presented at the Conference - Small Firms Policy and the Role of Research. Ashridge Management College, 1979.
Firn, J., and Swales, K. "The Formation of New Manufacturing Estabilshments in Central Clydeside and West Midlands Conurbations 1963-72: A Comparative Analysis." Regional Studies Volume 12. 1978
Gilroy, M.H., Growth, The Entrepreneur and the Small Firm, M.Eng. Dissertation, Glasgow, 1979
Huczynski, A.A., and Lewis, J.W., "An Empirical Study into the Learning Transfer Process in Management Training", Journal of Management Studies, May, 1980.
Knight, F.H., Risk, Uncertainty and Profit, Boston, Houghton Mifflin, 1921
Leveson, J., Small Business Education at the Undergraduate Level. Paper presented at the Conference - Small Firms Policy and the Role of Research. Ashridge Management College, 1979.
Mancuso, J., The Entrepreneur's Philosophy, Addison Wesley 1973.
McClelland, D.C., The Achieving Society, London Van Nostrand, 1961.

Schumpeter, J.A., **The Theory of Economic Development**, London, Oxford University Press, 1934

Scott, M.G., Entrepreneurs and Entrepreneurship, PH.D Thesis, Edinburgh, 1976

Scott, R.A., **Entrepreneurs in Scotland**, MBA Dissertation, Glasgow, 1979

Smith, N., **The Entrepreneur and His Firm**, Occasional Paper, Bureau of business and Economic Research. Division of Research. Michigan State University. 1967.

Stanworth M.J.K., and Curran, J. Management Motivation in the Smaller Business. London, Gower Press, 1973.

Storey, D., "Entrepreneurship and New Firm Formation in Cleveland." Paper presented at the Conference - Small Firms Policy and the Role of Research. Ashridge Management College, 1979.

Watkins, D.S., Entry into Independent Entrepreneurship: Towards a Model of the Business Initiation Process', Working Paper presented at the EIASM joint seminar on Entrepreneurship and Institution Building, Dansk Management Centre, Copenhagen, 1976.

7 UK Government support for entrepreneurship training and development

JOHN MORRIS AND DAVID WATKINS
Manchester Business School

ORIGINS OF THE NEW ENTERPRISE PROGRAMME

Before the successful sponsorship by Manpower Services Commission (MSC) of the initial New Enterprise Programme at Manchester Business School (MBS) in 1977, training for entrepreneurship was effectively unknown in the U.K. Since that time, the number and variety of initiatives to encourage new firm formation which include or are centred on a 'training' or 'development' programme has mushroomed. What then was the happy coincidence of factors which stimulated this growth? What considerations structured the first and subsequent programmes? And to what extent have these programmes met their initial objectives and the expectations of them?

One can perhaps identify three key factors which led to the first experimental New Enterprise Programme.

The first was a genuine concern for people. Although Manchester Business School has as its main clients the large corporations which seem to many people so impersonal, what we as teachers, trainers, and confidants deal with in our day-to-day work are specific individuals - at middle and senior management levels in such corporations. From early 1976 on, executive unemployment began to be a significant worry even among the managerial elite which forms our clientel. Moreover, the Manpower Services Commission began at about this time to sponsor a small number of people under the Training Opportunities Scheme (TOPS) on each of our major programmes - people who were registered with Professional Executive Register (PER) as seeking high level managerial employment. This brought MBS staff into close contact not only with the individuals thus sponsored (who were often vocal and articulate about the position in which they found themselves) but with the administrators and training advisors within TOPS and elsewhere in MSC who were seeking new solutions to a growing and worrying non-or misallocation of scarce managerial expertise.

The second factor, which will come more closely into focus as we describe the structure of the NEP and, in particular, the role of the management committee, was the creation and development at MBS of Joint Development Activities. In JDA'S, the providing institution and the sponsor work together both in designing and in managing the training/development activity, often with the active encouragement of the programme participants themselves to engage in these processes, too.

(See for example Morris & Burgoyne 1973 and Morris 1980.)

The third factor, superficially the most obvious one, was the pre-existence at MBS of perhaps one of the best developed (but still small) corpus of research and training expertise on the formation and development of new businesses. For throughout the 70's as concern mounted over the role and position of the small business in British Society and the apparent relative decline of the small business sector in the UK, the consistent MBS view was that the root of the problem lay in differential rates of formation of new firms rather than in unexpectedly high rates of failure. The greater part of the School's research and teaching effort in the small business area had been concerned with the mitigation of this problem (Watkins, 1976).

That this third factor was a necessary but insufficient one is shown by examining briefly the other entrepreneurship - directed activities at MBS which pre-dated NEP against a simple model of the pre-conditions for successful business formation.

It's an unfortunate fact of life that the establishment of a successful new firm requires far more that a bright idea - the traditional 'better mousetrap'. Indeed, new firms which see their competitive edge simply in terms of a 'better' product are almost doomed to fail; for hardly anyone ever does beat an Emersonian path to one's door. In fact, the success of a new enterprise demands the coincidence of three groups of factors: adequate technical and managerial skills, an appropriate motivational mix, and the existence of genuine opportunity. Figure 1 shows diagramatically how one might expect relatively few individuals to meet the pre-condition necessary for success at any given time. For example, one would expect that those with appropriate skills and opportunity but lacking in motivation (area 1) would normally continue happily in employment.

But redundancy, its threat, or some other discontinuity, could easily propel them into area 4, where individuals are both most likely to begin an enterprise and more likely to succeed.

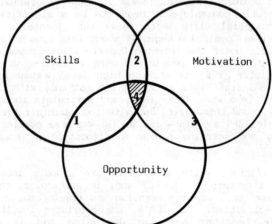

Figure 1 The pre-conditions for successful business formation

86

In the past, MBS had run a series of short programmes aimed specifically at individuals teetering on the brink between 1 and 4 - the 'Founding Your Own Business' series of weekend conferences of the late 60's and early 70's.

Similarly, the entrepreneurship project undertaken by all MBA students at MBS in their second year focusses largely on one area of Figure 1 - developing skills. The project is based on learning by doing which may explain the fact that there are strong indications that participation motivates many students to establish an independent business at a later stage in their career (or even on graduation). This however is not the major objective.

Thus in our pre-existing programmes we were unable, in particular, to deal specifically and extensively with the analysis (and creation) of real opportunities for new owner managers. Indeed, one can look at the establishment of NEP itself as a new activity in terms of the same model: it was the heightened motivation due to Factor One, together with the opportunity created by both Factor One and the credibility of Factor Two as a means of reducing risk to both sponsor and providing institution (itself an opportunity factor) which finally created the necessary pre-conditions for a successful launch of the New Enterprise Programme.

STRUCTURE AND OBJECTIVES OF THE PROGRAMME

The original conception of NEP was of a training programme which might lead to the establishment of a significant number of new businesses. Our hope was that from 16 participants, 4 businesses might emerge. To this end, we tried to select a fruitful mix of participants in terms of age, personal background, skills, industrial backgrounds, etc. Our belief was that these might be encouraged to evolve into a small number of teams which would select and evaluate business ideas that could perhaps form the basis of ongoing enterprises. At the selection stage we were pleased to recognise individuals who had a specific venture idea which they wished to investigate on an individual basis. This provided a fall-back position. However, many of the entrants did not have this fall-back position and we did not insist on it, although we explained that this increased the risk of participation. This is an important point, as we have always made it clear that we could not provide inidividuals or groups with ideas to evaluate. We have always believed that such ideas must come from the participants or their commitment would not be secured. If, at the end of the project phase, the idea was shown not to be viable or the person(s) involved did not wish to proceed our aim was that the programme would have provided useful training in new business evaluation/development for those re-entering large-scale industry, together with significant enhancement of job prospects in the business development functions of larger firms.

Although this latter sub-objective has been met for several individuals, the emphasis in the preceding paragraph has to be very firmly on the word 'original'. As the joint programme management of provider and sponsor has gained in experience and confidence, so have we all been able to be very much more open about our main aim: that people who a priori have a good idea, commitment and appropriate resources should undertake a feasibility study of their proposed new venture and, if appropriate, initiate that business with all reasonable speed.

As programmes are participative but shaped in large measure by the potential owner-managers' expectations of them it is perhaps most appropriate to outline the current programme structure and objectives in terms of the notes sent to all potential participants.

Objective

New Enterprise programme (NEP) provides a framework within which individuals or prospective business partners seeking to start a new business can test out the feasibility of their ideas, modifying these and implementing them accordingly. Each programme comprises about sixteen individuals - women and men - who learn not only from experienced MBS Faculty and outside experts but also from one another. The businesses formed should have the potential to employ others besides the initiator and his immediate family.

Location, Duration and Structure

Participation in the Programme lasts a maximum of sixteen weeks of which the first month is spent in residence at MBS. Almost certainly, other periods will be spent 'on the road' in the UK or abroad. Workspace, telephone, telex and secretarial backing are provided at MBS during Phase II.

Financial Support

During Phase II each participant has access to an individually negotiated research budget in order to undertake the feasibility study. These budgets are typically measured in hundred of pounds rather than tens or thousands. They are intended for travel and accommodation in researching markets, premises, suppliers, sources of finance etc. They may be used for direct product development for professional fees or for normal trading purposes. In addition, TOPS Training Allowances are payable for the whole sixteen weeks. Course fees are also met in full by TOPS, not by individual participants.

Programme Management

NEP is managed by a joint MBS/TSD Management Committee. This makes decisions on entry to NEP, acceptance of individuals into Phase II of the Programme, allocation of individual research budgets and periodic reviews of progress towards the aim of establishing a viable enterprise. This Committee is the custodian of public funds and reserves the right, which it has exercised on rare occasions, to withdraw support from individuals at any stage if circumstances warrant it.

Nature of Business Idea

There is no sectorial bias: The basis of the proposed business may be the manufacture of a product; the assembly, repair or distribution of a product; or the provision of a service. The business must, however, be commercially viable and also be likely to create employment for others. NEP does not appear to be a very helpful vehicle for initiating consultancy businesses.

Eligibility

Any citizen of the EEC resident in the UK and wishing to establish a business in the UK is eligible. Personal ability and commitment are more important than formal qualifications.

There is a lower age limit of 19. We would expect the Programme to appeal most strongly to those between 25 and 50.

Women are as welcome as men. It has also concerned us that very few applications have been from immigrants to Britain, a traditional source of vigour and enterprise in business.

Success Rate

The main factor in the success of businesses emerging from NEP is undoubtedly the personal qualities, skills, and commitment of the individual participants. Nevertheless, most new businesses fail. Our expectation was that the sixteen participants in NEP 1 might give rise to four new enterprises. As a result of spontaneous partnership formation eight enterprises embracing 14 of the original 16 people were formed. One year from the end of the programme (in Autumn 1978) these businesses had all survived, to employ between them more than sixty individuals, and to have turned over in excess of £3/4m. This rate of progress has since been maintained. There is firm evidence that some of these businesses would not have been started or would have had very different histories had NEP not intervened. Furthermore, preliminary indications are that subsequent programmes run by other institutions have enjoyed equal success.

From these abbreviated participants' notes the emphasis is clear; what is offered is not a traditional training programme (the formal contents of even the first four weeks are barely discussed; rather, the emphasis is on the work to be done.

This is new work for each participant, since it is concerned with the possible establishment of a new business. The emphasis is strongly on 'learning from one another' as well as from staff consultants. Although the first four weeks do reveal some of the familiar features of conventional training courses - lectures, group discussions, case studies, exercises and simulation projects - even here, the time available for programming by the participants to meet their individual and group needs, steadily grows from the first to the fourth week. The view is strongly expressed; 'This is your programme; take a hand in organising it'! In practice, the fourth week and most of the fifth are taken up with detailed planning of the final, crucial stage; the feasibility testing. Plans for this are discussed with fellow participants before being presented in confidential meetings with the Management Committee, at which point agreement is reached on how the time and the budget is going to be used. In the next three months, each participant works to the agreed plan, with whatever modifications experience shows to be necessary. Every three or four weeks, there are further meetings with members of the Management Committee in order to review progress. Although tutorial support is provided, virtually on demand, through this period, it is within the Management Committee that many of the key issues are most clearly brought to a focus, attitudes changed and thus, ultimately, behaviour perhaps brought more into accord with the stated objectives of the individual.

THE PARTICIPANTS

By now it must be clear that New Enterprise Programmes are shaped by the characteristics of the participants and their ideas to a far greater extent than could be conceived of in most traditional management development activities. Let us turn now to look at the characteristics of the people and their ideas.

One might expect people who are interested in forming an independent business to themselves be independent and highly individualistic. And so they are. A glance at the business ideas put forward by participants in a single programme covers an impressive range, even though it is limited to ideas that might have some chance of being launched with limited resources in a short time. On one programme alone, the following ideas were among those being worked on; toys and games, audio-visual materials for industry and commerce, micro-computer marketing information systems, PVC shower-curtains, country wines, a professional journal publishing house, assembly and sale of safety equipment, buoyancy apparatus for submersibles, pipe linings for food processing equipment, and small-scale textile finishing. This by no means exhausts the list for one programme of 16 people, but it may give some impression of the variety.

Our participants are from very mixed backgrounds, and have varied in age from their mid-twenties to the seventies (the oldest member of the programme so far has been perhaps the most successful in his business venture, in partnership with one of the youngest members). The programmes have always taken people at different stages in business development and this has proved a decided advantage, since it greatly increases the opportunities for participants learning with and from each other about the problems of business formation.

In the New Enterprise Programme notes cited earlier, a special comment is made to the effect that '. . . women are as welcome as men.' It has also concerned us that very few applications have been from immigrants to Britain, a traditional source of vigour and enterprise in business'. Despite these encouraging noises, we have never had more than two women on any programme, and only a very modest number of immigrants.

Despite the diversity of the participants, a few general observations can be made. They have a strong drive to independence and to being free from close supervision, but have a keen sense of business realities. They accept objective constraints much more readily than those embodied in 'authority'. Many of them are quite willing to control others, as employees or associates, but feel oppressed by the thought of complex legislation and 'industrial relations'. Their feeling is that if their companies can provide a continuing sense of growth and opportunity, many of the 'labour relations' problems of which British owner-managers complain will solve themselves.

They tend to be practical and outward-looking, rather than analytical and inward-looking. If asked what issues they want help on, answers come quickly; marketing and sales, sources of funds, premises, accounting on a realistic 'cash flow' basis, and details of business formation. There is not much sense of 'organisation' or 'relationships' as presenting problems; these, one suspects are thankfully deferred until success forces them on the owner-manager's attention at a later stage of business development. The nature of one's own motivation, and how it will stand up to the day-to-day stresses and strains of business operation, is of interest, but it is rightly felt to constitute a very different kind of problem from the practical 'nuts and bolts' that can be offered in other problem-areas.

Even with a four-month programme at their disposal,those taking part in the various activities feel a constant pressure of time. This means that they often want the fruits of professional expertise, rather than the drudgery of acquiring the expertise for themselves. Not surprisingly, they are greatly impressed by people who have established themselves in a successful business, but are still close enough to recollection of their own early stages of development to be able to pass on their experience, in an unpretentious, down-to-earth fashion.

The emotional problems of reaching a decision with such far-reaching consequences for oneself and one's family as starting a business are considerable. The decision to take part in the programme is an important one: but it permits a deferment for some weeks or months of the actual decision to begin trading. At such crucial points of decision, people are swayed between varying moods: excitement and depression: dependence and aggressive independence. The programme and its management must be sensitive to these changing states as well as to the more obvious needs of participants for information and basic techniques. The very mention of 'management' of a programme for would-be entrepreneurs raises quite fundamental questions. How does one manage those who - to be successful - must be self-managing? This again focusses attention on the role and responsibility of the Management Committee.

THE ROLE OF THE MANAGEMENT COMMITTEE

As previously noted, the idea of having a Management Committee for each of the Programmes was drawn from the 'joint development' line of work for which MBS is well known. One advantage of such a structure is that a management committe composed of sponsors and staff consultants can start a programme with a group of participants without the providers having to set up a 'selling apparatus' of a glossy brochure, a fixed offering, and lengthy statements about staff qualifications. The working management group can set its own standards of effectiveness, in close collaboration with the interested parties with whom it is managing. They can use 'audits' and 'evaluation' as flexible devices for improving current and future effectiveness, rather than as formal monuments to research endeavour. If circumstances change, so can the programme. Instead of being a fixed commitment, the programme is seen as part of a network of agreements between people who have a personal stake in it. They are people who want the programme to be effective because it is an important part of their lives.

This, of course, is a statement of an ideal. Programmes often become rigid control devices, dominating the activities of those who are part of them, rather than fallible human arrangement for getting things done in a difficult world. One has only to look at the programmes in numberless training centres to see how rigidity rules the day. Split off from the hurly-burly of everyday life, they prescribe the course of each day with fantastic precision. This point is often missed by those taking part in them because they are replete with dramatic and ritual elements that obscure the formal rigidity of the whole arrangement. Because many of us expect education and training to be a combination of heart-stirring and technical instruction, the fundamental irrelevance of much of the activity is obscured. It is left to the outside observer to note that the marvellous orderliness and efficient use of resources that are the pride of the company training centre and the business college are achieved by shutting out the world that we are supposed to be dealing with. Reality only breaks in when the budget is cut or the support staff go out on strike. Bad practice in management development; inconceivable as a aid to entrepreneurship development.

This fundamental task of the management committee is to help maintain and develop a flexible programme that helps us to understand and cope with the world while at no point losing touch with it. The purpose of the programme is to help us as human beings move purposefully towards an agreed objective in a confusing world. Moreover, the format of the management committee is a way of enabling the nature of the agreement to be open to inspection and worked with as a key issue rather than being taken for granted.

The realities of managing the programmes can perhaps be seen more clearly if we again regard them as very much 'new enterprises' in their own right. They have had their own problems of securing adequate funds, suitable premises, and initial staff. They are a continuing test of the commitment and of the competence of the small group of people at the centre. There is much the same sense of initiative and ownership of the activity as in the new enterprises that are being fostered. But there are important differences. The New Enterprise Programmes are joint ventures, rather than independent businesses. Shrewd observers have not failed to notice the nature of the parent institutions and to ask, 'how can a university business school and a government agency do anything useful for entrepreneurs?'

Closer inspection of the people working on the programmes, and the nature of the parent institutions reveals some reassuring features. The Manpower Service Commission is a relatively new 'executive arm' of national manpower policy, and displays much of the imagination and energy of an enterprise in its pioneering phase. Those who have joined the management committee from the sponsoring side have been willing to lend their energies as well as their skills to progressing the programmes. And they have been enterprising people, with wide-ranging experience outside as well as inside public service. Manchester Business School, for its part, has a strong commitment to innovate development programmes, and has a form of organisation which favours rapid grouping of staff into programme management and support teams. There are no academic departments, and even the degree programmes are focussed on options and on projects - including the popular entrepreneurship project mentioned briefly before rather than on traditional disciplines.

STAFFING THE NEW ENTERPRISE PROGRAMME

One useful way of looking at staff working on New Enterprise Programmes is to see them as a combination of programme managers and project consultants. Since each participant in a programme is usually deeply concerned with being the unchallenged manager of his or her own business, as a personal project, there is not much scope for consultants to be project managers in an immediate sense: though as they warm to the opportunites that they see in a proposed new business, they often fall into the role of a partner rather than a consultant ('we could do it this way' or 'if I were you, I would go for the second product at least six months later than you've got it in the plan'........and it became apparent that in every such consultant, there is an independent businessman halfway into a business of his own; indeed, most of the staff associated with the programmes have live or potential business projects of their own bubbling away all the time!)

Both the programme manager and project consultant have a difficult job: and for much the same reason. New enterprise is a matter of getting a lot of different people and things to come together at a particular place and time, to meet a particular need. There is no end to the specialist expertise that the new enterprise could use, from filling in export documentation to knowing the best source of supplies of a rare commodity. But the key task is getting it all together, and through the largely untested new agency of the owner-manager and the very small group of people with whom he works. Much of the subject-matter of academic disciplines and business specialisms is made up of well-ordered materials, in the form of theoretical frameworks, analytical techniques, cumulative research, custom-and-practice and so on. The teacher of an academic discipline and the staff specialist working within a big company are much more alike then they care to recognise. They are working with bodies of knowledge and well-established procedures. They know what they know, and exude the air of self-confidence proper to one who treads familiar paths in a well-ordered domain.

Part of the work of the owner-manager may be well-established and familiar, though not usually in the early days of business formation. But even when he has become 'established' there is little in his head in the form of explicit knowledge. In its place is a vast array of rules of thumb, detailed understanding of complex and changing situations, a sense of the continuing need to keep a small number of key people satisfied. And, above all, an over-riding sense of purpose and personal commitment.

If the consultant tries to respond to this kind of business reality, he is faced with a dilemma. The safest course is to be a recognised expert in a general-purpose business specialism, such as marketing or accounting. Not necessarily the kind of expert who would be valued highly in a 'centre of excellence' in the educational world, but one who has developed a broad understanding of small-business life, with its flux of opportunities and problems. A valuable but less appreciated expertise is in being able to think clearly about priorities, the oddities of human personality, the tortuous paths through which we move in everyday life. Such thinking might earn the consultant the label of 'useful sound-board' or 'catalyst', but it will often be seen as 'just common sense.'

Many of these difficulties would be mitigated if one gave up the attempt to model the form of development activities - the New Enterprise Programmes - on the form of new enterprise itself. One is reminded of the way in which many well-run management training centres deal with the challenges of an increasingly turbulent world by bringing bits of that world into the training centre, but always in a form that does not disturb the tidiness of the programme. Thus, it is commonplace to find exercises in the 'management of uncertainty' which are guaranteed to end one minute before the scheduled coffee-break; and simulations of aggression, deceit, and rivalry which leave the syndicate members in good fettle for getting together in the bar for an agreeable evening's discussion! 'Self-development' can also be neatly encapsulated within a programme that is conceived and managed in a fashion which allows little room for the participation of the members. In the New Enterprise Programmes of the kind described here such dilemmas are revealed rather than concealed by the design and management of the activities. The difficult switch from 'support' to 'control' the painful oscillation between trust and mistrust, become glaringly obvious when real time, real funds and real outcomes are the focus of the activities, and not a complex web of real and unreal issues, resources, roles and relationships.

IMPRESSIONS OF THE EFFECTIVENESS OF THE PROGRAMME

It is possible at this stage in the development of the programme to establish the nature of their contribution to fostering new enterprise? The most obvious indicator, which the objective of the programmes makes possible, is the actual number of independent enterprises established, and their survival and growth rates. Table 1 gives some impression of the outcome of the first programme (NEP 1) which ended in late 1977. The evaluation exercise was conducted in late 1978. The alphabetical letters in the first column of the table refer to the 14 participants who established independent businesses.

Approximately 20% of first years production was in exported goods and services. This is likely todouble in year two. If current expectations are confirmed, total turnover in year two will be £1.75 m and employment about 100.

An initial evaluation of NEP II, (which ended in mid-1978), showed that 9 companies had been formed, with a total employment level by the

94

Table 1

Selected characteristics of NEP enterprises at the end of 1978

	Turnover in first year £ P.A.	Full Time (or equiv) Employees (Excl. Directors)	Number Employees Previously Unemployed	Break-even achieved	Pre-tax Profits + Total Directors Drawings
h,i	31,200	4 (all unskilled)	2 or 3	x	
m	4,000	0	-	x	
d,c	260,000	13 (all unskilled)	13		
c	60,000	2 (one unskilled)	1		
n,o,p	204,000	20 (one unskilled)	Few if any		
a,b	12-15,000	2 (all unskilled)	1/2		
f,g	120,000	4 (one unskilled) (one semi-skilled)	2		
j	95,000+	15+casuals (all unskilled) started with 5 1/3	13		
Approx Total	3/4M+	60	30 - 35	6 out of 8	£115,000 plus 8 company cars

end of 1979 of III (full-time or full-time equivalent. The turnover of the NEP II companies was significantly smaller than those of NEP 1, but this is very much a function of the type of product, many of which had long development, lead times before sales built up. The range of products and services in the companies so far established is very wide, fashion lingerie, micro-processor applications, photo copier refurbishing, specialist wall-coverings, emergency industrial repairs, specialist adhesives, site electrical installations, roof insulation, furniture design manufacture, stainless steel stockholding, vinyl plastic products, carpet weavings, clothing, sawmilling and brewing.

However, short-term evaluations of New Enterprise Programmes in terms of simple parameters such as initial gross employment creation could be very misleading. There are a number of reasons for this.

First, we are dealing with a process over time, not a point event (Watkins 1977). The four months of a New Enterprise Programme cannot compromise even all the pre-start-up procedures of all the businesses which the programme has helped people to initiate. For example, two participants in NEP II entered into partnership while in residence at MBS (although previously unknown to each other) in November 1977. The nature of their chosen business - softwood saw milling - was such that it was not possible to begin production for some two years. The intervening period was spent in identifying a site, raising substantial sums of venture capital, building a specialised factory, purchasing stands of timber for later delivery, and so on.

Secondly, employment, turnover and profit are by no means the only dimensions with which a full evaluation would concern itself. One firm started by participants who met on an early programme re-builds photocopying machines. Each machine re-built (which would previously have been scrapped) not only provides turnover, profit and employment within the U.K., it substitutes more than its own re-sale value in the balance of trade (as there is no indigenous producer of small photocopiers), while providing equivalent benefit to its end user at lower cost than would otherwise be the case. It might also, as a result of its lower price, expand the total market for photocopiers in the U.K. Clearly in this case, as in many others (1), the cost benefit calculations are complex.

But along one dimension at least it is easy to claim substantial success. Not only has the success of the early MBS programmes led directly to the establishment of MSC supported NEPs in several other centres, the success of the programmes as a whole has completely opened up the field of new enterprise development programmes in the U.K. MSC has itself sponsored an extensive programme of shorter, less complex small business courses in different parts of the country. In addition, localised programmes of various kinds have been promoted, with or without MSC support, in many parts of the country.

When one considers the national programme as a whole, the outcomes are impressive. There have now been 19 NEP's run in four centres (Durham, London, Glasgow and Manchester). The results for the first seven of these, one year after course completion, are now available. 76 per cent of participants completing a programme initiated a business and its average scale at that time was an employment level of 8. Forty-two small business courses have now been run, of which figures are available for the first 18. 70 per cent of trainees completing a course started in business within one year, with the year-end average employment being four people (including the trainee). The implication is that, taken together, the NEP's and SBC's between them have assisted 536 otherwise non-employed people to create more then 500 new businesses providing employment in their first year alone for 2857 people (Watkins, 1981). Moreover, the somewhat more limited evidence yet available indicates (a) continuing growth beyond year one, (b) above average survival rates and (c) acceptable early levels of profitability.

But in conclusion we must again switch the focus: from the macro to the micro, from the programme of programmes to the individual and his or her new enterprise.(2).

What then is it that programmes such as ours seem to offer the participants? they are very much aware of the value of constructive criticism of their business ideas, of a clear statement of the success and failure factors in new enterprise, and of helpful, specific pieces of advice, or useful contacts on premises, sources of funds and other vital resources. if one had to pull together the essential contribution of the activities, it seems to be a sustained opportunity to bring together (3) (or find that one has not brought together) two tasks:

(i)   the task of establishing the business idea as a feasible proposition, with the available time, competence and other resources available, and

(ii)   the task of confirming one's own commitment to establishing or joining an independent business, with this idea. and not only one's own commitment, but also that of the key people with whom one would be associated - as family, partners, key workers, etc.

When these two tasks have been related positively, and a decision is made to go ahead, there is a sense of having reached a crucial turning point in one's career, and a flood of self confidence and heightened awareness. It is at this point that the management committee and staff consultants need to try very hard to keep a balance between a stringent reality-testing and enthusiastic boosting of the participants, self esteem. This is not always an easy task, for it is still at the individual level that our success (or otherwise) is at its most apparent ...... and most rewarding.

NOTES

(1) The sawmill above is another example. It processes to higher grade use British softwood which would otherwise go to paper-making or burning. Again, this has interesting implications for the balance of trade, employment of different labour skills in this country versus other, etc.
(2) See the papers by Dyson, Jackson and Lessem in this volume.
(3) Cf. Entrepreneur - he who stands between and brings together the different factors of production.

REFERENCES

Morris, J.F. and Burgoyne, J.G. Developing Resourceful Managers, I.P.M. London, 1973.
Morris, J.F., 'Joint Development Activities: from Practice to 'Theory'' in Advance in Management Development (ed. C.L. Cox, and J. Beck), Wiley, London, 1980.
Watkins, D.S. 'Education for Entrepreneurship, is it Possible' 6th Annual EFMD Small Business Seminar Milan, 1976.
Watkins, D.S. 'Grundlagen einer offentlichen politik zungunsten von grundung und ausbau gewerblicher betrieve, Internationales Gewerbearchiv 25 (2), 1977.
Watkins, D.S. Private Communication, Manpower Services Commission, February 1981.

8 The position of New Enterprise Programmes in the process of start-up: an approach to matching enterprise founding programmes to different categories of business founder

JERRY DYSON
Small Business Centre,
Durham University Business School

INTRODUCTION

In the last three or four years there has been growing interest in this country in various types of 'training programme' (1) aimed at fostering the start up of new businesses. Approaches to this basic aim have included the 19 New Enterprise Programmes financed by the Manpower Services Commission which have been run at four business schools, programmes provided by, for example, URBED, (see the following paper by Ronnie Lessem), the Welsh Development Agency, and the Highlands and Islands Development Board, and a series of Start Your Own Business Courses provided by seven polytechnics.

These programmes are not just concerned with developing the managerial capability to found a business, but also have the particular objective of leading to the actual formation of new businesses. Thus the programmes are to some extent "results orientated" which means that they must intervene at the right point in the founding process and must provide the right kind of support to allow individuals to develop sufficiently to start their own businesses.

To achieve the "results objective" enterprise founding programmes require careful positioning with particular attention to the selection of candidates, and to programme design, administration and execution.

This paper looks at the problems of positioning the programme and of identifying the 'support needs' of the would-be business starters so that an appropriate programme structure and content can be determined. It is based largely on experience of running six New Enterprise Programmes at Durham University Business School (2) and attempts first to develop a general model for identifying and designing enterprise founding support programmes and then looks at how this model is applied to the way NEP's are run at Durham.

Finding the right point in the founding process and providing the right kind of support have to be done in the context of a number of constraints. One constraint is that enterprise programmes tend to work in a partial vacuum. However well the managerial capability is developed the enterprise needs resourcing. Allan Gibb (1980) has argued for example that starting an enterprise is such a vulnerable and high risk prospect that for the government and other agencies to be serious about wanting to encourage new enterprise creation then special preferential support, possibly similar to that provided in Germany, is required. Apart from counselling and perhaps information, however, the provision of resources is outside the scope of new enterprise programmes.

A further constraint is that the programmes are centreed on the would-be founder. Whilst this person's motivation and ability are key elements in the founding process the commercial and competitive viability of the business idea cannot be ignored. If the programme is orientated towards results in terms of businesses started judgements about viability have to be made. Where the funding of the programme is related to the need to create employment, as with the NEP's, then these judgements are even more critical.

The risks involved for the individual who is dedicating time and money in order to prepare to found a business also puts a particular kind of responsibility on those selecting people for, and running, the programme. (The stakes are of a very different order from those of passing or failing an exam.)

Finally, to justify the resources spent on programmes like the NEP, it is important to select those with a real need for the programme, and who will be most likely to benefit from it, but at the same time to avoid the self fulfilling prophecy of selecting people who can start a business without any sort of help.

Background and structure of new enterprise programmes

Before turning to these issues, it is useful to look briefly at the background to, and typical structure of, the New Enterprise Programmes.

New Enterprise Programmes are funded by the Training Services Division (TSD) of the Manpower Services Commission, who provide the cost of the programme to the Business Schools and a training allowance, plus some approved research costs to the would-be starters (3).

The Programmes were developed out of research concerned with whether it would be possible to train people in founding enterprises and if so, what the content of this training should be.

Research in this area had been conducted independently by both the Manchester and Durham Business Schools (Watkins, 1976, Gibb & Ritchie, 1977) and the findings discussed with the Manpower Services Commission. The idea of New Enterprise Programmes was then developed and financial support won, so enabling a pilot programme at Manchester Business School in May 1977 and at Durham University Business School in May 1978. Between then and the end of 1980, Manchester Business School will have completed eight programmes; Durham University Business School, six; the London Business School, three (starting in April 1979); and the Scottish Business School, two (starting in March 1980). Each Business School normally runs two programmes a year, aiming to take about 15 people on each.

The first part of a typical programme, say four and a half weeks, is residential and concerned with what needs to be done to set up a sound new business (4). It focuses on the specific business ideas of people on the programme, rather than on any abstract model of the start up process. Important elements include extensive counselling with each individual concerning his or her business proposal and contact with representatives of relevant support agencies (such as banks, accountants, local authorities, CoSIRA and so on). The main output sought from this first part of the programme is the would-be starter's draft plan of the founding and early stages of his or her new business. The drafting of this plan also identifies any critical gaps in the would-be starter's knowledge and/or resources, and so establishes the priorities which have to be worked on.

The second part of the programme, (about three months) involves the business starters in working 'on site' preparing to set up the business (researching markets and suppliers, finding adequate finance, establishing a location and so on). During this period they receive continuous counselling support from the Business School and discuss their plans and progress at monthly intervals with a panel of people experienced in helping new businesses.

In general one can expect all but one or two of the people on the programmes to start some sort of business, with most becoming self supporting within, say the first three months and with the majority employing three or four people by the end of the first year (with a few employing many more).

POSITIONING THE PROGRAMME

Because of the dual results and training objectives of New Enterprise Programmes, it is essential to have guidance on what kind of support programme will both accelerate the founding process and ensure that the business established is sound and capable of future growth.

(a) A model of the process.

Insights into the founding process are provided by Shapero (1977). He identifies the following four critical interdependent elements which relate to the impetus to act, the person's motivations and aspirations and the environment conducive to starting an enterprise.

1.   Displacement: the disruption of a normal pattern, a change in the person's attitudes or in his environment, an impetus that might produce a response to act in an 'entrepreneurial' way. (For an interesting form of displacement: refusing career promotion that would mean having to leave a locality, see 'Independence and the Flight from Large Scale: Some Sociological Factors in the Founding Process', M. G. Scott, 1980.)

2.   A disposition to act: seen most importantly as a strong internal locus of control; a belief that the individual is in control of his own life and that his fate results from his own actions.

3.   Credibility of the act: within the individual's society models of behaviour must be available that allow him to

see running a business as an acceptable and appropriate way of life that is open to him.

4.   Availability of resources: the availability of the various specific kinds of support needed to form an enterprise.

When displacement of some kind occurs such as loss of job, a break in a life style or removal of status, only those who are relatively autonomous, self confident, resourceful and disposed to act will respond by seriously considering starting a business. To proceed, however, it is necessary for the business idea to be attractive and credible, and for the person to have a realistic view of himself starting and owning a business. As a final step, he must be able to draw together the necessary resources.

In a process of this kind 'training' programmes can probably have only a quite limited and indirect role. As far as the Durham NEP is concerned, for example, three of the above are regarded as essential 'preconditions' for anyone hoping to use the programme to help them start a business. To be serious about wanting to start a business, some kind of stimulus will already have occurred and the idea of starting a business will be both believable and attractive. There will also be a distinct 'disposition to act' to start a business, although this is quite consistent with a recognition on the part of the individual that there may be gaps in his knowledge and abilities and perhaps even fairly serious doubts about whether he can, in reality, succeed in starting a business (5).

In order to identify the appropriate forms of support for business founders attention must be focused on what has to happen to convert the firm desire to start the business into a capability to bring together the right resources. Experience of would-be starters at Durham suggests that there are six important requirements involved in turning the intention into a preparedness to start (Figure 1).

To some extent these preparation needs have to be developed sequentially.

Commitment might ebb and flow and motivation will become directed toward different ends, but it needs to be evident throughout the whole of the founding process.

The idea might come first as something that seems technically feasible and even be developed into a prototype before it is translated into an achievable market opportunity, or the business idea might start as the recognition of market demand inadequately supplied, with a 'product' to fill this gap developed later. In reality there might well be a number of ideas, with or without their corresponding products or market opportunities, that are taken up and abandoned and then replaced.

To some extent, however, the business idea must precede the development of managerial capability. Thinking about and working on this business idea (or sequence of ideas) can be an important influence on the development of the would-be starter's capability to start and manage the business since relatively risk free learning can take place by thinking about the idea, planning, getting other people's reactions, and recognising any weaknesses. (This risk free learning is an important basis of the NEPs as discussed below.)

1. Commitment: determination to start the business, possibly with continuous reassurance of the likely outcome.

2. Business Idea - This might be:

either	or
The product/service, developed to the point where it 'works' with production/operations thought to be feasible	A perceived market gap, potential demand unsatisfied or inadequately supported

3. Opportunity - Which is then:

either	or
Adequate attainable market demand for the product/service	A product/service developed to be capable of satisfying the perceived demand

4. Capability: relevant management knowledge, the specific skills and attitudes required to start and establish the business.

5. Plan: possibly quite informal but identifying what needs to be done in order to start the business. Some form of plan might be needed as support for getting resources.

6. Resourcing: adequate availability of the necessary time, information, money, possibly additional funds, people, premises and so on.

Figure 1 Preparation needs

Resourcing the business is consequent on some form of plan and the quality of this plan and the capacity to acquire the resources will also have been influenced by how far the 'managerial' capability has been developed.

The preparation needs in the model are therefore rationally linked in a sequence, although in practice development may be more iterative and they could not be termed 'stages'. All six must, however, reach a point of adequate development before the business can be started. How far development of the six preparation needs has to go will depend on a number of factors. Some are inherent in the chosen business idea such as the technical novelty of the product, the riskiness of that particular market or the complexity of the resources needed while others are determined by how far and how fast it is envisaged the business should be taken in its first few years.

In general it can be said that more preparation and development will be required to start a sound business with a high chance of survival than is needed 'just' to start a business. It seems likely therefore that attention to the sound development of these preparation needs in the start-up phase will have an important effect on the enterprise's capacity to grow in the early years (see Figure 2).

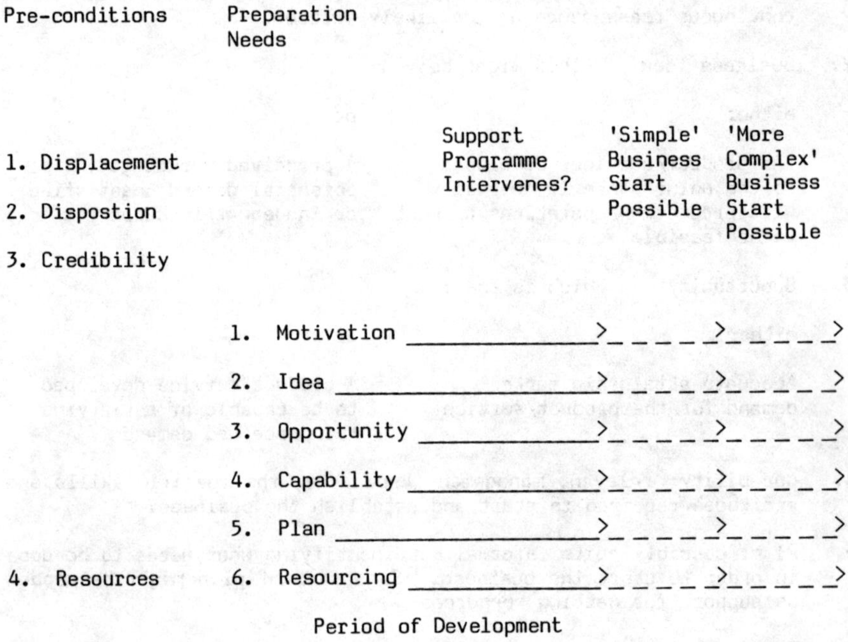

Pre-conditions   Preparation
                 Needs

		Support Programme Intervenes?	'Simple' Business Start Possible	'More Complex' Business Start Possible
1. Displacement				
2. Dispostion				
3. Credibility				
	1. Motivation _____	> _ _ _ _	> _ _ _ _	>
	2. Idea _____	> _ _ _ _	> _ _ _ _	>
	3. Opportunity _____	> _ _ _ _	> _ _ _ _	>
	4. Capability _____	> _ _ _ _	> _ _ _ _	>
	5. Plan _____	> _ _ _ _	> _ _ _ _	>
4. Resources	6. Resourcing _____	> _ _ _ _	> _ _ _ _	>

Period of Development

Figure 2 Preparation needs in the enterprise founding process.

(b) Application of the model

The model as set out in Figure 2 can be used to determine both the point of intervention and the broad content of a new enterprise support programme. By and large at Durham University Business School the NEP's are seen to intervene during the preparation phase and aim to accelerate the founding process and improve the survival and growth capabilities of the nascent enterprises. The pre-conditions of displacement, disposition and credibility must largely have been fulfilled by the would be starters, (although the programme to a small extent fosters and develops both the disposition towards and belief in the capability to found and to run a business). Different kinds of programme might be designed to operate at the level of the first three 'pre-conditions' aiming to increase the number of people who might seriously consider founding an enterprise.

As far as content is concerned, programmes aimed at the preparation phase might, like the NEPs, be 'inclusive' dealing with all six basic needs. Alternatively they might concentrate on particular aspects such as the creation of business ideas, or investigating and appraising markets. For some specific needs 'courses' closer to mainstream management teaching, and concerned with techniques in functional areas, can have a place as long as they are made relevant to small business and are put in the context of developing the range of preparation needs specific to starting a business.

Selection of would-be starters

The model outlined in Figure 2 is also useful in drawing attention to the timing of support programmes. As Johnson and Cathcart (1980) have pointed out the establishment of a business is often a long and drawn out process with involvement gradually increasing so that it may not be clear when the business can be said to be 'founded'. Where (as in the NEP) there is a 'results' objective, the timing of intervention is critcally important in this lengthy founding process: too soon and the business cannot be started quickly after the end of the programme, but too late and the support resources of the NEP would be unnecessarily extravagant (and deprive someone else who might derive more benefit). The question then of just how under-developed the six preparation needs can be and still reach the target point of start-up is a complex of the relative development required in these six areas, the capability of the programme to accelerate the individual's development and the requirements of that specific form of business.

Offering places on an NEP is, not surprisingly, one of the most problematic aspects of the programme and improving 'selection' has become a major focus for further development. If, however, particular needs are common to distinguishable groups of people, and if identifiers can be found for these groups, then there is a means both of knowing what to concentrate on in the design of a programme, and of matching the appropriate programme to a particular individual.

Experience of the 250 or so would-be starters who have been inter- viewed for NEP's at Durham suggests that they can be usefully cate- gorised. Subsequent analysis of the people interested in starting a business who receive support from Enterprise North (6) confirms that the following categories can identify people with different support needs (although in practice these categories are not used by Enterprise North panels).

Eight categories have been distinguished by examining the particular kinds of assistance that people look for when they are preparing to start a business. These categories may not be fixed for the same individual for in some cases someone who is in one category at one stage of preparing to start the business will move into a different category at another stage. The categories do not therefore generalise different 'types' of business starter, but they identify different groups of support needs that can form the basis of a variety of specific, appropriate programmes. Of considerable practical importance is the fact that it is usually possible to identify the predominant character- istics and so the would-be starter in a category on the basis of discussion of his business idea and how it has been developed (or is proposed to be developed).

The eight categories are termed: 'starters', 'learners', 'confirmers', 'perfectors', 'searchers', 'players', 'rejectors' and 'the needy'.

The 'starter' has a clear commitment to starting a business and already possesses the drive, essential skills and knowledge to be able to start. This kind of 'entrepreneur' might well want to use some support agency to fill a specific perceived gap in his knowledge (even if some guidance is required in defining the real gap) or to obtain help in acquiring resources. Such a person, however, does not need a prolonged training programme in order to get the business established.

The second category of would-be starter; the 'learner', is someone who is committed to starting a business and has a fairly clear idea of the product or service. The 'learner', quite importantly, lacks knowledge about how to proceed and about how to run the new business in its early stages.

The third category is the 'confirmer'. This person not only has quite a clear idea of the product or service, but might even have much of the ability and knowledge needed to found and run the business. What is most lacking is the confidence to proceed. It is not uncommon for this kind of person to be seeking reassurance on the major decision of whether to try to start a business but to cloak this in looking for often quite detailed confirmation of the many minor decisions (thus putting off making the final commitment).

'Perfectors' are the fourth distinguishable category. These are people who have an idea that might be quite novel and which involves technical development. For the 'perfector' this development is the main interest. Although there is an intention to turn the idea into a business eventually, the 'product' is clearly their priority for time and resources. The common preoccupation with security of the idea is often a block to testing its commercial feasibility, but the knowledge and ability to start and run a business seems, in any case, very variable for people in this category.

In a fifth category is the 'searcher'; a person who commonly is not merely interested in starting a business, but quite firmly committed to starting and who may also have the basic knowledge and resources. The 'searcher' has, however, no finally developed idea of what the product/ service will be. Often a series of ideas is considered and discarded one by one.

The sixth category is the 'player'. This person often not only has an idea, but an immaculately worked out idea supported by reports, flow charts, independent tests, copies of correspondence, long term financial forecasts and so on, but in the end, the planning, the dreaming, is what it is all about. There is ultimately no intention to turn the idea into a business.

The seventh distinguishable category is the 'rejector', someone who starts to seek assistance but then turns it down. In the view of the 'counsellors' this person may be in category two, the 'learner', but he seems to consider himself to be category one, a 'starter'. Or looked at another way, this person finds the assistance offered does not match what he wants and moves on.

The eighth category consists of people suffering from the gap in financing new businesses identified by the Wilson Committee's (1979) review of the functioning of financial institutions. In this category is the person who looks capable of starting a worthwhile business (immediately, or perhaps after knowledge/confidence needs have been

supported) but who is blocked because he cannot attract the necessary
finance. These are 'the needy' (7).

Different kinds of assistance and, hence programme, are appropriate to
the different needs of people in these eight categories. As a means of
identifying more closely the kinds of support required (and therefore of
determining the appropriate programmes and their content) the six
preparation needs that lead up to the founding of an enterprise can be
applied to each of these categories. Putting the two together gives a
generalised profile of the typical assistance needs of each kind of
business starter. As suggested earlier and as indicated by Figure 3,
the 'starter' is virtually ready to found his business. Where there are
gaps they are likely to be limited and concerned mainly with resourcing
or possibly with some particular aspects of knowledge or managerial
skill. Thus for the 'starter', counselling might help him get a better
sense of priorities and he may value talking a problem through and
getting a different viewpoint. Counselling is an element of an NEP, but
the particular needs of this kind of person are usually quite specific
and, most importantly, they are usually limited to a few fairly well
defined problems. The 'starter' does not need an inclusive programme of
the NEP type: indeed there is a risk that such a programme would be
counter-productive, holding back rather than accelerating the start of
the business. Counselling of the sort that is provided, for example, by
Enterprise North seems an appropriate form of support for the 'starter'.
(For some 'starters', a very different kind of programme focusing on the
growth of their businesses once established might be productive at a
later date; a TSD sponsored pilot programme of this kind is planned to
be run at Durham University Business School in 1981/2).

The 'learners' needs are different; his motivation might be quite
strong and the business idea and opportunity broadly determined but
still requiring development. His major learning needs are, however,
likely to be developing the relevant 'management' knowledge and skills,
knowing how to proceed to start the business and, probably quite
significantly, getting the various resources together (since those are
dependent on a plan of what needs doing).

This category of person is most likely to benefit from an NEP and the
relevant learning and support needs are considered in more detail
towards the end of this paper.

The 'confirmer' usually has a quite well developed idea, but a relative lack of final motivation. This might be influenced by doubts about
the conversion of the idea into an adequate opportunity. The need for
confirmation is, however, more likely to be a reflection of doubts,
sometimes not well founded, about the capacity to found and run a
business. There will usually be associated gaps in planning and
resourcing. If such reasons are the cause of the need for confirmation
and if development needs to take place in a number of areas a programme
of the NEP type will be an appropriate form of support.

The 'perfector' is strongly motivated to develop the idea, but might
be ambivalent about turning it into a business; it is at least not his
current pre-occupation. The reason for seeking support other than for
technical assistance might well be to do with protection and security of
the idea, or with acquiring resources that are primarily for development. There are a number of areas where 'management' support programmes

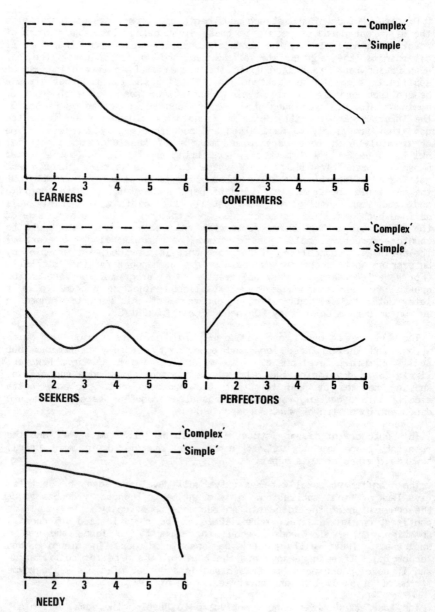

The vertical axis indicates the extent of development needed to start a 'simple' or a 'complex' business. The horizontal axis shows the six development needs (1. commitment, 2. idea, 3. opportunity, 4. capability, 5. plan, 6. resourcing).

Figure 3   Categories of enterprise founder: typical profiles

might be helpful in, for example, keying product development with market opportunities, understanding the implications of different scales of operation and more generally developing or re-orientating existing management capability to the requirements of founding a business. A comprehensive programme such as the NEP that aims at an early business start is unlikely, therefore, to be suited to the 'perfector'.

The 'searcher' again has different support needs; his motivation to start a business might be strong, but so far there is no settled business idea. The idea is not only essential to development of the opportunity, and resourcing it, but thinking about and working on the business idea is also the usual medium for developing an understanding of what it means to run a business. Hence development of the capability to start and manage the business will tend to be retarded without an idea to work on.

Lack of a business idea which can form a basis for the development of other attributes makes an NEP an unsuitable support programme for people in this category. In addition the objective of achieving an early start of a business makes the 'searcher' a high risk individual for inclusion on such programmes. The chances of his finding an adequate easily developed business idea that matches his preferences and aptitudes and which he can utilise on the programme are far too low. Nevertheless the critically important factor determining the number of new businesses founded is the supply of 'entrepreneurs' rather than the availability of marketable ideas. Furthermore, when a business is still small its continuing success and growth almost certainly depends more on the person(s) running it than on the original business ideas (excepting those occasions when an unusual growth opportunity is unexpectedly 'presented' to a company).

Some kind of support programme is therefore desirable for 'searchers' who have the motivation to start a new business, the three preconditions (of an impetus and disposition to found a business and a belief that this is a realistic aim) and who also have the capacity to develop the other attributes they will need. The solution seems not so much to intervene to provide someone with an idea (which then becomes their risk) as to help him recognise business ideas that match his aims and resources and learn how to evaluate them. Alternatively training might be provided in developing creativity or attempts might be made to bring together these would-be starters with people who have potential ideas, but who are not interested in running a business. Whatever the solution 'searchers' seem to represent a group that could benefit from assistance.

Programmes are not seen as suitable for 'players' and while 'rejectors' might benefit from some kind of support, counselling is possibly the only acceptable form. The 'needy' would benefit from a programme only if this was a route to their being able to acquire resources.

One use of this framework is therefore to identify a number of kinds of 'support programme' appropriate to different types of business starter and different stages of preparation. It can also, however, be used to identify the sort of people who will benefit from a particular kind of programme.

Thus, 'starters' are too advanced for the NEP. 'Learners' and many 'confirmers', who have developed or thought out a business idea are the prime target market. 'Perfectors' and 'searchers' are almost certainly too far away from starting to meet the 'results objective' and only in those few cases where the NEP is the means to acquiring resources should 'the needy' be considered.

Looking then at the preparation needs for these target categories and taking into account the prime objectives of the programme, a 'specification' can be drawn up so that people suited to an NEP should:

- be committed to the idea of starting a business (although there may still be some doubts),

- have a business idea that appears to offer an adequate opportunity for a new business and that does not need prolonged further product development,

- be capable of acquiring the knowledge and skills to plan and start the business,

- be able to get together the resources required both to start and establish the enterprise,

- be capable of running the young business in a way which at least increases its chances of survival and preferably makes it possible to take advantage of growth opportunities.

In addition the purpose of the NEPs requires that the business should be capable of creating new employment within the first year.

Specifications could similarly be drawn up for programmes designed to meet the needs of 'starters', 'searchers' or 'perfectors' with the scope of the programme modified according to any 'results objectives'.

Before looking finally at how these identified areas of need translate into the content and structure of the NEP, a further set of needs, those of style, have to be taken into account.

PROGRAMME STYLE NEEDS

Experience of running six NEP's at Durham has confirmed many of the particular attitudes to learning that have become apparent in running a variety of programmes for established small businessmen (with 'programmes' taken to include counselling as well as courses). In some ways this has been surprising. People joining the NEP have come from a variety of backgrounds - from small enterprise drifters to administrators from highly structured organisations - and with a wide spectrum of formal education. The typical small business attitudes to learning (see, for example, Deeks 1976 and McGivern and Overton 1980) are nevertheless very prevalent and have to be regarded as style needs in designing the programmes.

The more important for the NEP can be summarised as:

- Overt relevance of the course to helping get the business established is essential: disbelief is only briefly suspended.

- Specific, concrete inputs are expected. These are by no means the same as 'how-to-do-it' and factual details. Principles and theory that can be applied are welcomed: but abstractions are not.

- A progression must be evident in the would-be starters' own work; they are generally conscious of the value of time, and pressure is self-applied. In running the Programme it is more important to build in time for reflection than keep up pressure artificially.

- 'Lecturing' is not easily tolerated, neither are long periods of being passive. Some form of active 'teaching' style with participation is required.

- Would-be starters are, however, capable of quite long application. Their stamina is sometimes remarkable.

- Would-be starters value comment and learning about the experiences of their peers. A great deal of learning from each other takes place in the residential period 'out of hours'.

- They seek feedback, reassurance and opinions from those they regard as knowledgeable: counselling from tutors they trust becomes increasingly important as the programme develops.

- Although there is often quite intense psychological ownership of their own business idea, and this is what they mostly want to centre on, they are usually quite supportively prepared to discuss and even work on other people's business ideas.

- There is a variable disposition to learn from practitioners (solicitors, accountants, bank managers et al). Generally, the contact is valued, but if they find the practitioners do not share their pre-occupations, they may reject rather than learn about the way resource providers see things.

THE NEP AT DURHAM

The learning needs of those would-be starters for whom an NEP is considered both suitable and likely to lead to fulfilment of the 'results objective' of the programmes, together with the style needs, are reflected in the strands which run through the programme at Durham. Perhaps the most important is discussion of an individual's business idea, helping him form a realistic appraisal of its strengths and weaknesses, suggesting ways it can be developed, guidance on how other parts of the programme might be applied and considering the implications of the business for the individual. These discussions generally take the form of a tutorial. In terms of the scheduled time spent in the residential phase they amount to about 15 per cent. With five people often working as tutors the man hours spent on these individual discussions approaches half of the total 'contact' time.

This figure is still, however, an underestimate, since a great deal of discussion on business ideas continues between the individuals on the programme and it is normal for these business ideas to be taken as the illustrations when other topics are being 'taught'.

What might be termed the management functions, take a little over 20 per cent of the scheduled time. The main focus is on aspects of marketing and finance. The aim here is not just to concentrate on what needs to be known to start a business, but to develop an understanding that will contribute to establishing the business on a sound basis, capable of growth. To some extent, training in techniques is required (such as low-resource market research or producing and using cash flow forecasts) but most emphasis is given to understanding the principles with examples of how they can be applied to the development of the specific business ideas.

About a further 20 per cent of the time is allocated to finding out about the small business environment and in particular sources of assistance and resources. The usual approach is a talk given by a practitioner, followed by discussion. People on the programme not only learn what might be provided (in terms of premises or overdrafts or help with accounts and so on) they also learn something about the attitudes and pre-occupations of the 'providers', what to look for in employing an accountant or solicitor, and what to expect when seeking a loan.

The three areas mentioned so far - scrutiny and development of the business idea, starting to learn where management knowledge can be applied, and some awareness of the sources of help and resources - start to form the basis of a business plan which in turn becomes the main output of the residential phase.

Attention is however given to two other topics before any serious start to developing a plan is attempted. One of these is concerned with orientating the individual toward owning a small business, developing an understanding of management styles and of what running a business will mean in terms of their own lives and priorities. This orientation takes about ten per cent of the time but might well be taken further during the 'tutorials'. The other topic is the development of an overall strategy for forming and establishing the business (about 15 per cent of the time). It is common to find that forming a strategy has been neglected in favour of development of the idea and some components of a plan. The need for a strategy is often approached by drawing up a framework for the business and then examining how the specific chosen elements do or do not fit together.

About a further ten per cent of the time is spent on a form of skills training in negotiation, presenting a case and basic selling. In general it has been found that skills here are lacking and seldom adequate for the task of getting together, over a short period, the resources necessary to form a complex business. This kind of training has been given more attention in the recent programmes but might still require more emphasis.

'Legal requirements' not covered elsewhere (e.g. consumer credit, VAT) take about five per cent of the time as do matters concerned with planning, reviewing and evaluating the programme as it proceeds.

The method of approaching all these topics is determined by the style-needs so that while there is a definite set down structure to each programme there is a great deal of flexibility in the way that the separate components are managed. Although there is little need to apply pressure artificially quite specific outputs are required by the end of the residential phase. These take the form of the 'business plan' which serves to direct the preparation of the business on-site during the counselling phase, specifies the critical gaps in knowledge which need to be filled, sets down the strategy and plan for the business in at least the first two years of its existence, and forms the basic business proposal which can be used in seeking major resources.

(Durham has so far, like London and Manchester, taken all the residential period together. For its next NEP, however, it is to follow the approach chosen by the Scottish Business School of running the residential in two phases. The main advantage of this is to give the course members an opportunity to research certain critical elements and have time to reconsider and restructure parts of the basic plan with the chance to have further major playback and comment on their revisions.)

After this residential phase the would-be business starters return home to start work on implementing the plan. During this period there is regular counselling contact with the Business School and each member of the programme also returns to Durham three times to discuss progress with a panel normally consisting of one of the TSD people responsible for NEPs, an experienced consultant, a banker, a representative of the Department of Industry and one or two of their Business School 'counsellors'. This panel works sometimes creatively - suggesting different approaches, contacts, ways round obstacles - and sometimes critically to keep the preparation of the business on track.

CONCLUSIONS

This paper has set out to consider new enterprise support programmes and in particular the NEPs. It has been suggested that unlike the majority of other post experience training or education the NEPs have dual objectives; a training objective: to develop the managerial capabilities of would-be starters, and a results objective: to ensure the practical translation of such capabilities into viable new businesses by the end of the programme. The results objective thus clearly colours the training objective; the question becomes not simply, "who would benefit?", but "who would benefit to the extent that they are able to achieve a specific goal within a specific time period?"

The dual objectives have lead to two vital considerations which have been expressed in terms of a simple model that helps formulate the content and structure of the NEP conducted at Durham. These considerations are firstly the positioning of new enterprise support programmes in the founding process, and secondly the selection of candidates. The NEP at Durham University Business School quite firmly takes the stance that it is primarily concerned with developing the six preparation needs in the founding process, but this is acknowledged as only one approach.

Each of the four business schools running NEPs have particular organisational strengths that influence the design and presentation of their own programmes. In the case of Durham for example, a local support network has been built up over time so that it is now possible to call on a large number of specialist practitioners who are prepared to talk, often very frankly, about the way they see their own professions and about how they regard the particular presentations of the business ideas. The three year old New Enterprise Development Project also means that there is a group of teachers and researchers specialising in new business formation so that there is a particular capability for individual counselling.

The utility of developing frameworks of both the founding process and categories of would-be starters lies not only in enabling the structure and content of new enterprise support programmes to be thought out more clearly, and thus have a more rational basis, but also in highlighting some potentially contentious issues surrounding the NEP's in particular. A first issue is the results objective itself. How far is it justified?

Employment creation is the basic, if rather simplistic criterion, and on a straight pay-out basis an NEP is justified if it leads to the creation of fewer than a dozen jobs (that is the cost of a programme compared with savings of unemployment benefit paid before the new jobs were created plus, strictly, the extra revenue effects of new income tax and national insurance payments). Even on this basis the Programme pays for itself in less than one year. The expectation is however, that more new businesses and jobs than this will be 'produced': a working target for each NEP might be something like a dozen new businesses employing on average three or four people within their first year.

The value of these programmes is however by no means seen only in terms of businesses started and jobs created and it is worth drawing attention to just two of the spin-off results of this group of business starter programmes. One of these is concerned with learning more about the start-up process, about the sort of people and business ideas that combine to produce sound new enterprises and about the difficulties that are commonly experienced in this process. Some applications to various types of training programme have already been indicated in this paper. But there is a wider effect and increased understanding of start-up needs is also guiding the provision of such resources as premises, counselling services, start-up finance and so on: there has, as an example, been some collaboration with major banks on the development of recently introduced schemes to apply more appropriate financing criteria to the founding of a new enterprise. Learning about the start-up process from NEPs is also one source of information being used to influence small business policy.

More generally there is a need to de-mystify common impressions about the sort of character and talents that are required to start and run a business and a need to review the commonly un-examined assumptions and conventional wisdoms about enterprise founding.

As a second spin-off, Enterprise founding programmes are also making a contribution in a different direction. It was stated earlier that strong commitment to starting a business has to be regarded as a necessary pre-condition of participating in an NEP. But programmes of this sort can still have an important role in demonstrating to other potential business founders that people like themselves can make a success of starting a business. In other words there is a contribution to increasing the supply of would-be starters by helping create the necessary credibility of the act of being a business founder that was noted by Shapero.

A second issue concerns the relatively narrow band of would-be starters catered for by the NEP. Although the model draws attention to the timing of support programmes, and points to the option of developing the preparation needs, empirical evidence suggests that both the gestation of a business idea, and the actual establishment of a business are often long drawn out 'processes which may also be iterative. Thus, to some extent NEPs seek not only to accelerate the development phase, but also to channel it. In so doing they perhaps ignore, again because of the results objective, certain categories of would-be starter. This raises the question of what might be done to assist the categories of would-be starter for whom an NEP is not suitable, or who would not benefit to the extent of being able to form a business quickly. As suggested earlier these categories are not necessarily different types of people, but may be would-be starters at a different stage.

Whilst therefore, the NEPs mark a milestone in the provision of support and training for new enterprises, it has to be recognised that the peculiar constraints under which they operate means that such provision remains narrowly based. But with the NEPs demonstrating that certain kinds of business founder are not necessarily 'born entrepreneurs', but can be developed, there is a scope for seeing if other kinds of training programme can help realise the potential of people at other points in the enterprise founding process.

NOTES

(1)   'Programme' as used throughout this paper refers to management education or training of a kind more flexible and with more components than are usually associated with a 'course'. But the support provided by the 'Programme' is concerned with development of the individual wanting to start the business and does not, for example, include provision of finance or physical resources.
(2)   The present Programme Director is John Eversley, a member of the New Enterprise Development Project at Durham University Business School.
(3)   In this paper the term entrepreneur is avoided because it is so difficult to know what the word signifies to someone else. The terms used here are 'enterprise founder' or 'would-be starter'. This person then becomes the 'owner-manager' having the major ownership stake and being responsible for strategic decisions.
(4)   The term 'business' applies equally well as far as the NEP is concerned to manufacturing or service and has included co-operative ventures.
(5)   Just as the enterprise founder's typical attitude to risk leans more toward calculated success than gambling so his self-confidence will probably be based more on a fairly cautious self-assessment than bravado.
(6)   Enterprise North consists of voluntary panels of established

businessmen in the Northern Region of England who discuss and advise on
a variety of proposals for new businesses. The scheme is entirely free
to the would-be business starter. Durham University Business School
administers Enterprise North and gives further counselling before and
after the panel discussions.
(7) These people exist. One person's conclusion that the business
project has sound potential to succeed might not of course, also be the
conclusion of a potential investor. But the reasons for turning down
these new businesses have often been based not on a scrutiny of the
business proposal nor of the person, but rather on such standard grounds
as lack of security. This is not to say that normal lending policy is
'wrong', but that it is not particularly designed to help business
start-ups. The major banks are now experimenting with schemes to apply
different criteria. But for the present this funding gap for new
business starters certainly exists.

REFERENCES

Deeks, J., 'The Small Firm Owner-Manager', Praeger, 1976.
Gibb, A.A. and Ritchie, J., 'A Management Development Programme for the
  'Would-be-Entrepreneur', A report to the Training Services Division of
  the Manpower Services Commission. November 1977.
Gibb, A.A., 'A Study of the Institutional Framework for Small Firms
  Development in Baden Winterberg'. A report to the Department of
  Industry. June 1980.
Johnson, P. and Cathcart, G., 'Manufacturing Firms and Regional
  Development. Some Evidence fom the Northern Region.' in Gibb, A.A. and
  Webb, T.D.(Eds.) 'Policy Issues in Small Business Research'. Saxon
  House 1980.
McGivern, C. and Overton, D., 'A Study of Small Firms and Their
  Management Development Needs' in Gibb, A.A. and Webb, T.D. (Eds.)
  Policy Issues in Small Business Research. Saxon House 1980.
Scott, M.G., 'Independence and the Flight from Large Scale: Some
  Sociological Factors in the Founding Process' in Gibb, A.A. and Webb,
  T.D. (Eds.), Policy Issues in Small Business Research, Saxon House
  1980.
Shapero, A., 'The Role of Entrepreneurship in Economic Development at
  the less than national level' prepared for the Economic Development
  Administration, US Department of Commerce, January 1977.
Watkins, D.S., 'Entry into the Independent Entrepreneurship Towards a
  Model of the Business Initiation Process' Working Paper presented at
  the EIASM joint seminar on Entrepreneurship and Institution Building,
  Dansk Management Centre, Copenhagen 1976.
Wilson Committee to Review the Functioning of Financial Institutions
  Interim report. 'The Financing of Small Firms', HMSO 1979.

Setting up in Business	Registration, Incorporation,
Your Business Premises	Accommodation, Addresses, Offices, Shops and Factories, Decorating and Furnishing
Communications & Security	Post, Telephone, Telex, Fire Precautions, Office Equipment, Printing, Processes
Advertising	Press, Magazines, Posters, Media
Public Relations	Conferences, Exhibitions, Personnel, PR
Finance Organisation & Banking	What do you need the money for?
Budgeting & Accounts	Estimating, Petty Cash, V.A.T., Wages
Buying a Going Concern	Franchises
Professional Advice You Need	Accountants, Solicitors, Insurance
Employing Staff	Part, and full-time; wages, salaries and N.H.I.

Figure 3.   The administrative bias of small firm text books: chapter headings from Douglas, P. Run Your Own Business, Dent, 1973.

How to increase profits	Management techniques for the Smaller Firm; Marketing Budgeting, and Production Control, costing and Work Study
Managing for Profits	Manage for results, pricing, creating an image, selling, advertising and sales promotion
Accounting for Profit	Classifying costs, standard costing, marginal costing and decision making
Productivity for Profit	Work study and measurement, management controls
Profit is not Enough	How to stay solvent; cash flow budgeting; control of profits; debtors, creditors, stocks.

Figure 4.   The business technique bias in small firm text books: chapter headings from, Wood, E.G., Bigger Profits for the Smaller Firm, Business Books, 1972.

Wood's approach (see Figure 4), however, does serve as a bridge between the language of business techniques and that of 'management'. In the transition from one to the other, the emphasis switches from technique and analytical method, to insight and to involvement with people. Whereas the business technician deals with an impersonal business, the manager deals with an 'organisation'. John Deeks' Small Firm Owner Manager is one British work with a managerial emphasis (Deeks, 1975). Using the conventional terminology of management, he differentiates between the 'entrepreneur' and the 'administrator' (see Figure 5).

`Entrepreneur'   'Administrator'

Innovating   Objective Setting
Risk-taking   Policy Formulation
Tactical planning   Strategic Planning
Negotiating   Organising
Inter-personal communications   Formal Communication
Troubleshooting   Control

Figure 5.   The distinction between the entrepreneur and the
            administrator. Adapted from John Deeks, The Small
            Firm Owner Manager, Praeger, 1975.

Whereas writers like Deeks (1975), describe an entrepreneurial approach to management, they offer little advice on how to stimulate its development. Little seems to have been written on this since the classic American work on `Enterprising Men' (Collins et al, 1964), made a serious attempt to link entrepreneurial and enterprise development. Having conducted intensive interviews with some 200 entrepreneurs in their localities, they found:

> `the act of entrepreneurship to be that
> of bringing ideas, skills, money,
> equipment and markets together into a
> profitable combination. The economist,
> the accountant and the banker tend to
> look at these arrangements in terms of
> the financial and material resources
> involved. The entrepreneur sees always
> the bringing together of people into a
> new arrangement'.

They also concluded that formal education and entrepreneurship were poles apart. The `school for entrepreneurs', as far as they were concerned, needed to offer `coursework' in Drifting, Basic Dealing and Protegeship, over many, many years. First, through a long period of `Drifting' the entrepreneur picked up a wide repertoire of technical skills and abilities; he broadened his grasp of the "transactional nature of personal relationships". Secondly, through "Protegeship" he became an intense student of entrepreneurial behaviour, watching his sponsor's every movement and learned the rudiments of bringing resources together, of setting up structures, of creating and severing relationships. Finally, having graduated from Drifting and Protegeship, he was ready for the 'course' in Basic Dealing; he learned how to bring together ideas, skills, money, and facilities in a 'deal'.

The conclusion from this brief analysis (summarised in Figure 6) appears to be that, as far as textbooks on starting a business are concerned, the language of administration predominates. The indications are, however, that while the enterprising man has been left behind, the business technician (to a greater extent) and the manager/entrepreneur (to a lesser extent) are gradually entering the picture.

Language	Orientation	Focus Person	Unit	Key Exponent	Emphasis Today
1. Administrative	Know-how	Administrator	Company	Douglas (1973)	Very Strong
2. Business	Technique	Businessman	Business	Wood (1972)	Rapidly Increasing
3. Management	Insight	Manager	Organisation	Deeks (1978)	Slowly Increasing
4. Entrepreneurship	Personal Development	Entrepreneur	Enterprise	Collins (1964)	Very Weak

Figure 6. The languages of entrepreneurship

b) Training programmes

(i) For small business - Whereas Start Your Own Business texts provide administrative know-how, small business courses appear to emphasise business techniques. Recently, Bennett and Reynier (1980) published the results of an extensive study of educational programmes for small businesses. They mailed 265 relevant establishments and discovered that 142 of these offered some form of provision. The most significant provider was further education, including Polytechnics, with 37 per cent. Universities were responsible for 18 per cent and Industrial Training Boards for some 15 per cent.

Classifying the courses cited by Bennett and Reynier under the headings of Administrative Know How, Business Techniques, Managerial Insights and Person/Entrepreneur Development, yields the picture illustrated in Figure 7.

Administrative Know-how	30%	Legislation (29) Sources of finance (15) Personnel (12), Sales (10) Exporting (9), Starting up (3)
Business Techniques	47%	Finance (28), Production (19), Marketing (18), Personnel (12), Start Up (3), Management Techniques (22)
Managerial Insights	22%	General Management (37), Relations at Work (14)
Person/Entrepreneur Development	1%	Start up (2)

Figure 7. Classification of courses offered by categories of information and knowledge required by small businessmen

Not unexpectedly perhaps, it appears that within academic establishments, business techniques have become predominant. Of these, finance and marketing/sales seem to be the most popular. In addition general management appears to be much more popular than in the texts. This is probably because it is often the generalists who are drawn to small business, because of their broad view of the organisation. Finally, and not surprisingly, the entrepreneur, in the true sense of the word, seems to be undervalued.

(ii) For new enterprise - Only one per cent of the courses offered by the establishments surveyed by Bennett and Reynier, explicitly dealt with new business formation. The main exceptions are the New Enterprise Programmes (N.E.P's). These have all been sponsored by the Training Services Division of the Manpower Services Commission, and have taken place in the last two years in six locations. The longest standing have been those run by Manchester and Durham University Business School in the North of England. More recent ones have been run by the Welsh

126

Development Agency, by Sundridge Park Management Centre, London Business School and URBED/City University in London. All have followed more or less a similar basic programme with the exception of URBED's approach.

The conventional New Enterprise Programme(6) starts with a one month taught course, in which business techniques and administrative know-how predominate. For the remaining 12 weeks, prospective entrepreneurs develop their businesses in the field, whilst getting tutorial support from staff members. Participants also develop a business plan, which is vetted periodically by a panel of experts.

Thus courses for both existing and new small firms are strong on instruction, covering administrative know-how and business techniques. The N.E.P.'s involve much more fieldwork than most other programmes. How much management insight and entrepreneurial aptitude is gained in the process however, is open to question, and to further research. This paper only attempts to answer the questions with respect to the URBED programme.

HOW DOES URBED'S APPROACH WORK?

a) Aims

URBED, as an organisation, concentrates on finding practical solutions to the economic problems of run-down urban areas. Thus the development of training programmes is a means toward the creation of viable employment and the encouragement of new enterprise. The joint sponsors of the first programme, the Training Services Division and Hackney Business Promotion Centre (7), reflected URBED's dual aims. By involving City University Business School, Shell (UK) and two of the clearing banks, URBED gained insight into the supportive environment.

The philosophy underpinning the URBED programme has been that training, to be effective, needs to involve learning by and through experience. As Lao-Tse put it, "I hear and I forget; I see and I remember; I do and I understand". Furthermore, that a programme needs to extend over the natural development period of a business, both 'pre and post natal'. Finally, that a programme should offer scope for integrating the person and the business.

b) Content

The initial programme offered by URBED had three distinct features. First there was a strong emphasis on learning while doing, and in association with others. Second, the different kind of levels of business and personal development were catered for by operating in stages, (which were both linked and self contained, as shown in Figure 8). Third there was an emphasis on getting into business; having helped prospective entrepreneur's to acquire the administrative know-how required in starting up (Stage 1), the programme moved on to the development of the entrepreneur's business idea (Stage 2) The business techniques introduced at Stage 3 were then put into practice (Stage 4) as participants began to take the 'plunge into business'.

The following sections deal basically with the scope and results of each stage.

1.	THINKING ABOUT IT Saturday 27th January, 1979	One day Conference	Introduction to sources of assistance; basic administrative know how.
2.	ASSESSING THE PROSPECTS Saturday & Sunday 24th & 25th February, 1979	Week-end session for those whose ideas are not yet firm	A more clearly worked out business plan; greater insight into entrepreneurial aptitudes and market opportunities
3.	PREPARING TO GO 2nd-5th April, 1979	Four day course on basic business techniques	An understanding of what it takes to start and run a successful business
4.	TAKING THE PLUNGE April to June 1979	12 weeks to get going, with one day a week in the classroom	A realistic business plan, and the first steps taken towards starting a business

Figure 8. URBED's start your own business programme

Stage 1 - Thinking About It: One Day Conference

a) The experience of January, 1979.

The 'conference' was run in partnership with the Hackney Business Promotion Centre and URBED, with the former acting as host and providing the speakers and the latter preparing an information package and co-ordinating the publicity. The event was symbolic of the borough's attempt to stimulate indigenous entrepreneurship and thus was seen to be much more than a 'training day'. It was also to provide an initial pool of Hackney - Islington based entrepreneurs from which future stages of the programme could be drawn.

As a course of instruction with limited objectives, the event was very well received. The fact that the majority of speakers were practitioners and professionals rather than academics was appreciated. The lectures were much more effective than the group discussions, where the absence of skilled 'group facilitators' was noticeable. Suggestions for improvement from participants, which are well worth repeating, included;

"Could you explain the sequence of running a business".

"Could you provide a notice board for people to make contact on".

"Could you include some women and black experts rather than all white males".

As a promotional activity, the event was only partially successful. Although extensive publicity was carried out (through advertisements in local papers; posters and cards in the streets, libraries and confectioners; as well as through letters to bank managers, estate agents and college teachers), only 44 out of the 100 who attended were actual or prospective entrepreneurs. The remainder were advisors, educators and local and London based interested parties. Not only do these statistics reveal the difficulties of reaching potential entrepreneurs in a large city, but they also high-light the importance of prior publicity, especially when one is focussing upon a particular locality.

b) Stage 1 re-design for 1980.(8)

As a result of this initial experience it was decided that for subsequent programmes the one day conference would be replaced by a two day workshop. (The first of these modified workshops was scheduled for May 1980). The overall aim was to remain unchanged, that is to attract people with an interest in self employment who have, as yet, no definite idea upon which to base a business. The modified approach, however, was to be based more closely on the 'SELF-BUSINESS TRIANGLE' illustrated in Figure 9.

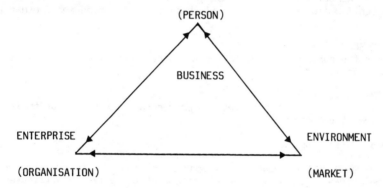

Figure 9]: The self-business triangle

The thinking behind this concept is that a match has to be created between the person and -

      i)   a business idea, as well as
     ii)   their business activities.

The first relates the business to its external environment and the second to its internal functions.

To create a match in this area, the programme aims to do two things. First, to get workshop participants to generate thoughts about what is going on in the world around them. For this purpose brainstorming techniques will be used to outline ideas. Secondly, participants are encouraged to focus upon their own background, interests, and intentions as shown in Figure 10.

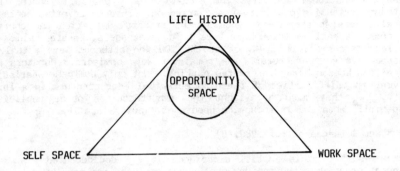

- LIFE HISTORY or personal 'biography';
highlighting themes, events and experiences from the past that have
relevance to a future business

- SELF SPACE or 'leisure' pursuits;
highlighting important features of their current occupations, other than
work

- WORK SPACE;
that is the content of their present and/or recently work experience and
organisation, and

- OPPORTUNITY SPACE;
that is their future intentions and prospects, arising out of their past
and present situations.

Figure 10. Idea space

It is within the 'opportunity space' (9) that it is believed a new
business idea is born. It is an amalgam of the person's attributes and
society's needs; it knits together past, present and future. The next
step is to assist the person to develop the idea into a business
proposition.

The author agrees with Low(1976) that a business is an idea in a 'Form
with a Demand'. No matter how attractive the idea to the public, until
it is given a tangible form it cannot actually reach them. For example,
until Edison had set up a laboratory, acquired materials and a work
force, and created a phonograph that worked, his idea of a phonograph
got him nowhere. The idea of an 'instrument that could mimic' needed a
form before it could be marketed as a product. It only became a 'phonograph business' once people demonstrated their willingness and ability
to pay for it. Having been turned into a business, it needed to be
operated, staffed, administered, financed, and the product sold. These
are the 'activities' of business.

Different types of people/entrepreneurs approach these activities in
different ways, depending on their backgrounds, motivations and attitudes. Some people see themselves as 'sales people'; others as 'techni-

cally minded'. URBED's workshop uses a 'Relationships Awareness Test' (10) through which people can identify their personal motivations, strengths and weaknesses. Basically there are four prevailing attitudinal types:

- the caring type, corresponding often with the outgoing craftsmen (see Figure 1)

- the assertive type, who may have something in common with the classical entrepreneur

- the analytical type, who is often a professional person

- the hub type, who has something in common with the gamesman or outgoing opportunist.

The 'analytical' type, for example, may see himself as good at finance and poor at selling. Yet he should be able to develop an approach to marketing that draws on his analytical bent. Similarly, the 'caring' type may be good with people and poor with books. Yet again, he should be able to find a way of caring for paperwork. So this part of the workshop is concerned with fitting the person to the business activities he must undertake and, where appropriate, indicating where delegation and collaboration are required; for it is the people in the business who develop and maintain its activities.

Stage II Assessing the prospects: developing your business idea

The aim of the weekend session on 'assessing prospects' is summarised in Figure 11.

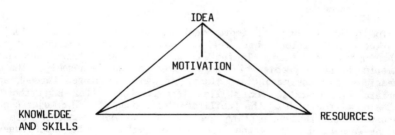

Figure 11: Assessing your prospects

Participants were divided into six to eight small groups according to the stage of development of their business idea: vague idea, taken first steps, part time or full time business. Within these small groups, stimulated by one of the programme facilitators, they worked through their idea, their knowledge and skills, their resources, and their motivation. They alternated between self assessment, on pre-set worksheets, and interaction with others in the group. Prior to these group sessions, talks were given by both academics and practitioners on all of the above key aspects. Entrepreneurs from previous programmes were deliberately involved as trainers, to ensure that a link between work and education was maintained, and to provide the basis of a New Entrerprise Network that has brought about a continuing exchange of information, contacts and ideas.

Thus this stage of the programme was more 'educational' (personal development) than 'instructional' (knowledge and skills).

Responses received from more than half of the 28 participants in Stage II endorsed the achievement of these objectives; 13 of the 15 respondents found the weekend to be very worthwhile. They found it helped them to a greater or lesser extent to work through their business plan, clarify their ideas, and identify their strengths and weaknesses. (See Table 1)

Table 1
Assessing the prospects: course evaluation

Objective	Completely Fulfilled	Partly Fulfilled	Not Fulfilled
Clarify market opportunity	42%	33%	25%
Work through business plan (1st steps)	45%	33%	22%
Identification of strengths/ weaknesses	40%	38%	22%

The greatest room for improvement appeared to lie with 'clarifying market opportunities' where reliance was placed on 'instruction' rather than upon interaction. In fact it was the group interactions and the meeting of other people which were looked on most favourably. The group sessions were not mere discussions, but were structured through appropriate 'instruments' and skilled 'facilitators' (for a further discussion of the role of the facilitator, see page 23). The major conflict arose between those expecting specific help - "more concrete help, less wishy-washy", and those who expected the weekend to be about assessing prospects. The major unfulfilled need was expressed by five respondents: "we would appreciate more individual attention". Thus, not only were small groups appreciated, but individual attention was also desired.

Stage III. Preparing to Go: Acquiring Business Techniques

The four day intensive programme on 'business techniques' served as the knowledge and skill base for the action learning programme to follow. Thus it was both part of an overall 13 week package, for 15 carefully selected participants, and was also offered as a self contained course for four non-sponsored people. Participants sponsored by the TSD had to be unemployed or only 'marginally' employed (just starting in business). Fifteen out of some 40 applicants were selected on the basis of 'the person' and 'the idea'. The business ideas worksheet, used in the weekend, doubled as a selection form.

The intensity and brevity of this induction course, distinguished it from other N.E.P's. The programme was divided between Marketing (concept and techniques), Finance (sources and applications), Administration (paperwork, people, premises) and Planning (information sources and problem solving). All 19 participants found the intensive course helpful (8 quite helpful, 11 very helpful). The most successful day, on finance, was the best co-ordinated, most clearly structured, contained a good variety of experts and practitioners, and focussed largely on a single technique - cash flow.

The main conclusions of the first course of this kind were that -

- speakers should be well briefed in advance;

- the day's convenor should play an active co-ordinating role;

- people want to be spoon-fed at this stage of the game;

- but they appreciate a variety of people to do it, and a mixture of lecture and discussion, information and reflection;

- and continual reference both to their own situations and also to an on-going case study, is very valuable.

Again building on this experience the course has been redesigned to move away from the conventional form - finance, marketing and administration and to bring it more in line with SELF=BUSINESS philosophy (see Figure 13 - page 20).

Use will be made in future of Marks and Spencers as a case study because this offers an opportunity to analyse the evolution of the company from 1863-1980. This, it is hoped, will facilitate the demonstration of the basic processes - innovation, organisation and collaboration - occurring and reoccurring. Participants will be taken through a process of reflection whereby their own prospective business evolution can be compared with that of Marks and Spencer's especially at the early stages of this organisation's development.

Stage IV. Taking the plunge: developing your business

In many ways the 'action learning' programme represented the core of URBED's educational activity and philosophy.

THEME	TOPICS
1 Creating a Business	Business Evolution,
2 Finding a Market	Marketing Concept
3 Planning Ahead	The Cash Flow Merry Go Round, Sources and Uses of Finance
4 Getting Organiseed	Business as a System, Coping with Paperwork, Business Activities
5 Involving People	Personal Motivation Selling and Promotion
6 Doing Deals	Negotiation
7 Committing Yourself	Defining the Business, Action Learning.

Figure 12. Preparing to go course structure.

a) Action learning in theory

The idea of action learning has largely been developed by Reg Revans: (11)

> "Managers are not employed to describe, nor even to recommend; they are employed to act. They learn to do this more effectively only after they know the result of their own, worked out plans, implemented by themselves. In the risky situation of being accepted by others or not, each manager needs the support, not of confident experts, but of those who are themselves going through the same tricky process". (Revans 1980).

Action learning is contained within a cycle of action and reflection. As illustrated in Figure 13., learning takes place as a person moves from action to an observation of the results of such action, onto the formulation of hypotheses about the causes of such results. These hypotheses will affect the future actions we take, and so the cycle goes around and around. As David Kolb of M.I.T.(1974) has explained, this learning cycle in fact conforms with scientific method.

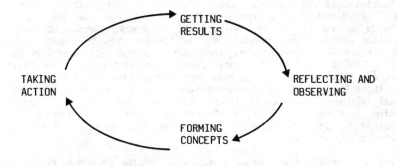

Figure 13:   The learning cycle

The basic tenets of action learning are:

- **you learn from and through others** by listening to them; learning to respect their opinions; giving and taking advice, support and criticism; accepting and comparing one another's values; and allowing oneself to become dependent on others.

- **you learn from and through experience** by looking critically at, assessing the relevance of, and looking afresh into, past experience.

- **you learn to deal with information** by asking useful questions; describing situations as well as acting upon them; conceiving of people, information and things in relation to each other; predicting the consequences of actions, and comparing predictions against actuality.

- **you learn to turn words into actions** by taking risks; learning while doing; carrying out actions as well as describing them; but changing your behaviour only when you wish to.

b) Action learning in URBED practice

i) Introduction - At the end of the four day course, the 15 participants were divided into sets of five. The allocation was based on two major considerations:

-       mix of personality/entrepreneurial types, based on the 'Relationship Awareness Test'.(This was administered during Stage II). Basically the attempt was made to include craftsmen and opportunists, and introspective and outgoing types in each set.

-       maximum diversity of type, business, age, and stage of development in two of the sets and as a control, restricted diversity in the third.

135

Participants subsequently spent one day a week within these sets, together with a 'set advisor'. The intention was that the set should provide the vehicle through which 'reflection complimented action'. The function of the 'set advisor' or 'facilitator' was to ensure that such reflections were appropriately focussed and that the exchange between SELF=BUSINESS was a fertile one. Each set advisor clearly had their own particular personality, interests and back-ground and although each of the three had worked with groups extensively, and was also familiar with small business, inevitably there were variations in the approach to action learning. Figure 14 demonstrates these differences as they appeared to the participants in the respective groups and to the set advisors themselves.

The set therefore served as a microcosm of the business world. Within it the individual entrepreneur could innovate, organise and collaborate; he could use others to develop and test out ideas, to help organise him or her and to negotiate and trade with others.

c) The limits of action learning

The action learning method appeared to offer plenty of scope for entrepreneurial development, given the right educational structure and atmosphere. More specifically:

- the method stimulated participant's desire to co-operate, thus providing for an informal, supportive environment. Such co-operation both provided access to resources and to extend market opportunities. The desire, however, for collaboration needed to be reinforced if full advantage was to be gained from it.

- the set advisor needed to intervene in the group to help, organise, stimulate and channel the interactions. First, because the opportunities that existed for combining ideas across the different businesses were often not taken up; secondly, because the scope for the setting up of imaginary situations and negotiations between set members was much greater than was realised; finally, because entrepreneurs, who may be skilled in developing their business ideas, were often unskilled in organising group activity.

- reporting back needed to be centred upon key issues or problems, and to involve objective setting and monitoring. Unless participants set a time, space, and direction for each person's activity meetings became rambling and purposeless. Fresh injections of method, tempo and setting were also desirable.

Set	Respondent	Comments on the Advisors Role
1	Members	"He **animated** the group, **reflecting** back and **organising** what was said, though there were some sterile periods". "He organised the group and gave **advice here and there**". "Our 'advisor' was an **integral part** of the set". "He **made** the group work and set a **direction**".
	'Advisor'	"I see myself as an organiser of the group's interactions, primarily in relation to setting direction, processing their **thinking**, and facilitating the building up of **connections** between one person's train of thought and anothers".
2	Members	"He was good on **networks, contacts, tips** and **amiability**". "Has **credibility** as a self-employed person". "His **incisive** mind is applied to solving problems". "He acted as a **co-ordinator**". "He opened my mind to a new **way** of **looking** at things".
	'Advisor'	"I saw myself initially as a processor of interactions, and later as a **resource person** and atmosphere builder". "I had intended to be quiet and let it happen, but in practice, I intervened a great deal".
3	Members	"His role was not a dominating one, but he kept us on the right lines, **insisting on objectives, pointing out** needs, and instructing when required". "He used his **expert knowledge** throughout". "He helped solve **my problems** and **guide** me on the right lines". "By not **dominating**, he made us lead ourselves".
	'Advisor'	"I saw myself as a **clarifier** and critic (no-one else challenged people much), and as an **organiser** and **resource** person".

Figure 14. Set characteristics

- the action learning set was not the complete answer to new enterprise development. Whereas it served most of URBED's educational objectives, and provided a supportive environment, it needed reinforcing on the instructional side.

Action learning therefore, for all its strengths had one major weakness. Because the reflection took place in groups, the scope for rigorous application of business techniques, and for critical appraisal of them, was very restricted. Such rigorous analysis is probably best accomplished by individuals on their own, with an expert, or in response to appropriate challenges. These were offered in the form of a meeting with a bank manager, a written business plan, and an oral presentation of the plan to a panel of experts.

Two thirds of the way through the course, participants were invited to make an imaginary presentation to a bank manager. Three quarters responded, and a representative from the Midland Bank offered to co-operate. This highlighted the value for both parties of simulating a negotiation which is real in terms of the people involved, and yet not real in terms of the exchange of resources. The simulation was also opened up to student on-lookers for discussion of the process involved.

Bank managers and Business Schools alike, nowadays, are placing increasing emphasis on the business plan. This is very much a reflection of a logical, analytical approach to starting a business. It parallels the emerging emphasis on business techniques. The URBED programme tried to bring plan and reality as close together as possible. For example, it was suggested that people incorporate actual brochures, letterheads, plans of premises, invoices, articles of association, names of witnesses and suppliers, and so forth, in the final plan. Given the range of educational background on the programme, it was not surprising to find that the length of plan varied from three to 53 pages.

The conventional N.E.P. incorporates a series of reports on progress made to a panel of experts. In URBED's programme, the group interaction replaced the majority of these. It was seen as important, however, to lay emphasis on a final presentation with two panels made up of representatives from TSD, URBED, City University Business School, The London Enterprise Agency, Hackney Business Promotion Centre and the local banking community. The intention was to provide as much feedback to participants as possible. In fact the presentation culminated in an open discussion between the two sides on how the interaction could be improved.

d) The Learners' Perceptions of Action Learning

So far, this paper has only considered what action learning is, both in theory, and as adopted for URBED's practice. It is now important to look at the way the participants conceived of the programme as a whole. In other words, what did they feel they gained out of the learning situation? In response to the specific question "What do you think makes for a successful programme?" the replies shown in Table 2 were given (13 responses):

Table 2
Perception of action learning

Orientation	Criteria	%	Total %
Instruction: imparting knowledge and skills	Business techniques Bringing bits together	16 10	26
Education: personal and entrepreneur development	Gaining confidence Acquiring discipline Self-organisation Widening ideas Gaining commercial attitudes Developing Self- knowledge	9 9 9 6 4 2	39
Supportive environment	Support/encouragement Space Networks Learning from others	10 10 9 6	35

On the basis of the summary comments tabulated above, some conclusions can be drawn. First, although 'business techniques' remains the single most important category, as an overall proportion, it only represents 16 per cent, the balance of the responses very much emphasise personal and entrepreneur development. Second, there is a category of responses that needs to be included that relates to the supportive environment. Third, the actual elements specified under what URBED terms 'personal develop- ment', are revealing in themselves: confidence, discipline, widening of ideas, networks, commercial attitudes, and self-knowledge.

In summary, instruction, education, and a supportive environment appear to play a critical part with the sort of training that the prospective entrepreneur who participated in URBED's programme considered effective.

STAGES OF BUSINESS DEVELOPMENT

a) Embryo Business Development

The relatively flexible programme of activities offers an opportunity to observe respective development paths; for each participant was encour- aged, subject to advice and criticism by 'set advisors' and peers, to follow his or her own direction and pacing. The only significant constraint was the business plan, required at the end of the three month period.

For this purpose the growth of five embryo businesses within one particular set was monitored over the three month period (12). Thus, for example, Brian (see Figure 15) having out-lined his business opportunity, moved straight into selling. At the same time he was forced, by the group, to undergo some kind of self analysis. This 'analysis' was related to Brian`s desire to remain independent from the influence and advice of others. The analysis was followed, through chance or logical development, by a series of diversifications. Brian's business moved from Contract Computer Staff to Sales Agency.

The starting point, for all five of our prospective entrepreneurs was the market opportunity. For the three opportunists (Brian, Joe and Oliver) this represented a launching pad into personal and business development. For the craftsmen, Maurice, the opportunity was reflected in the uniqueness and quality of his product. Moreover, for out-going Brian and Oliver, the respective roles of gamesman and social entrepreneur were fitting. In contrast, Joe was much more the classical entrepreneur, battling his way into position.

Almost as important as the opportunity is the partnership, formal or informal. Whereas Brian had a conventional business partner who was supplying working capital, both Maurice and Oliver had wives who were playing significant parts. Maurice's wife had a very logical mind which she applied to the development of his business plan. Oliver's spouse served both as a designer, drawing pictures to present to local authorities, and as a sounding board. The fact that neither Joe nor Gill had partners involved in their businesses accelerated their need to find associates. The entrepreneur and his or her market opportunity had thus to be complemented by a supportive network of partners, collaborators and advisors.

Having identified market opportunities, and gathered together associates, the participants then began to consolidate upon entrepreneurial strengths. Brian and Joe began selling and negotiating, the former relying on his experience as a salesman and the latter on his background as a 'hustler'. Oliver displayed his abilities as an intermediary, bringing people and ideas together in imaginative ways. Maurice immersed himself in his product, producing a menu, as did Gill in hers - starting to research the market for word processing machines. Entrepreneurial strengths thus spanned trading, negotiating and selling ability; powers of imagination; personal commitment and product knowledge.

From strengths, the prospective entrepreneurs, through chance or necessity, moved into personal and business weaknesses. Maurice discovered that all the competitors in his street had 'long faces' as business was bad. Brian, following his selling routine, was upbraided for not opening up to the group. Joe showed himself to be very disorganised. Oliver revealed his personal doubts as to whether he wanted to become a social or business entrepreneur. Gill suffered a credibility crisis. Thereafter, a strategy for alleviating weaknesses was developed. Maurice conducted some market research and found a supposed market niche. Brian became the group's professional advisor. Joe withdrew from selling and began setting up his administration. Oliver secured a first customer, and Gill followed up potential collaborators.

Name and Business	Phase 1 --------->	2 --------->	3 --------->	4 --------->
Brian (Contract Computer Staff)	Describing business opportunity	Selling and Self Analysis	Diversification and business re-definition	
Gill (Word Processing Typing Service)	Testing out the business she may be in	Setting up the operation securing contacts, gaining credibility	Channelling commitment: estimating cash flow; segmenting the market; developing an image	
Joe (Distributing Drinks Dispensers)	Marketing: consolidating on strengths	Administ'n: alleviating weaknesses	Breaking through the technique barrier: costing, and budgeting	Integrating person and business
Maurice (Snack Bar)	Product differentiation Establishing husband/wife roles	Matching capabilities and possibilities	Preparing the Business Plan Seeking Planning Permission	Developing a business image; Preparing facilities
Oliver (Land Management Services)	Developing his market opportunity; Forming a husband/wife partnership	Integrating himself, the business and society	Collecting options for himself and others	Moving from dreams to reality market research; developing a business image

Figure 15: The development of five embryo businesses

Only after asserting both their strengths, and also alleviating weaknesses, did participants break through the 'business technique barrier'. Personal and entrepreneurial development, as well as the harnessing of a supportive environment, preceded the systematic application of business skills. Thereafter, Maurice developed his

business plan; Brian diversified; Joe prepared his first budget; Gill did a cash flow analysis; and only Oliver remained collecting options, having not yet resolved his business-society conflict.

(6) The training role at specific stages of business development

When the trainer's role at different stages of the embryo business development was examined, the person as entrepreneur appeared very much in the foreground, and comparitively speaking, administrative know-how and business skill receded into the background. Table 3 shows an actual ordering of business elements as they applied to the five prospective entrepreneurs studied in detail. As can be seen people returned again and again to their market opportunity and the definition of their business, as well as to an organisation and planning of their own activities.

To-ing and fro-ing apart, participants followed very different development paths. For example, Brian (outgoing opportunist) secured collaborators early and Maurice (introspective craftsman) secured them late. Gill and Joe launched quickly into paperwork and Oliver left the books very much to the end. There was, however, a general tendency for premises and finance to be sought later rather than earlier.

There are two major conclusions that can be drawn as a result of this analysis. First, a training programme needs to cater for the different development paths of individual businesses. This is something, in fact, to which action learning is particularly well suited. Second, informa- tion, techniques and insights dealing with product/market development and self-organisation (planning and motivation) are particularly important. So the aspects given most consideration in recent texts and courses - administration (paperwork) and finance (cash flow) - remain in the background, as far as the embryo business development is concerned.

Indeed, as already mentioned, all 15 participants in the URBED programme found that factors relating to personal development and to a supportive environment were at least as important as business techniques.

LESSONS FOR EDUCATING AND TRAINING THE ENTREPRENEUR

a) Providing vertical and horizontal linkages.

At the start of this paper it was argued that the education and training of entrepreneurs should involve vertical and horizontal linkages. In this concluding section some of the lessons that can be drawn about these dimensions are set out.

(i)   Vertical Linkages (Matching Courses with the Stages of Business Development) - A business is an evolving organism, like any other. Fertilisation precedes conception; conception precedes birth; birth precedes infancy. Even before fertilisation takes place there needs to be a period of courtship between the SELF=BUSINESS. The better the 'love match' the more healthy an upbringing the infant business will receive. This is why URBED placed special emphasis on a phased programme, taking people through from courtship with an idea to giving birth to a business enterprise.

Table 3
The ordering of business elements

ELEMENT	SEQUENTIAL ORDER IN WHICH ELEMENT WAS CONSIDERED AND RE-CONSIDERED				
	B	G	J	M	O
Business/Product/ Market	1,3,7,9	1,4	1,12	1,4,7,12	1,6,9,13
Marketing (pricing), selling, promoting	4,6	12	2	2,3,8	4
Operations (systems)	11	5	9	11	13
Premises* (and facilities)	10	7	10	6,10	-
Paperwork (books, legal, VAT)	-	3	4	-	12
People (collaborators, advisors, employees)	2	6,9	6	9,13	2,8
Finance (sources and applications)	12	2,11	7	8	7
Management (planning, self-organisation)	8	8,10	3,5,8,11	5	3,5,10

Note to Table

*None of the five participants monitored were in manu-
facturing, and Maurice had secured premises before the
course began. Premises could well have been an early
concern for a group of manufacturers/craftsmen.

On the evidence of the action learning programme, and the embryo
business development contained therein, the person entrepreneur and his
supportive environment appear to lie at the heart of new enterprise
development. The key tasks that emerge are the identification of the
business (personal motivation combined with market opportunity),
collaboration and transactions with others, and the planning and
directing of one's own activities (self-organisation). In fact, as
shown in Figure 16 all business elements could be placed under these
three major headings, with the primary entrepreneurial capabilities at a
higher level, and the secondary skills and knowledge lower down.

	Matching You and Your Business	Organising Yourself	Collaboration and Negotiation
Entrepreneur- ial Develop- ing	Harnessing motivation Developing creativity and imagination Developing self-asserti- veness Establishing a self- business identity	Increasing one's ability to: Plan tactics Set goals Solve problems Troubleshoot	Developing negotiating skills Developing an ability to take calculated risks Gaining skills in conflict resolution
Business Techniques & Management Insights	Forming a business strategy Developing marketing knowledge/ skills Diagnosing one's business strengths/ weaknesses	Developing knowledge and skills in: Work study/ measurement costing, budgeting, pricing, Inventory/ quality control cash flow analysis	Increasing one's ability to motivate people to communicate in person and on paper to bring people together in novel and effective ways
Administrative Know-how	Gaining know- ledge about: business incorporation and registra- tion; premises and accommodation; advertising and public relations;	Gaining know- how in: Office procedures; basic equip- ment books and stationary; book-keeping;	Getting to know about: Professional advisors employing staff, finance and banking;

Figure 16: An educational design for business development

For example, before starting up a business, the entrepreneur needs to know where to find premises and of what kind; whether to form a limited company, and how to publicise his activities. Yet all this admini- strative know-how must form part of a wider business and marketing strategy. Finally, unless the person has the motivation, commitment and assertiveness to 'make things happen', no business will be established.

Such commitment arises out of a matching between the person (motivation) and the business (market opportunity).

(ii) Horizontal linkages (between the enterprise and the entrepreneur
on the one hand and between the business and the environment on the
other) - Taking the four key resources of information, premises, people
and finance to which it was argued small businessmen will need to gain
access it can be argued that the kind of course offered by URBED was and
can be useful in creating horizontal linkages for the following reasons.

Information: Small firms tend to be sceptical of the value of a
government sponsored, centralised information service like the Small
Firms Information Service (SFIS). Similarly, people within the SFIS
sometimes see themselves as being under-valued (13). A training programme could provide the context and the stimulus for the establishment
of a locally based service, through which resources and needs could be
gradually matched. Similarly, the proverbial accountant or solicitor,
so often maligned and so seldom praised, could be brought into the
programme, not only for his expertise, but also to learn.

Premises: Premises are of more than physical value. They serve as a
symbol of emergence and a source of credibility. Often the lack of
their availability prevents the prospective entrepreneur from moving on
to more important things like finding customers. Yet, at the same time,
he may be exaggerating his needs for premises. He may not realise that,
at an early stage of development, he could operate quite comfortably
from his home. The role of the Planning or Industrial Development
Officer, in a local authority should be interactive, rather than active
or reactive. Mediated through the training programme, he would not
merely provide for, or discourage the practitioner from the acquisition
of premises. Rather he would come up with a solution to the entrepreneur's problem - whether or not the local authority have the premises
themselves - through engaging in a dialogue with him.

Finance: A very similar situation applies with finance. The banks are
increasingly seeing their role with regard to small firms, as providers
of both advice and resources. To do this combined job well, they need
to find out exactly what makes the business tick. So the branch bank
manager has as much to gain from learning about the entrepreneur's
business as the entrepreneur has from learning about the bank's. Branch
managers, in the context of a training programme, can challenge the
participant to produce the cash flow analyses that they require and then
comment on the result. There is nothing like a realistic challenge to
evoke an appropriate response. As for the customer, especially if it is
big business, the educational context is particularly appropriate. On
the one hand Purchasing Officers can get a real feel for their prospective customers, without needing to commit themselves 'for real'. While
on the other hand, the entrepreneur can get much needed information
about, and practice in, selling to big business. For organisations
feeling their way towards a shift in their procurement policies, this
provides for a gradual evolution.

People: In the same way as bank managers and information, planning and
purchasing officers can be brought together with the entrepreneur under

the guise of a training programme, so can a School or College Careers Officer. 'Personnel', however, as far as the individual starting in a business is concerned, is much more to do with partners, collaborators and advisors, than with employees. In that sense, a Business Promotion Centre, like that in Hackney, can both serve and benefit from a New Enterprise Programme.

The business expertise brought together under its wing, can interact with the entrepreneurs on the training programme; conversely, such a programme may provide the springboard for the development of a Business Promotion Centre, or small business club. In the URBED case a new Enterprise Network was sponsored. The most important 'Person' in the business, is the entrepreneur himself or herself. In that context a local community (local authority, banks, colleges, large firms, chambers of commerce, trades councils, community workers) have a vital role to play in 'trawling for entrepreneurs' to feed the courses. Unfortunately, too seldom is a 'Start up Conference' seen as a continuing process, from active marketing long before the event, to continuing involvement long after.

b) The implications for educators and trainers.

(i) The role of the educator and trainer - People involved in educating and training entrepreneurs act out two roles: planning and implementing the programmes; and creating and representing their establishments. In first role the main concern is with the business entrepreneur; in the second, with the business environment. In educating and training potential entrepreneurs, a programme needs to provide administrative know-how and business techniques, as well as managerial insights and scope for entrepreneurial development. In addition a supportive environment, which can offer informal support and encouragement as well as specific access to resources, is required. In general terms, a combined programme for formal teaching and action learning can offer all of these things. More specifically, however, trainers need to take account of the different types of entrepreneurs and the stages of their business development.

(ii) The role of the education and training establishment - All education and training establishments identify themselves with a region of concern. In some cases this may be national and international, in URBED's case it has been local and metropolitan (London, inner city). The need to identify in this way arises out of the relationship between a business and its environment. Big business is intimately associated, for example, with banking headquarters, and central govern-ment (for money); and higher education and employment bureaux (for people). Small businesses interact with a more localised network of branch bank managers, local authority planning officers, as well as professional advisors of one kind or another. Unfortunately this 'supportive environment' is sometimes reputed to be more of a hindrance than a help. Imagine banks and employment bureaux being perceived as a hindrance to large companies!

This problem can be overcome, however, by the educator or trainer acting in three ways. First, in the Start a New Business Programme, URBED acted as an intermediary between the Training Services Division, the Borough of Hackney, City University Business School, and prospective entrepreneurs in the London area. In addition, Barclays Bank and the

Midland Bank as well as Shell (UK) were involved. For in the same way as the educator and trainer needs to help the entrepreneur become more responsive to his environment, so the education and training establishment needs to help the environment become more responsive to the entrepreneur.

This mutual interaction can be most easily established when there are clear benefits to be realised on each side. For example, the banks gain access to customers, while the entrepreneurs gain access to finance. Large companies might develop new sources of supply, while the small company meets potential customers. For such interaction to occur, the supportive environment needs to be involved in the design, implementation and follow up of the training programme. The role of the intermediary is to bring people together at the appropriate times in appropriate ways.

Second, whereas the psychotherapist deals with his clients on a one to one basis, the family therapist deals with the family group (14). The psychological health of a particular child is clearly affected by his relationships with his parents. Similarly the well-being of the parents is reflected in their dealings with their children. By analogy, the psychological health of a new, and growing enterprise is strongly affected by its relationships with the institutional environment. In many ways, big companies and banks act as parents to new businesses, whilst fellow entrepreneurs might act as brothers and sisters.

The role of family therapist, or educator and trainer of entrepreneurs, is to get the parents and the children to understand each other better. Subsequently, they should be in a better position to respond to each other's needs. Again, the educator and trainer has a part to play in encouraging this response. For example, once banker and entrepreneur have met on neutral ground and discussed each other's needs and resources, they may well leave it at that. The educator and trainer, as facilitators, need to encourage them to go beyond this new found understanding, and to a set up mutually beneficial arrangements.

Third, like parents and children, institutions and entrepreneurs need to learn from each other, if their relationship is to be a healthy one. A lack of communication between 'advisors' and 'practitioners' is often caused by a lack of mutual understanding. The so-called 'helping agencies' also need to see themselves as 'being helped', or else an imbalance arises. The educator or trainer has a part to play in adjusting this imbalance between the entrepreneurs and the different resource providers or helping agencies.

In conclusion, therefore, it is proposed that programmes aimed at helping small firms into being should take greater cognizance of the SELF=BUSINESS concept described in this paper, such that the traditional inputs - administrative know how, business techniques and managerial insight take second place to the personal development of the entrepreneur in relation to the market opportunity that they have identified.

NOTES

(1) URBED is an independent training, research and consultancy group concerned with the regeneration of inner city economies.

(2) See for example Lovett, I. <u>Financial Advice for the Smaller Company</u> in Gibb, A. and Webb, T. <u>Policy Issues in Small Business Research</u>. Saxon House. 1980.
(3) Technical Development Capital Limited a branch of ICFC specialising in developing businesses based on new technologies.
(4) See the paper which appears later in this book by Ritchie, J. et al. <u>Arousing Aspiring Entrepreneurs</u>.
(5) See for example Stanworth, M.J.K., and Curran, J. <u>Management Motivations in the Smaller Business</u>. London, Gower, 1973.
(6) For further information on the objectives and structure of New Enterprise Programmes see the paper by Jerry Dyson that follows.
(7) Hackney Business Promotion Centre sponsored the weekend event entitled "Assessing your Prospects" and the Training Services Division the three month programme: Preparing to Go and Taking the Plunge.
(8) Information on the success of the modifications to the original programme can be obtained from Ronnie Lessem at the City University. A relevant article describing some of these modifications entitled '<u>Midwifery: Conceiving a Business Idea</u>' can be found in the Business Graduate 1980.
(9) See Edward De Bono's recent (1980) paperback entitled '<u>Opportunities</u>' published by Penguin for some interesting thoughts and practices concerned with creating opportunities.
(10) This test is administered in this country by Tony Morrison and is devised by the American phsycologist Elias Porter.
(11) See Reg Revons booklet by <u>The ABC of Action Learning</u> published by Reg Revons and printed by F.H. Wakelin.
(12) For some further thoughts on the development of the embryo business, as reflected in subsequent programmes to the one described here see the author's article entitled '<u>What it Really Takes to Start a Business</u>' Industrial and Commercial Training, July, 1980.
(13) For an alternative evaluation of the Small Firms Information Service see the paper in this book by John Howdle.
(14) The model of the 'family' and the entrepreneurial context has been developed by the author in an article that appeared in the Small Business Guardian on 10th October, 1980.

REFERENCES

Bennet, R. <u>The Provision of Management Education and Development for Small Firms</u> in Gibb, A. and Webb, T. <u>Policy Issues in Small Business Research</u>, Saxon House, 1980.
Boswell J. <u>The Rise and Fall of Small Firms</u>, Allen and Unwin's, 1971.
Collins, O.F., Moore D.G., & Unwalla, D.B., <u>Enterprising Man</u> Michigan State University, 1964
De Bono E. <u>Opportunities</u> Penguin, 1980
Deeks J. <u>The Small Firm Owner Manager</u>, Praeger, 1975
Douglas P. <u>Run Your Own Business</u> Dent, 1973
Drucker P. <u>Management</u>, Pan Paperback, 1978.
Kolb D. <u>Organisational Psychology</u> - Prentice Hall, 1974
Lievegood B. <u>Phases</u> - Rudolph Steiner Press 1979
Low A. <u>Zenard Creative Management</u> - Doubleday 1976
Macrae N. <u>The Coming Entrepreneurial Revolution</u>, The Economist, 1976
Schumacher E.F. <u>Small is Beautiful</u>, Abacus 1973.
Smith N. <u>The Entrepreneur</u>, Michigan State University, 1968

Steiner R. The World Economy, Rudolph Steiner Press, 1972
Teillard de Chardin The Future of Man, Fontana.
Tucker & Swayne, The Effective Entrepreneur - General Learning Press,
    1973
Watkins D.   The New Enterprise Programme - Manchester Business School
    Journal, 1979
Wood E.G. Bigger Profits for the Smaller Firm - Business Books, 1972
Woodcock C. Time to stop talking and get off the bandwagon, Small
    Business Guardian, August 24th, 1979.

10 The identification and development of entrepreneurs: experience from new enterprise promotion in rural Wales

GRENVILLE JACKSON
Development Board for Rural Wales

INTRODUCTION

The points made in this paper relate to the author's experience in the Development Board for Rural Wales and views expressed should be considered as personal and not the policy of the Development Board for Rural Wales.

The Development Board for Rural Wales (DBRW), which began operations in April 1977, was created by the Development of Rural Wales Act 1976. It is the second specialist regional development board in the United Kingdom. The first was the Highlands and Island Development Board, established 11 years earlier.

The Act gave the Board the general responsibility to promote the economic and social well-being of the people living in the local authority districts of Ceredigion in Dyfed, Meirionnydd in Gwynedd, and the three districts of Brecknock, Montgomery and Radnor in Powys. This area is traditionally referred to as Mid Wales.

On the economic side the Board sees its main job as the encouragement of manufacturing industry as a main provider of employment.

In the Board's first three years there has been an unprecedented flow of new industries to Mid Wales. 130 factories have been let and a potential of 1,850 job opportunities created. This level of activity is greater than previously achieved during 20 years of various local and central government interest in the economy of Mid Wales. Industrial enquiries are running at an average of 100 per month. The current factory programme will provide 75 factories totalling 300,000 square feet for this year. The Board is confident these will be quickly filled. This page briefly summarises the Boards' efforts to bring in industry but even more challenging is how to get development from within the region.

ENTREPRENEURIAL ACTIVITY IN MID WALES

The Board recognises that if the economy of Mid Wales is to achieve self-sustaining growth there must be continuous production of new enterprises from within its area. There is national concern about the shortage of entrepreneurs and the factors discouraging new enterprise. In Mid Wales the problems are compounded because there is no tradition of indigenous entrepreneurial activity. This suggests it could be a long haul but early results indicate much can be achieved.

"Why are entrepreneurs so scarce in Mid Wales?" It is important to try to answer this question. Board action and programme designs must take account of "factors in the environment". Also, only from a full appreciation of the circumstances which have led to a lack of indigenous new enterprise formation is it possible to judge achievements to date.

The successful entrepreneur requires confidence and motivation, an opportunity and business skills. Certain circumstances in Mid Wales have had a deleterious effect on all three of these critical components.

Confidence and motivation

There has been a steady loss of population until the early 1970's. In this century alone the population has fallen by 25 per cent. The major factor causing this has been the shedding of labour by the agricultural industry coupled with a lack of alternative employment opportunities and the consequential migration of economically active people away from Mid Wales. This helped speed the secondary decline of the community - shops are no longer profitable, pubs, post offices and garages have closed for lack of business. This decline in the community has in itself discouraged any new activity from being established in the area because it has not encouraged confidence in the future of new enterprise. Indeed, it has been de-motivating.

In contrast, self employment is common in Mid Wales. Approximately one in six members of the labour force is self employed. Although this largely reflects the economic structure of the area it is true to say that there are exceptionally strong aspirations to become self employed. Possibly a linked factor is an important social constraint: whilst rural communities readily acknowledge successful business people who have migrated from the area they do not like to see local people getting "above their station" by forming new local enterprise.

Market opportunity

The entrepreneur close to a market can generally recognise and respond more quickly to opportunities. The geography of Mid Wales has been a major inhibiting factor in new enterprise growth. Mid Wales remains one of the most sparsely populated areas of Great Britain with a population density of 0.2 per hectare. The area covers 40 per cent of the land of Wales with 7.1 per cent of its population. The largest town is Aberystwyth with a population of just over 10,000 people. For local people the big towns and conurbations are considered remote. There is little opportunity to see or seek market openings and the absolute decline of the community, to less than 200,000 people, has reduced the number of local opportunities for new enterprise.

The economic structure of the area, particularly the poor representation of manufacturing industry, which until recently accounted for less than 1 in 10 jobs, has not brought market opportunities to people's attention. In Ceredigion and Meirionnydd districts manufacturing accounts for less than 5 per cent of employment.

Skills

The typical entrepreneur possesses business and/or technical skills. The selective outward migration of high ability young persons and skilled workers has dramatically reduced those members of the Mid Wales population most likely to possess these skills and therefore to form new enterprise. This has been re-inforced by the education system in Mid Wales, which has concentrated, and possibly more so than in other areas, on the development of job seekers particularly in academic pursuits. There has been a total absence of teaching of career opportunities in the area of small business ownership and management. Abraham Maslow has written that "the most valuable 100 people to bring into a deteriorating society would not be economists, or politicians, or engineers, but rather entrepreneurs". (Maslow, 1968) In Mid Wales the education system's response to the decline of the area has been largely to produce teachers and preachers.

NEW ENTERPRISE PROMOTION

To stimulate and assist local entrepreneurial activity the Board quickly established a programme of small factory construction, a Business Advisory Service and various other services. This included research into local opportunities for new enterprise. The findings only served to highlight the absence of local entrepreneurial initiative

- visitors to Mid Wales annually spend £7 million on giftware and souvenirs. Less than 15 per cent of this market is satisfied by local production despite strong consumer preference for locally made items.

- productive forests cover 10 per cent of the land area of Mid Wales and these are fast reaching full output yet 85 per cent of timber grown in Mid Wales is processed outside the region.

- fatsheep and cattle are the major product of Mid Wales yet local slaughtering and food products is negligible with 80 per cent of output exported to England for processing.

These measures have proved useful ways of helping existing entrepreneurs and encouraged some new entrepreneurs to come forward. The Board soon appreciated, however, that a new initiative was required to identify and develop more local entrepreneurial talent. Attention focussed on the pilot New Enterprise Programmes run successfully by the Manchester Business School (MBS) for the Manpower Services Commission. It was felt that the experience, gained in the creation of entrepreneurs from 'redundant' managers could be translated to the particular needs of Mid Wales. MBS accepted the Board's invitation to run a modified New Enterprise Programme in Mid Wales. To distinguish it from the national programme the Mid Wales course is called "New Enterprise Promotion."

The programme design reflects the particular needs of Mid Wales. It is a three-stage programme and progresses through a general training course of value to a large number and wide variety of people to the specific encouragement of a small collection of individuals committed to the establishment of new enterprises.

Stage One aims to provide opportunities for participants to consider some of the main factors associated with success and failure in small-scale enterprise. A number of owner/founders of successful enterprises in Mid Wales open the workshop, after which participants examine the main opportunities and problems that they have encountered or expect to encounter in their own businesses. Several sessions are then devoted to examining these. Information is also provided on financial and other opportunities for small enterprise.

The main objective of this stage is to develop motivation and commitment. The workshop does not aim to provide training in the skills of operating small enterprises but provides an opportunity of sharing experience, examining the findings of research studies on small enterprise, and acquiring useful information about opportunities for new enterprise in rural Wales. The workshop allows participants to identify their individual skill deficiencies, and the Board and MBS to recognise the needs of the group. Furthermore, it allows a preliminary assessment to be made of an individual's commitment to new enterprise. Stage One is held over two days.

Stage Two aims to develop the opportunity - seeking skills of participants and refining the skills required to develop and run a successful business. Emphasis is given to skill deficiencies identified previously such as marketing, financial control and business planning. The design of the course is highly participative through action-learning. There is a continuous process of review of the development of individuals and the group.

This stage is designed also to provide a useful training in general business management for those participants who do not wish to proceed to or are considered unsuitable, for the final stage.

Stage Two is held over 3-4 days one month after Stage One.

Stage Three provides a small number of highly motivated participants with the opportunity to select, evaluate and develop a proposal for establishing a new small enterprise. Participants have access to a budget to allow them to undertake necessary research. It is hoped that at the end of this programme each participant will have formulated a formal business plan and that some of the projects will be implemented.

This stage lasts 16 weeks with the group meeting on a regular fortnightly basis. These meetings consider progress to date and allow the skills of the group to be used to benefit individual problems. In addition there are some formal inputs designed to improve skills in running a small enterprise. Individuals meet with the course management team on a six weekly basis to assess individual progress and terminate participation if necessary.

IDENTIFICATION OF PARTICIPANTS

The programme is intended to be of value to those persons who have a project idea or feel they have some of the capabilities or commitment to establish a new enterprise and persons who have been running a small business for less than 12 months and whose business is trading marginally.

The Board aims to reach and encourage as many local people as possible to come forward irrespective of whether they have a particular business opportunity in mind. This is achieved by widespread local newspaper advertising, mailings to target groups and posters in Job Centres and Post Offices. Advertising and promotion accounts for approximately 15 per cent of total course cost. Interested persons need complete only a very brief application form to be considered for Stage One. Entry fees are kept to a bare minimum (50 per cent of accommodation costs) to eliminate lack of finance as a reason for not joining the course.

Selection of participants for Stage One is based primarily on their place of residence and the type of business proposed, preference being given to manufacturing activities. A maximum of 75-80 persons are accommodated at Stage One. The staged programme then acts as a `natural filter' identifying entrepreneurs, but at the same time encouraging as many as possible to proceed to the next stage. Stage One participants motivated to take their idea forward then apply by letter to join Stage Two. They are asked to complete a Business Planning Framework which permits self assessment and assists the course organisers in the selection process.

ACHIEVEMENT TO DATE

Demand to attend the New Enterprise Promotions has exceeded expectations. The first two pilot programmes were heavily over-subscribed, each attracting between 150-200 formal applications from 400-500 enquiries for Stage One of the course. There was only slightly fewer applications for the third programme. This could suggest there is considerable latent entrepreneurial potential in the area and that the product we are offering is right for the market at this time. On the other hand a large proportion of applicants are recent immigrants to the area which suggests there is still much to be achieved as far as persons born in Mid Wales are concerned.

Participants on Stage One of the three courses have exhibited the following characteristics

- relatively few people under the age of 24
- persons over 35 years of age account for nearly 50 per cent of all participants
- a gradual fall off in the number of female participants from 42 per cent to 22 per cent
- an increasing proportion of participants are not in business
- few persons have a production background
- of those not in business about one in five have no specific business idea

- giftware, woodproducts, clothing and textiles are the major business activities.

27 persons attended all three stages of the two pilot programmes. With only two exceptions new enterprises were identified and developed. This includes persons who attended Stage One without a specific business idea. They employed Board research to identify product opportunities and developed the idea fully in Stage Three. Although it is much too early to judge the success of the courses between 75-100 jobs have so far been created. The level of confidence and motivation of partici- pants compared with other producers in the area impresses all who come into contact with them. Moreover, each new enterprise stimulated by the course is an example for others to follow. This factor features strongly in the Board's in-region promotions.

POST COURSE ASSISTANCE

On completion of the formal programme each participant is attached to one of the Board's Business Advisory Officers, to progress business development and continue to meet `training needs'. Each new enterprise can then avail itself of a larger number of Board services.

Market opportunities - the Board recognises the importance of bringing to people's attention the existence of local market opportunities. These are identified through independent market research. For example, the survey of tourist spending on giftware and souvenirs identified market size and opportunities within a large number of product categories.

Product marketing - the sale of Mid Wales products is vigourously promoted. Companies are encouraged to take part in stands with the Board at major exhibitions. The Board has launched its Canolbarth Cymru/Mid Wales Mark to denote products made in its area. Here is a new concept to identify products from Mid Wales and expand both their production and markets. The Board publishes a full colour Buyers Guide to products made within Mid Wales. This is distributed to buyers throughout the world. The Board brings buyers to Mid Wales.

Financial services - firms can call on a Business Advisory Accountant to assist them with financial controls and forecasting. Help is given to put the best package of financial assistance together. Loans are available from the Board.

Premises - small starter factories of 750 square feet each are being constructed. They offer the new entrepreneur an opportunity to develop a business in a purpose-built small factory. `Instant starters' or portacabins are being deployed to meet the urgent needs of new small businesses. For approximately £25 per week the entrepreneur can lease both the small factory and rent attractive housing accommodation from the Board. This permits the release of private money.

FUTURE DIRECTIONS

Whilst the response to the first two New Enterprise Promotions was better than expected it is felt that the response from certain population groups could be greater, for example, young persons and skilled workers. Initiatives to release and develop the entrepreneurial talents of these groups are now under consideration.

Marketing strategy

It is worth making the general point that it is important to seek professional marketing advice when defining course recruitment campaigns. Variations in marketing strategy will stimulate differing response rates from population groups. For the third New Enterprise Promotion, the local advertising campaign was switched from a neutral-broad appeal to an appeal to inventors/creators. This resulted in fewer applications overall, less people with a well-advanced business idea more engineering projects compared with giftware and noticeably fewer women. Also for the third course everyone who had attended earlier programmes received details and application forms to pass to associates who they considered might be interested in new enterprise.

Education and entrepreneurship

The development of entrepreneurship characteristics and interest in small business ownership has been a neglected part of the curriculum of schools and higher education. If specific personal characteristics are essential to business success, then "the education of the potential entrepreneur must not wait until he has grown up, by which time he has acquired non-entrepreneurial habits". (Poh, 1976) Entrepreneurial concepts must be integrated into vocational programmes at all educational levels, during formative years in primary and secondary schools and on into college education. Young people must be encouraged to develop their entrepreneurial talents. To say this is to recognise that long-run regional economic growth is more likely to be determined by the motivations, attitudes and skills of local entrepreneurs than by other factors.

The question of "education for entrepreneurship" should not be treated as a purely national issue. There is much to be achieved at the regional level.

In August 1979, the Board launched a Schools/Industry Programme with the support of a grant from the Industry/Education Unit, Department of Industry. A major element of this programme is to encourage school children to become involved in entrepreneurial activities. Five Young Enterprise Companies have been established. These are miniature manufacturing companies and though scaled down every major activity in the manufacturing process is imitated by the companies, from the election of their own managerial staff to the issuing of dividends to shareholders. The principal aim of the year's exercise was to provide pupils of all ranges of ability with a practical experience of running a business and to give them an opportunity to develop qualities of leadership, initiative, manual skills and self confidence. For all schools and for all age ranges the Board is running a competition. The objective was to increase awareness and stimulate interest in manufacturing industry, by submitting written, visual or prototypes of a potential marketable product.

So far the Schools/Industry Programme has received excellent support from headmasters, teachers and careers advisers. This is equally as important as the successful involvement of children in the various ventures. This is the first step in achieving a move within the education programme away from its sole concern with job seekers to job creators and producers.

Each year the colleges of further education in Mid Wales turn out several hundred young persons with craft skills. Some have enterprising and innovative ideas. In others innovation and enterprise have been suppressed. Students are taught how to be managers or to become employees.

Persons completing craft courses within the last five years at one local college have been the subject of a direct-mail campaign to join the New Enterprise Promotion courses. The response was low and those who did come forward were self employed and commited to continuing in their present job. This suggests alternative intitiatives, courses or facilities, could be more relevant to this group at least.

The Board wishes to inauguerate a New Enterprise type course for these young people which they would join immediately on completion of their skill training. Marketing of the course would commence early during formal skill training to stimulate interest and to encourage students to think about marketable products and new enterprise in their college projects. Unfortunately there are few precedents for this type of training. TOPS rule of no training assistance within two years of completing full-time education' is an important limitation to this type of course getting off the ground.

Encouraging skilled workers

Many skilled or semi-skilled workers have the manufacturing experience and production skills to identify production opportunities. There is often a strong desire to be rid of the frustration of subordinate or unchallenging jobs. The New Enterprise Promotions have attracted little interest, however, from this group. This may be a function of the marketing strategy or the infancy of the manufacturing sector in Mid Wales. It may simply be a daunting prospect to attend a course or travel to a course.

There are several possiblities for identifying and releasing the entrepreneurial potential of the skilled and semi-skilled manual worker under consideration within the Board. Many have been tried elsewhere. These include holding Stage One of the New Enterprise Promotion on a local area rather than regional basis to maximise its informal appeal.

A particularly attractive idea is the establishment of New Enterprise Workshops, as pioneered in Scotland by Stratclyde Regional Council and Glasgow District Council. These provide the working person with the facilities to develop prototypes at low cost and for Business Advisors to help evaluate product potential. They would be an ideal seedbed for participants for New Enterprise Promotion courses. Another possibility is a competition for new product ideas which is marketed strongly at the factory worker.

CONCLUSIONS

The New Enterprise Promotions have shown that people with entrepreneurial potential or entrepreneurial aspirations are not as scarce as previously thought. It is possible to improve motivation and commitment, knowledge of market opportunities and skills to exploit these opportunities.

A mass training approach at the regional and local level can assist identification of entrepreneurs who would be dissuaded from coming forward by national programmes. Considerable thought needs to be given to the identification of potential entrepreneurs. Target groups should be clearly identified and appropriate marketing strategies developed.

Knowledge of the availability of post-courses advice and services and maintenance of personal contact can be an important motivating factor during the early stages of formal training.

Business or industry experience is not critical to confidence, motivation and skill development. A sense of frustration can be sufficient to motivate a person to look for market opportunities.

Lengthy surveys are not needed. The problems are well understood and plentiful good ideas already exist for new enterprise development programmes. For example in the sacrosanct field of secondary education there is scope for initiatives to develop entrepreneurial traits. What is needed is positive action to implement the ideas which do exist.

REFERENCES

Maslow, A. Readings in the Economics of Education. United Nations. UNESCO. 1968. p. 623.
Poh, Y.B. Entrepreneurs in Economic Development. Malaysian Business. February, 1976.

11 The Small Business Development Centre Programme in the USA: The network concept

ALLAN GIBB
Small Business Centre,
Durham University Business School

INTRODUCTION

The small firm population of any developed country embraces a wide variety of forms of organisation, products, processes, size, management characteristics, rates of growth and objectives. Its needs from the supporting environment are equally varied and diverse. Thus it is scarcely surprising that there are often numerous services in any one region seeking to meet these needs.

These services have arisen in response to the highly fragmented nature of small firm's demands. Indeed, the dominant characteristics of the 'market' for services for small firms, (including management training and development) are precisely those in which small organisations are likely to enter and survive. In particular they include:

   (i)   The absence of any massive prospective demand on a general scale which would lend itself to a standardised service.

   (ii)   The difficulty of identifying clear and organised market segments of any size.

   (iii) The importance of tailor made products and services.

   (iv)   The need for personal communication to overcome consumer resistance.

   (v)   The difficulty in demanding a good price for the service.

   (vi)   The relatively local market horizon of consumers.

The prevalence of these kinds of conditions and the varied response that has emerged makes the market place look 'untidy' to those who survey the small firms' scene. With the growing interest in small firms at a national level there has developed a lobby advocating the rationalisation and centralisation of the services to small firms under an umbrella organisation. The aim would be to bring 'software' (advice, information counselling and training) together with 'hardware' (finance and other resource provision) under one authority. In this context the establishment of national and regional agencies of one sort or another

161

has been proposed. While undoubtedly there may be a case for making more visible the supportive environment to the small firm the 'all service' bureaucratic agency is only one possible model. An alternative is to seek to provide a form of organisation that facilitates cooperation between existing services, retains local initiative and energy and yet presents a clearer picture of assistance available to the small businessman.

It is in this context that the Small Business Development Centre concept which is very actively pursued in the U.S.A., is of some interest. This paper is based on an examination of the Development Centre concept in the U.S.A. which was carried out for the Department of Industry in 1979. It embodies the findings resulting from a detailed analysis of four of the eight experimental centres operating at that time; at the University of Chico in Northern California, the Polytechnic University of California at Pomona, the University of Nebraska, Omaha, and Howard University, Washington. The Smaller Business Development Centre Programme in the U.S.A. is of relatively recent origin. At the time of the visit the SBDC experiment was being evaluated by the Small Business Administration and a Bill was before Congress seeking authorisation for the establishment of a network of such Centres throughout the country. This programme is now going ahead.

A BRIEF DESCRIPTION OF THE SBDC PROGRAMME

The overall practical aim of the SBDC is to bring together, at a minimum cost and without large elements of bureaucracy, all important services for small firms existing in a region. This is achieved through a control centre based on a University School of Business. The Centre acts as a basis for facilitating, promoting and controlling (to a limited degree) activities, analysing needs, developing the network of small business services in the region and acting as a central point for client reception and registration and ultimate referral.

At a basic level a Centre is charged with disseminating business management information; developing entrepreneurs; undertaking management audits, marketing studies, financial analyses, feasibility studies, and business planning for small firm clients, providing business management counselling and training, and follow-on resources for on site implementation of recommendations. In addition to this the SBDC may provide a wider range of specialist services included in Figure 1.

As Figure 1 indicates, the Centre's activities can be divided into Basic Services and Special Services. Basic Services are those relating to management training and counselling. The SBDC may choose to assume primary responsibility for developing and conducting training programmes with limited assistance from other sources. It may, alternatively, or additionally, initiate training through other organisations such as Chambers of Commerce, other colleges, trade or professional organisation or SCORE Chapters (1). Final responsibility for the quality of the training, however, rests with the SBDC.

In addition to training, the Centres are responsible for management counselling, described officially as "A Service provided to small business firms to identify management problems, develop corrective measures, plan alternative solutions and advise and assist in implementation as appropriate". Counselling activities are divided into 'Contacts' and 'Actions'. 'Contacts' denote all non-substantive

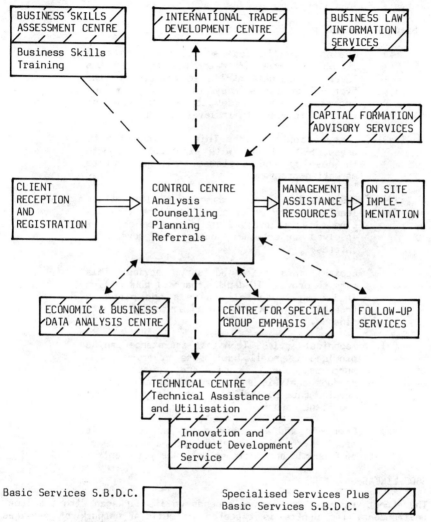

Figure 1 Small Business Development Centre Client Services

counselling activity including brief discussions, telephone advice, responses to requests for publications, referrals to other services, etc. 'Action' denotes any substantive business management counselling session over approximately one hour in length between an SBDC resource and a small firm or person. Any client who receives over twelve hours or more of counselling is described as an 'in-depth counselling client'. Counselling may be undertaken directly by a number of the SBDC staff, by a member of the Faculty of the University, by personnel in SCORE or ACE (the core of counsellors currently still in business), by the Management

Assistance Officer (MAO) of the SBA, (who is usually located with the SBDC), or indeed by a variety of other persons organised through the Centre's various links.

Special services may include the following:

(i)   Business skills assessment. Under this an attempt is made to determine the client's level of business skills in relation to the type of business they intend to, or are operating, and to develop a programme of training to raise their level of skill.

(ii) International trade. This service aims to assist SBDC clients with exportable products to develop and implement an appropriate marketing programme.

(iii) Business law information service. This offers legal advisory information to clients excluding clients involved in litigation or those involved in actions 'against the government interest'.

(iv) Capital information advisory service. This aims to provide in-depth financial counselling including financial analysis and planning together with information on sources of equity finance.

(v)   Technical advice. Technical assistance can be provided to small businesses covering areas such as: energy audit and conservation; product analysis and improvement; new product development; innovation - technology transfer; and plant layout.

(vi) Economic and business data analysis. This provides for the operation and maintenance of an Economic and Business Data Analysis Centre.

SBDC LINKAGES

The effectiveness of the Centre depends on its linkages with the local environment. The Centre is expected to build a network of services linking with all other facilities for small firms in the region. It thus joins forces with official SBA backed counselling and information services, other universities and colleges, banks, solicitors, accountants, planners, official and unofficial agencies, etc. Figure 2 describes this network system albeit in general terms.

The Centres operate with relatively small staffs, usually of no more than seven front line persons. Staffing is very dependent upon the degree to which outside funds are available and the number of specialist services offered. The Director of the SBDC is usually responsible directly to the President of the University through an Operations or Management Policy Board consisting of the Deans of the relevant Schools of the University. There is also usually a Regional Advisory Board which

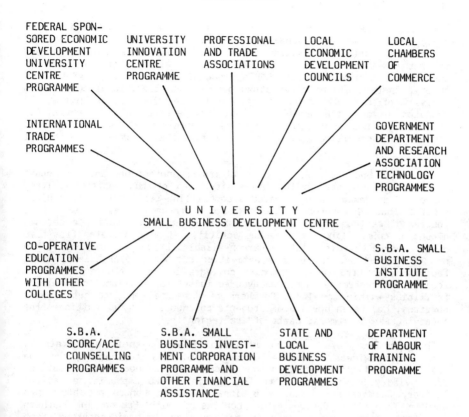

A LINK-UP OF

FEDERAL SPON-
SORED ECONOMIC   UNIVERSITY   PROFESSIONAL   LOCAL   LOCAL
DEVELOPMENT   INNOVATION   AND TRADE   ECONOMIC   CHAMBERS
UNIVERSITY   CENTRE   ASSOCIATIONS   DEVELOPMENT   OF
CENTRE   PROGRAMME   COUNCILS   COMMERCE
PROGRAMME

INTERNATIONAL   GOVERNMENT
TRADE   DEPARTMENT
PROGRAMMES   AND RESEARCH
                                                             ASSOCIATION
                                                             TECHNOLOGY
                                                             PROGRAMMES

                         U N I V E R S I T Y
                  SMALL BUSINESS DEVELOPMENT CENTRE

CO-OPERATIVE   S.B.A. SMALL
EDUCATION   BUSINESS
PROGRAMMES   INSTITUTE
WITH OTHER   PROGRAMME
COLLEGES

    S.B.A.   S.B.A. SMALL   STATE AND   DEPARTMENT
    SCORE/ACE   BUSINESS INVEST- LOCAL   OF LABOUR
    COUNSELLING   MENT CORPORATION BUSINESS   TRAINING
    PROGRAMMES   PROGRAMME AND   DEVELOPMENT   PROGRAMME
                    OTHER FINANCIAL   PROGRAMMES
                    ASSISTANCE

Figure 2   The Small Business Development Centre

might consist of both politicians and business and commercial representatives. The Director of the SBDC usually has senior status equivalent
to a Professor. He is not necessarily, however, of a pure academic
background.

    The University must enter into a formal agreement with the SBA to act
as a Centre. The SBA in turn provides basic finance but wishes this to
be used as a lever for wider funding. Centres are therefore funded from
a variety of sources depending upon the mix of their acitivities.

THE OPERATION OF THE CENTRE IN PRACTICE

All the centres visited had established basic links with organisations in their regions although the degree of linkage varied substantially. This, of course, depended on the nature of the small business support environment in that region, and the degree to which traditionally the university had developed specialist services or worked with the local small business environment.

It was common practice for the centres to have an SBA man on the campus. He organised counselling referralls while frequently also undertaking certain activities which traditionally had been organised under the umbrella of the local SBA, for example, workshops. In three of the centres there were also SCORE personnel on the campus, so that in theory, there could be close links between the traditional counselling activity of the SBA and that of the Centre. The SBI programme (2) operated in, and drew cases from enquiries, received by each Centre. All the Centres had also made substantial attempts to involve faculty members in counselling (through payments from their budgets, and the SBI programme).

One Centre had, 'on call', 30 to 40 staff; another had involved staff from ten departments in the University. Two of the centres visited, Chico and Nebraska, also operated a counselling service from subsidiary centres located throughout the region. Nebraska had established five 'outreach' centres which undertook, on a sub-contract basis, a certain amount of counselling and training activity. It also operated from five other Centres where facilities were available. Chico, in California, had not contracted out any of its activities but was, nevertheless, using facilities in five local community colleges in the northern California region. One centre had also endeavoured to set up additional counselling facilities within the local Chambers of Commerce, and, to get greater coverage, had taken parties of students on counselling 'expeditions' for several weeks to remoter parts of its region.

The operation of specialised services was rather more sketchy, depending considerably on the history of the institutions. By far the most developed in this respect was Chico which was operating a Business Law Advisory Service, a Centre for Special Group Emphasis, a Capital Advisory Formation Service, a Business Research Centre and had links with a Technology Centre. This contrasted with Pomona in Southern California which, as yet, provided no more than the basic services. Such provision could, nevertheless, be very substantial. Pomona, for example, dealt with 1,500 counselling clients in 1978 and had 500 longer consultations of four hours or more. In addition it organised 35 workshops.

The facilities of the centres, even in respect of basic services, varied substantially. Nebraska had a regular mailing of their management guide and information pamphlet to over 22,000 businesses. This was distributed through the Chambers of Commerce in the region and was a major source of counselling enquiries. The Capital Loan Advisory Service at Chico was of particular interest in view of the substantial involvement with the banks. All the referrals to the service came from the bank, the aim being for the service to provide an improved packaging of the loan, presenting the best possible financial case to the bank and helping the client to choose the most appropriate form of finance for expansion.

FUNDING

In two of the centres visited; Chico and Pomona, the base funding was
$130,000 each in 1978. Nevertheless the overall budget in Pomona was
$253,000 and in Chico $345,000 reflecting the 'gearing' from other
sources. Moreover, the University made a contribution in terms of
overheads which were usually waived, and, in addition, a certain amount
of staff time was given free. Most of the gearing funding in all centres
was, however, from other federal government departments. It was,
therefore, the stated intention in Washington to try to increase the
amount contributed from state and other sources and maximise the
leverage on government money. To this end it seems likely that SBDC
growth will be by means of a state plan with the state financing a major
part of the programme.

AREAS COVERED BY THE CENTRES

The scale and scope of the activities of the SBDC's visited varied. The
SBDC at Omaha, Nebraska, aimed to cover the whole state of Nebraska and
involved a 'population' of 40,000 small businesses. The Centre estimated
that it was in touch with over 20,000 of these. The farthest distance
travelled was 450 miles, although the average distance was less than
five miles because the Centre operated from five regional Centres and
five other sub-Centres.

In contrast Pomona, on the fringe of Los Angeles, had some 34,000
small businesses within ten miles travelling distance and 73,000 within
a radius of 20 miles.

SMALL BUSINESS DEVELOPMENT CENTRE PROGRAMME OBJECTIVES

Having outlined the activities undertaken by the Centres, it is
appropriate to consider how far these activities are meeting the
objectives of the programme, before examining its relevance to the UK.

The overall official aim of the Small Business Development Centre
Programme is:

"The comprehensive development of management and technical assistance
for the small firms in a region."

This objective, however, embodies the philosophy of harnessing
existing sources of assistance within a region and promoting others
where gaps exist. This the central task of the co-ordinating and control
centre is to provide links between basic counselling and training
services in a region. Equally importantly the control centre must plan
to build up a range of specialist services which it can coordinate, but
not necessarily own. The centering of this co-ordination on a University
Business School (the education sector) is deliberate, in that it is
regarded as a means of forcing links between the community and
education, bringing together colleges and universities in a region to
participate in the programme.

SUCCESS IN MEETING OBJECTIVES

Undoubtedly there are problems in defining the types of output that might be expected from an SBDC programme. The emphasis by the SBA in terms of both evaluation and control seems to be on numbers. The centres in their operating plans have, therefore, to indicate numbers of workshops, other training sessions, consultancies, publications and research outputs. This is a major problem in itself in that those operating the centres become highly conscious of numbers and the need to ensure that they meet 'targets'. This affects the types of programmes operated. For example, it is easier to get large numbers of companies to attend training events by having a large number of very short programmes. Automatically emphasis is placed on running clinics or conferences with can either be many in number or attract many clients at one time. Thus the total figure at the end of the year of those in attendance and of the number of events will be very high. This says nothing, however, about the quality, depth or effectiveness of programme inputs. On the counselling side every effort is made to count the total number of enquiries and to build these numbers up. In at least one centre visited, a form had been developed to make sure that every telephone call was monitored and classified. The need to 'play the numbers game' was recognised by each of the institutions visited and was obviously reflected in turn by the need of the SBA to justify expenditures in terms of 'numbers of events' and ultimately the 'price of the event per dollar invested'. Consequently the paperwork involved was substantial. The directors of the centres realised that numbers did not give a true picture of their effectiveness and this, together with the paperwork involved was resented.

A better starting point for evaluation of the SBDC's might have been the objectives of the SBA in fostering them.

Translated into final outputs these might be as follows:

To encourage:

(i)	more small business start-ups.
(ii)	the expansion of existing businesses.
(iii)	increased technology transfer and utilisation.
(iv)	greater student practice in small business management.
(v)	more students setting up small businesses.
(vi)	the development of research services and a data bank and dissemination to relevant agencies.
(vii)	improved marketing and export assistance.
(viii)	more entrepreneurs from socially and economically disadvantaged classes.
(ix)	more viable small businesses.

Whilst the institutions themselves had not organised their information so as to enable these outputs to be measured easily, some comment on progress towards meeting them can be made.

Encouraging more start-ups and the expansion of existing businesses: certain, but not all, of the centres visited were involved in pre-business programmes. These were, however, of only one-day duration. No attempt had been made to investigate the number of start-ups following the programmes or indeed the nature of the client population attending them. It was unlikely that much could be achieved by a one-day programme over and above informing the participants of the support available in the environment and summarising the aspects which ought to be considered when starting up.

Information concerning the expansion of existing businesses merely comprised records of the number of counselling sessions, workshops, etc. There were course assessments, but no detailed follow-ups appeared to be undertaken.

Encouraging increased technology transfer and utilisation: none of the centres visited were involved substantially in this area. They had, as yet, failed to involve the engineering and scientific departments of their universities. Although technology enquiries were handled, they were usually referred elsewhere. There did not seem to be strong links in any of the Centres visited between the university and private or public research and development organisations. Nor were specific activities geared to the higher technology firms. Any criticism in this respect is unfair since the Centres had been operating for less than two years and had concentrated their efforts on developing basic counselling and workshop activity and consolidating existing relationships with the environment.

Encouraging the development of small business awareness for students: the main vehicle for this was the SBI student programme. It was significant that the Centres visited had all managed to extend the SBI programme among several of the faculty staff and into several departments. Thus the numbers of students involved had increased although this had produced corresponding difficulties for the SBI Director. Outside of the SBI programme, few additional initiatives had been taken to meet this objective.

Developing research facilities and data banks: this was most advanced at Chico where there was a Centre for Economics and Business Research financed through the university. A number of studies had been undertaken not only for local authority clients, but also for individual companies or groups of companies. Nebraska was also attempting to develop this activity, but was concentrating on the dissemination of information pamphlets. It is significant however, that the research base at Chico existed prior to the Small Business Developmemt Centre. In the other locations, research funds had yet to be found from the university or other sources.

Improving marketing and export assistance: this had not been substantially developed in any of the centres visited, nor had it existed prior to the visit. This was nevertheless covered in workshops, seminars and in counselling. The former usually amounted to only a few hours, or at the most, a day. While nationally there are a few international trade centres sponsored by the Department of Commerce, there was only one currently based at a Small Business Development Centre.

Improving opportunities for socially and economically disadvantaged entrepreneurs: this service depended on the existence of a separately funded Minority Programme known as a Centre for Special Group Emphasis. There had been such a centre at Chico which was being wound up and incorporated into the SBDC. At the time of the visit Pomona was applying for funding for this activity. The Minority Programme basically seeks to undertake counselling and training workshop activities with minority groups in the area very much along the same lines as the SBDC. Special funds are however available for this.

Increasing business viability: this is very difficult to judge and no attempt at evaluation of this was discovered during the visits to the centres (3).

Because of the short period the Centres had been in operation, it is perhaps unfair to try to evaluate their activities against the above criteria. The Centres were immediately under pressure to create outputs of counselling and training. In this respect they were very differently prepared in terms of their resources and their previous track record. The same point can be made about the development of Specialised Services. These required considerable additional resources and probably a period of up to eighteen months to develop them into viable activities.

In the light of these kinds of problems the major outputs which could be looked for in the short run would be those relating to the degree to which the Centres had been able to establish ties with their appropriate environments. In the Centres visited the opportunities for linkage varied with the existence and capability of the local organisations and with the strength of the Centre's previous relationships.

Moreover, different strategies were being pursued: some centres were concerned to undertake most of their work through other organisations. For example Nebraska was financing the five out-reach centres it had established for basic secretarial and counselling activities; and it had budgeted these centres to undertake certain additional activities. Chico in contrast, while organising out-reach centres, had not budgeted them for any activity, since they merely provided facilities and were manned entirely by Chico staff or organisations relating to the Business Development Centre.

The centres also chose different channels through which to direct their energies depending upon their view of the degree of co-operation they would obtain and the capabilities of the local organisations. In Nebraska the Assistant Director and in Chico the Director had both had extended careers with Chambers of Commerce and business associations and therefore had a considerable network of contacts. A great deal of the work of each Centre was thus being channelled through these organisations. Nebraska was actually establishing counselling activity within the local Chambers of Commerce in its region and was using them to disseminate information and as locations for workshops. Trade associations presented more of a problem in terms of integration because they were naturally looking for industry specific counselling and training programmes. Howard University had, however, experimented in the development of local industry specific workshop groups. Relationships with other organisations including banks, accountants, other small

170

business associations and government departments were gradually being developed in all of the centres visited. Chico, which operated a Capital Formation Advisory Service, focused on loan packaging, and had developed extremely good relationships with banks. To accomplish this the Centre had had to demonstrate that it was providing an essential and useful service which would complement and benefit banking activity. Chico seemed to have achieved this and was involved in packaging in one year loans totalling $400 million.

Aside from establishing new activities the problems of the Centres in bringing together existing services in a region and establishing an element of control were significant. In particular, there were problems in integrating SCORE into the work of the Centres, especially where this involved moving an already established SCORE chapter away from its traditional independence. It was clear in both the Centres and in the other University Business Schools visited, that SCORE was becoming an independent organisation in its own right with its own chapters, undertaking its own recruitment, selection and training. Moreover, it was becoming a political force with a powerful lobby in Washington. In addition there were criticisms of SCORE personnel relating to their experience and consequently their ability to relate to the problems of small business, the variability of their capabilities, motivations and commitment, and the difficulties of integrating them into other programmes or activities.

It was anticipated that the Centres would experience difficulties in establishing links with other colleges, and in particular, overcoming the problems of resentment and suspicion of "control". These were confirmed but had largely been overcome by the fact that the Centre could provide funds to the college and that, as a result of the activities developed, there were spin-offs for the college in terms of increasing credibility within the local community. Obviously, in developing the Centre concept further, there will be major difficulties in determining where control should be located. This will particularly be the case in the development of state plans in those areas where there has been no Business Development Centre.

The views of SBA personnel were collected both in Washington and in the regions. In Washington the senior personnel interviewed were very supportive of the Business Development Centre concept. It was clear, however, that problems were caused in evaluation because there was no uniformity in the output and management potential of the Centres. This made the task of evaluating real achievements very difficult and obviously aggravated the SBA's problem in feeding back to Congress outputs in a standard form. This in turn was the source of pressure on the SBDC's for 'numbers' which as indicated earlier was resented and regarded as dysfunctional.

Other operational difficulties experienced by the Centres arose from the control, allocation and evaluation of counselling cases. Tradition- ally these activities had been undertaken by the local SBA Office, but had been transferred to the centres. These difficulties were partly overcome by the SBA Management Assistance Officer who liaised between the Centre and the local SBA Officer. Nevertheless some local SBA Office's felt that they had lost control.

In summary, it can be said that all the Centres visited had made considerable progress in the short time they had been in operation. This progress could, however, only be assessed in relation to the starting point of the centre, the circumstances of the local area and the funds available from other sources to complement those from the SBA. These factors varied considerably from one location to another. There were also difficulties in establishing clear evaluation and qualitative criteria so as to meet the SBA's requirements. Preoccupation with numbers and events was resented by the Centres. Finally, in building up an adequate co-ordinated network of activity with other organisations in the local region the Centres were faced with different problems and attitudes. Uniformly, however, the absorbtion of SCORE activity was a problem and although there was considerable goodwill between the SBA offices and the Centres, some operating responsibilities concerning counselling and training activity had still to be resolved.

RELEVANCE TO THE UK

It can be argued that the relevance of the SBDC programme to the UK depends upon:

(i)   Whether there is a need to co-ordinate exist-
        ing services and resources for small business
        assistance in the regions in order to avoid
        overlap and make it easier for the small
        business to see what is available.

(ii)   Whether the education sector needs to link
        more closely with the small business commun-
        ity.

(The latter issue has been dealt with briefly in an earlier paper in this book by the same author)

The co-ordination of small firm services in the UK.

The main context for the SBDC investigation was the presently rather fragmented assistance environment for small firms in the UK. The general concern with small firms as a means of providing more local employment opportunities has not only led organisations whose traditional interest is in the small firms' area to reappraise their existing policies and introduce new forms of assistance but has also encouraged institutions, which hitherto neglected the small firm, to introduce new measures. As a result there is a growing, if rather complex panorama, of small firms' assistance. Thus it is not uncommon to find in a region that over the past two years, the higher education community has rediscovered the small business with a variety of programmes of assistance and in some cases the setting up of small business centres. It has also joined in with its traditional research contribution. Local authorities and development corporations have also begun to make special provision of advisory and counselling services alongside other schemes or provided finance and/or premises. The Department of Industry itself has developed the role of its Small Firm Centres into counselling. In addition there has been a variety of initiatives under the aegis of the Special Programmes Division of the Manpower Services Commission. These and other services have added to the existing provision by official government bodies and the work of such other organisations as the Chambers of Commerce and productivity associations.

While many of the new initiatives in the environment are aimed at finding new ways of meeting the needs of the small business it can be argued that the resultant plethora of assistance sources makes it even more difficult for the small businessman. There is indeed evidence to suggest that he, typically, has real difficulties in scanning the environment outside of his own particular business interests: and even in this respect he may often have a very limited horizon.

The work of the Department of Industry's Small Firm Centres is, of course, a major force in signposting the small firm through the maze of assistance. It is not, however, responsible for co-ordinating the environment: and while in practice it may seek to influence developments, its resources are limited. What is clear to the observer is that there are overlaps and possible links between advice and information, counselling and consultancy and training and education services to small firms. A comprehensive training package for example, may encompass all these aspects. In turn such packages may well have links with the provision of finance and other forms of assistance.

The need which the Small Business Development Centre concept is designed to meet, is therefore probably of similar importance in the UK as in the United States. This need can be seen in terms of successfully integrating the variety of services available to the small firm into some form of coherent help within a particular location. The call is increasingly heard now, particularly in the press, for some kind of agency to bring together small firm services. One interpretation of this is the centralisation of services within a particular agency such as an English Development Agency, or indeed, an SBA. This argument merits careful scrutiny. It is possible, for example, to argue that there are major differences between regions and that the existing services have been developed in response to the needs of the local market. The setting up of a new agency to centralise small firms' assistance within a region, while giving all appearances of 'tidying up' the situation might have serious disadvantages in terms of losses in flexibility and restrictions on the ability of individuals to take initiatives. Moreover, the 'internalisation' of services in a region within a bureaucracy might be a possible source of discouragement to other local initiatives and sources of help. The concept of the SBDC might therefore be seen as an alternative to this with emphasis on the development of a network system aimed at bringing together through a small central agency the efforts of a variety of existing organisations. This concept is essentially regional in character and will bring out the differences in regional characteristics and opportunities.

Before concluding with the strengths and weaknesses of the SBDC concept it is worth noting that the American system has been based on university business schools. The reason for this in America is quite clear, namely that one of the major objectives of the Centres is the influencing of the education system; its staff and students to come to terms with small business. This objective is certainly met by placing the control within the education sector and, by the very nature of the contract, forcing links with the environment. The University or college must commit itself to a major environmental initiative in respect of small business in undertaking the contract. University business schools and polytechnics in the UK do not, by and large, have to take this kind of initiative.

The strengths of the concept

The idea of a network system based on an educational establishment has many strengths. If adequately organised it would help the education sector to develop closer relationships with the local environment. It would also be making maximum use of existing institutions and their skills and energies with the emphasis on co-operation in the region. It will thus only work if it succeeds in harnessing skills and energies and therefore achieves credibility with the relevant institutions and the business community. This, it must be noted, is a harder task to achieve than the operation of a simple bureaucratic system which will invariably tend towards producing its own 'success' data. If it succeeds, it will have the benefit of allowing flexibility for regional differences in needs and scope for individual judgement and initiative. Moreover, it will be relatively cheap because of its use of existing channels.

The weaknesses of the concept

The source of possible major weakness of the system can be found within its strengths. It is, for example, dependent upon the motivation and involvement of other organisations which cannot easily control and command in order to achieve outputs for it will have only limited funds.

Its success in the short run will therefore depend very much on the initial potential that already exists within a region, which may be small, and the careful selection of the centre. Without a sound potential base it would take a considerable time to build up a system particularly as there are certain to be jealousies between official agencies and other institutions and any new control centre.

If accepted in principle for implementation in the UK development would therefore require considerable patience, commitment, and funding. Key factors in the success of the experiment are likely to be:

- Careful selection of centres

- Careful monitoring of initial staffing in particular selection of a director

- Provision of government money and encouragement of local organisations in industry to provide additional support

- Full support from government officials and existing government systems

- The establishment of careful evaluation criteria linking to effectiveness and the monitoring of this rather than merely counting numbers of events

- The eventual evaluation of results by research among the small business community.

174

In practice building up the basic services of the centre would require close linkage with the Training Services Division and local Industry Training Board network in a region. Through this collaboration there will be some responsibility for the quality of the training and the development and dissemination of programmes.

In counselling the centre would have to link closely with the Small Firms Information Centre Counselling Services. Its links to the sign-posting service of the SFC's will also have to be close. Among the basic services might be training and education programmes for 'institutional personnel' within a region including accountants, bank managers, industrial planning officers, etc. In this there might be joint venture with the Small Firms Information Centres Counselling Service and other educational institutions.

The concept is ambitious and in the first instance involves some not inconsiderable outlay. The benefits, however, might be considerable, not only in providing a vehicle for helping the very small firm, but also in providing a major influence in business education.

NOTES

(1) The Small Business Counselling Service of Retired Executives.
(2) See the earlier paper by Allan Gibb in this book entitled "The Small Business Institute Programme in the USA and its relevance to the UK".

12 An evaluation of the Small Firms Counselling Service in the South West Region

JOHN HOWDLE
South West Regional Management Centre,
Bristol Polytechnic

INTRODUCTION

This paper is based on a survey which was conducted in response to a request by the Small Firms Division of the Department of Industry for an independent evaluation of the Small Firms Counselling Service in the South West. The Counselling Service is approximately three years old and it was felt that sufficient experience of counselling had been acquired to justify a thorough evaluation. The Counselling Service was pioneered in the South West and was first offered in November 1976. The survey interviews were conducted over a four month period from October 1978 to January 1979. The terms of reference emphasised the need "to concentrate on those firms which made use of the fee-paying, follow-up, Counselling Service". The investigation was intended to establish detailed information relating to:

(a) How and why contact with the Counselling Service was made, the nature of counselling and the method of work adopted by counsellors.

(b) Whether clients received written or verbal recommendations and whether they acted upon the advice received.

(c) The benefits which resulted from counselling help and the adverse consequences if any.

(d) Results in terms of measures of performance and the client's level of satisfaction with the counselling received.

(e) Whether clients would use the Service again, their views on pricing, their willingness to recommend the Service and the scope for improvement or extension.

Within the confines of this paper it is impossible to deal with all the categories listed above and all the issues analysed in the main report. Three main themes which arose out of the study have been chosen, therefore, for detailed examination here. These are respectively: the nature of counselling, the impact of counselling and the scope for improvement of the Counselling Service. Before proceeding to discuss these findings, however, it may prove helpful to describe the

177

principal characteristics of the Small Firms Counselling Service.

THE STRUCTURE OF THE COUNSELLING SERVICE

The Counselling Service is in part modelled on similar services offered in Canada and the USA (1). In the South West the Counselling Service is based upon seven areas. Counselling appointments are made in the first instance through the staff of the Small Firms Information Centre based in Bristol. There is a Freefone service available for the use of clients of the Counselling Service. The first counselling interview is free, but the client is expected to attend at the nearest Area Counselling Office. These area offices (2) are located in Bristol, Gloucester, Swindon, Exeter, Plymouth and Redruth. Interviews are time-tabled at two hourly intervals. The initial interview is intended to be exploratory in nature, an opportunity to define the nature of the problem.

Subsequent interviews involve fees. The second interview costs £5 and further interviews (up to a maximum of ten) attract a fee of £15 per session. It is important to note that, with the exception of the first interview, later counselling sessions will normally occur on the client's premises and do not involve any specified time limit. Thus it is quite normal for a counsellor to travel to the client's premises and to spend several hours or even a day investigating an enquiry.

There are currently 20 counsellors working in the South West Region. These counsellors have been selected for their ability to assist small businessmen on the basis of their own work experience. Their average age is 56 years and a majority have spent their working life in small businesses. Some counsellors currently own their own firms or are actively involved in a part-time capacity. One or two counsellors have a background in consultancy and several others have considerable experience of general management in medium and large sized companies. There is a spread of functional expertise available but emphasis has been placed upon the recruitment of individuals with a well rounded experience of business.

Field management of the counsellors is delegated to three area co-ordinators. One co-ordinator is responsible for the Bristol, Swindon and Gloucester centres, a second deals with centres at Truro, Plymouth and Exeter, and because of geographical separation, the third is responsible for the Poole centre.

Counsellors are remunerated on a fairly modest scale. Each counsellor receives £16 per day spent on counselling work.

The work of the counsellors is monitored by the area co-ordinators who report in turn to the Manager of the Small Firms Counselling Service in Bristol. The Bristol Office Manager is responsible for promoting the activities of the Counselling Service together with his other role as Manager of the Small Firms Information Centre. In addition, he has a third function which is concerned with information gathering in relation to the needs of small firms in the South West. In this capacity the Manager can exert some influence upon the development of small firms policy.

METHODOLOGY

In order to ensure the objectivity required by the terms of reference, the two samples employed in this survey were selected on a random basis. The main research effort was directed towards the sample of follow-up cases, since clearly follow-up clients have experienced more concentrated exposure to counselling.

Sample of follow-up cases

Follow up cases were defined to involve at least two counselling interviews, one of which will occur at the client's place of work. Sixty five firms were interviewed from a random sample of 88. The random sample was stratified in terms of three variables; area, size and type of industry. The sample of 88 firms was drawn from the 188 follow-up cases which had been completed by the Counselling Service by March 31st, 1978. This date was selected in order to allow a period of at least six months to elapse between completion of the case and the survey interview.

Sample of single-interview cases

Single interview cases were counselling interviews which did not involve any payment of fees or visits to the client's premises. A 6.5 per cent random sample was drawn from the records of all single interview cases maintained at the Bristol Office. This sample was stratified by area, but by no other characteristic.

The constitution of the two samples is shown in Table 1.

Table 1

Constitution of Samples

Area	Sample of Follow-up Cases	Sample of Single Interview Cases	Total Cases
Bristol	16	22	38
Gloucester	2	7	9
Swindon	2	7	9
Bournemouth*	21	3	24
Exeter	10	8	18
Plymouth	11	5	16
Redruth	3	10	13
	—	—	—
TOTAL	65	62	127

*The Area Counselling Office is now located at Poole

179

THE NATURE OF COUNSELLING

Types of counselling assistance

In the course of this survey, it has been possible to identify several types of counselling assistance.

(a) Pure counselling

This occurred when the client shared his problem with the counsellor and used him as a sounding board for ideas. The counsellor's role was one of evaluation and feedback, the client ultimately made the decision to act but his actions were often modified as a result of the counselling which had been given.

(b) Morale building counselling

In a substantial number of cases, the client approached the Counselling Service because he or she was extremely worried about some aspect of their business. The counselling interview consisted largely of the client telling the counsellor what they believed was the best course of action in response to the client's business situation. The counsellor's role in this case was frequently to rubber stamp the client's proposed course of action. The client was thus released from indecision and proceeded to implement the planned course of action.

(c) Action counselling

A number of counsellors in the South West are highly motivated individuals with considerable resources of energy. When a certain type of client approached the counselling service with urgent problems (typically financial or legal), a successful and confident counsellor could often achieve a great deal in a very short time. For example, the counsellor could release the client's power to act by generating optimism and enthusiasm for the business. On occasions a client's problems were often dissipated by the counsellor's deft use of personal contacts or pressure at the correct point.

(d) Analytical counselling

Action counselling as described above was found to be an anathema to a certain sort of client. Where a client was an established businessman or woman without immediate problems of survival, counselling needs tended to be more long term in nature. In such circumstances, the client tended to look for analytical counselling. Here the client required somebody with the ability to sift their way through a complex mass of information and to help generate some sensible solutions.

One client who was visited during the course of the survey interviews, approached the Counselling Service because he was suffering from severe pressure from creditors. The client in this case was a manufacturer of small lighting fittings. The counsellor immediately set to work on overdue accounts on the client's behalf. On the same morning that the counsellor became involved he visited the client's major customer and obtained a cheque for £7,000 for an overdue account and negotiated an 18 per cent price increase. The counsellor subsequently helped to arrange an increased overdraft limit for the business.

The nature of help offered by an individual counsellor depended upon his own particular talents and experience. Some counsellors excelled at the more reflective forms of counselling whilst others were better at generating optimism and activity. Certainly action counselling offered the most dramatic results and clients often achieved remarkable benefits in a very short space of time.

To the client, these interventions represented a very unexpected and welcome bonus. They were only possible because the counsellor was a respected local businessman with a lot of energy and a good network of contacts. In the example quoted, the counsellor was able to wield influence at the highest level in the organisation concerned.

Where clients were seeking, 'pure or analytical counselling', rather different talents appeared to be involved. Analytical counselling, for instance, seemed particularly demanding because it often required the counsellor to help devise a new strategy for the client's business. This form of counselling therefore, appears to share some of the characteristics of consultancy but to lack any element of prescription. Typically the client was well aware of the complexity of the issues involved and was seeking the assistance of an experienced individual who could retain an independent stance and put forward an objective view of any given proposal.

The Influence of the counsellor

Counsellors were able to operate in three closely related areas:

    (i)   analysis
    (ii)   contacts
    (iii)   influence

The first step was to analyse the situation. Once the situation was clearly understood, the counsellors efforts to resolve it might well depend more upon his or her personal contacts and status than on his or her intellectual skills.

Some enquiries were solved by internal re-organisation within the firm, by for example, releasing cash internally, or improving the utilisation of assets. Frequently the client was faced with external problems and this was where contacts and influence became very important. In a number of cases which were investigated the counsellor's ability to introduce the right contact proved fundamental to the successful conclusion of a given enquiry. Three examples of such contacts were respectively a retired local printer, a rather obscure source of venture capital, and a list of works managers (with specific interests).

Small firms tend to operate within the local commercial and industrial environment. Most of the counsellors in the South West draw their own experience from this same environment and between them they possess many contacts which may be tapped into by the small firm. This sort of assistance is not readily available from any other body and in this sense the counselling service is offering a unique form of help to the small firm.

The Counselling Service also appeared to be unique with respect to the level of involvement which some counsellors bring to their task. Many examples were discovered where the counsellors displayed levels of enthusiasm and commitment which would be rare in other forms of organisation. In quite a number of cases counsellors accompanied clients on visits to see bank managers, debtors or to buy premises. Frequently counsellors devoted considerable amounts of time during the evening and at weekends to help resolve particular problems. The clients drew great strength from such help and valued the assistance of individuals who were aware of what risk taking and financial strain involve.

Whereas specialist advisers such as accountants, solicitors and bank managers are subject to their own constraints and inhibitions, a counsellor does not have to consider bank lending criteria nor is he wholly concerned with financial reporting. The counsellor, therefore, is in a much better position to identify with the client's total situation and he has the time available to do so. Even if the accountant or bank manager has the will to help he rarely has enough time and is frequently obliged to charge quite heavily for such services.

The counsellor's influence appeared to depend largely upon the strength of his or her personality and social status. Some clients reported that the intervention of counsellors had an almost magical impact upon bank managers, reluctant payers and tardy accountants, others found the effect less dramatic. Most third parties appeared to take a client's arguments much more seriously once they realised that a counsellor, with a vague but official Department of Trade and Industry connection was involved. On occasions clients reported that bank managers and accountants were entirely unaware of the existence of the Counselling Service. Indeed some had to explain who the counsellors were and what their role was. This is disappointing in view of the considerable efforts made to publicise the service to this very group of people. Initially, it was hoped that bank managers might prove a valuable source of counselling cases. This has not proved to be the case, although there have been some notable exceptions.

It is worth pointing out however that counsellors have little real power to influence events if a third party chooses to ignore the rather tenuous government connections.

THE IMPACT OF COUNSELLING

Problem type

In order to establish the impact of counselling it is important to analyse what sort of issues lead the owners of small firms to seek counselling advice. There are, of course, dangers inherent in such analysis since not many problems can be strictly classified as falling into one particular area of business activity. Many of the issues raised by clients involve several aspects of the business. Financial problems are particularly misleading in this respect as invariably they are linked to other factors such as production or marketing. For the purposes of this survey the nature of the enquiry/ problem was classified under one major heading, although the enquirer may well have discussed related, but subordinate issues.

The main feature of Table 2 is the dominating position of financial enquiries. Both the sample of follow-up and the total number of follow-up cases up to end March 1978 showed that financial enquiries constituted almost 50 per cent of all further counselling. This was in marked contrast to an analysis of all enquiries (November 1976 - December 1978), which showed financial enquiries at only 27.8 per cent of the total and a higher incidence of start ups 20.5 per cent and management enquiries at 17.7 per cent.

Table 2.

Follow up Counselling by Problem Type

Nature of Enquiry/Problem	Sample Number	%	All cases* Number	%
Starting New	10	15.4	31	16.5
Finance	32	49.2	90	47.8
Management	3	4.6	22	11.7
Production	3	4.6	4	2.1
Marketing	12	18.5	24	12.8
Expansion	1	1.5	9	4.8
Diversification	2	3.1	3	1.6
Other	2	3.1	5	2.7
Total	65	100.0	188	100.0

* (November 1976 - March 31st 1978)

The greater frequency of financial problems and the lesser frequency of start-up enquiries in follow-up counselling appears logical. This suggests, as one would anticipate, that financial issues are difficult to ignore, that they rarely subside of their own accord and are thus great motivators to action. Once again, however, it is dangerous to over simplify the situation. The broad classification of 'finance' includes a wide range of issues from raising capital through standard costing and book-keeping to coping with a bad debt.

If the dominance of finance is predictable, the absence of production enquiries is rather less easy to explain. Production enquiries were rather over represented in the sample at 4.6 per cent, whereas they actually represented only 2.1 per cent of follow-up cases and 2.9 per cent of all enquiries. The predominance of enquiries from the service sector of industry goes some way to explain these low figures, but other explanations are called for. It is frequently argued that the insti-gators of small firms are often well versed from a technical and pro-duction point of view but are weak in the areas of finance and market-ing. The incidence of marketing enquiries appears to support this view. If the three related areas of marketing, expansion and diversification are added together they account for over 20 per cent of follow-up counselling. It is noticeable that marketing becomes a more potent factor as the size of firm increases.

It is encouraging that one in every six follow-up cases involved starting a new business. Whilst this was down on the one in five incidence of such enquiries at the initial interview stage, this was to be expected. Many of the start-up enquiries which are discussed at initial interviews lacked much substance. The enquirer either lacked the knowledge, the capital or the nerve to proceed. Indeed one of the counsellor's more unpleasant tasks was to disabuse enquirers with ill-conceived start-up plans.

During the course of this survey it became apparent that the level of satisfaction with the Counselling Service was closely related to the type of problems brought to counselling and the counsellor's power to assist with these problems. Given that counselling can prove helpful to client firms, what form do the benefits take and how can these be measured?

Difficulties in Measuring Satisfaction with Counselling

It was recognised from the outset that any attempt to measure the benefits from counselling would present a number of difficulties. This indeed proved to be the case. It was not difficult to identify clients who had instituted changes and who were convinced that they had enjoyed subsequent benefits from these changes. The problem arises when one attempts to measure the benefits. Measuring implies some sort of objective scale. It also implies that one can distinguish that part of any given change in a variable which emanates solely from counselling. Many of the clients could identify positive improvements in particular variables, but there were few who claimed they could accurately identify those changes which occurred as a result of counselling and those changes which were the result of other factors. The results achieved by any given business are related to a complex range of variables including the economic situation, the actions of competitors and the changing pattern of consumer demand.

In order to give a reasonably complete picture, it proved necessary to count the numbers of firms claiming benefits on particular given dimensions. It is recognised that this cannot be as convincing as a series of measurements on a particular scale but it does represent a first attempt at quantification. Table 3 provides a visual map of the results achieved from the analysis.

It was encouraging to find that, despite the difficulty of sorting out such cause and effect relationships, a sizeable percentage of the sample were able to point to specific measures and say with confidence that they had improved as a result of counselling help. A minority were prepared to estimate actual cost savings and to estimate percentage effects upon their profitability and turnover. It is probably not surprising that most of the benefits were seen in terms of financial criteria, as this is one area where there are some fairly clear measures available.

In many respects the empty columns are as interesting as the completed ones. It is possible to argue, that the empty areas in marketing and production are there because they are difficult aspects to measure. Alternatively, it may be that few enquiries were received relating to these aspects. This is certainly not the case with respect to Marketing and one of the recommendations made is the need for a greater capacity in this subject in the South West.

Analysis of significant and measureable benefits

* New start planned
** Will close loss-making branch

Table 3

COMPANY CODE	FINANCE					MARKETING				PRODUCTION					MANPOWER		
	PROFIT BEFORE TAX	CASH FLOW	SALES TURNOVER	INCREASED FINANCE	COST SAVINGS	NEW PRODUCT	NEW MARKET	EXPORT	DISTRIBUTION	OUTPUT	INCREASED PROD'TY	INCREASED INV'T	STOCKS/PURCHASING	IMPROVED LAYOUT	EMPLOYMENT	SURVIVAL	S/NEW/GO
02	▲												●				
03		▲															
04		▲													✻		✻
07			▲													✻	
08																	*
09		▲	▲		○										✻		
13				▲													
14		▲		▲	▲										✻		✻
17	▲	▲		▲											✻		
18		▲	▲	▲					○	●		●					
19	▲			▲											✻		
20	▲	▲	▲	▲											✻		
22				▲								●		●	✻		
23															✻		✻
26			▲	▲											✻		✻
27						○											
28	▲		▲	▲											✻		
29	▲		▲													✻	
30		▲														✻	
32													●				
34	▲	▲		▲									●				
37							○										
38			▲														
40	▲				▲												
41	▲		▲	▲			○								✻		
42			▲														
44					▲												
45		▲	▲														
46	▲				▲										✻		
48															✻		✻
49		▲											●				
50					**												
52							○										
54											●		●	●			
56					▲												
58	▲	▲	▲	▲			○							●		✻	
59		▲		▲	▲												
61	▲			▲	▲				○							✻	
63															✻		✻
TOTALS	12	13	9	12	14	1	4	1	2	1	1	2	5	3	12	7	6

On the basis of the benefits indicated in Table 3, 39 clients out of a random sample of 65 were able to identify one or more measureable benefits from follow-up counselling. This represents some 60 per cent of the sample, but excludes a number of individuals who claimed other non-quantifiable benefits. Of all those firms whose attitude was favourable to counselling, a very high proportion mentioned the morale boosting effect of their counselling experience. In a number of cases the client argued persuasively that a morale boosting visit from a counsellor released him from indecision and provided a spur to action.

The converse was also true. Where clients had a negative experience of counselling they found their energy sapped and a residue of depression to be overcome. One client's comment about counselling was that the counsellor - "contributed a bit of gloom".

Survivors and New Start-Ups

One potent measure of benefit which was not anticipated in the survey questionnaire was SURVIVAL. It became apparent during the course of the survey that a number of companies attributed their continued survival to the intervention of the Small Firms Counselling Service. One criteria of success to be borne in mind for the future, therefore, is the number of businesses and jobs saved. Unfortunately, however, the counselling service was often called in to assist clients a matter of days or hours before closure had become inevitable. Some of the firms represented in this sample, though, appeared to have requested help at a stage earlier on the downward cycle and the counsellor had been able to arrest the slide.

In addition to those clients who claimed that the Counselling Service had helped them survive, there was another group of clients who claimed that without counselling help they would not have commenced trading. The measure of counselling performance could then in the future be seen in terms of numbers of new businesses and in new jobs created. Once again these measures are rather superficial and do not pay any attention to the multiplier effects which extend to the local economy. No one, including the client, can be absolutely certain that without counselling assistance they would have gone bankrupt, or that they would not have started a new business but they can make a shrewd guess.

SCOPE FOR IMPROVING THE COUNSELLING SERVICE

If the Counselling Service is to make a significant impact upon the small firm sector it is important that counsellors should achieve real improvement in access to small firms. In this respect it is important that counsellors can attain a satisfactory level of conversions to follow-up counselling. If very few firms request more than one counselling session, there can be little impact.

At present there is a wide disparity in conversion rates from one area to another. A number of explanations are proposed for this phenomenon. For the purpose of this paper, it is interesting to examine those factors which determine the number of counselling sessions requested by clients.

Transferring Cases

Clients appeared to pursue further counselling until diminishing returns set in. So long as clients could clearly distinguish real benefits or the anticipation of benefits, further counselling was taken up. The cost element in further counselling becomes more important as the fee charged for the second session to the third increases from £5-£15. Even so, cost was still not a major factor, although it loomed much larger with clients in financial difficulties or start-up situations. If a counsellor was providing tangible help to the small firm then the client could easily save the cost of the counselling sessions in implementing the advice given.

As a business develops the client's problem areas change. A counsellor who is ideal for assisting with one aspect of the business may be out of his depth with another. Unless the counsellor is prompt to recognise his inability to provide the necessary counselling advice, the client may well look to other sources of help. If this happens, then the long term counselling relationship loses continuity and breaks. The solution in this situation requires a willingness on the part of the counsellor to introduce a colleague with more relevant experience and knowledge.

A number of follow-up clients explained during interviews that they found it difficult to ask their counsellor if they could be referred to someone else. This was often because they were reluctant to damage a friendly relationship with the counsellor which had been built up in stressful times. Larger firms in particular, looked for a level of expertise in a functional area which was often not available either from their original counsellor or any other counsellor from their local counselling office. Even if expertise was available in the right function it often needed to be specific to a given industry. At times this may mean that the client needs to see a counsellor from a different region of the country. Where counsellors have operated flexibly in this way, clients invariably benefited.

Marketing

One common problem faced by firms in the survey was how to sell their production once a reasonable volume had been achieved. In the very early days of a new firm, production is often the main difficulty but after a time the pressure moves over to the marketing function. As many small firms are started by individuals with good technical rather than management skills, marketing can represent a major obstacle.

Several clients approached the Counselling Service because they were interested in how to develop their talents for selling. Another group of clients were interested in how to identify potential customers. At the time the survey was conducted the Counselling Service did not appear to have any very clear answer to the selling question and the approach to the market research question also tended to be very piece-meal. Several clients reported dissatisfaction with the assistance which they received in relation to marketing problems. This may be associated with the fact that there are few short cuts available in order to obtain good reliable market research data, or to master the arts of salesmanship. Even so, there did appear to be a need to strengthen the provision of high level marketing expertise in the South West. The evidence that some of the larger companies experienced difficulties in the marketing area supports this view.

Financial Problems

The Counselling Service is in a front line position to cope with financial problems but has a rather uneven capacity to do so. At present the Counselling Service has no direct access to funds whatsoever (3). This means that whilst counsellors can help with certain categories of financial problems, they are left rather defenceless with others. Where the counsellors do have scope for action they appear to have acquitted themselves rather well.

Counsellors frequently managed to persuade bank managers not to foreclose on their clients. In quite a number of cases counsellors solved overdraft problems simply by moving the account to a more sympathetic branch. On some occasions, difficulties were resolved by changing the client's borrowing from an overdraft to a loan basis. Where relatively small amounts of short term finance were involved, counsellors enjoyed a reasonable success rate.

Searching for sources of medium and long term finance was a more difficult task for the counsellors. Like the client, they were forced to fall back on their knowledge of the commercial market. If the counsellor has good financial contacts and access to private sources of capital then he must guard these jealously. A counsellor will not retain such contacts for long unless he is very careful about the quality of the introductions he makes.

Other counsellors restricted their assistance to advice and lists of sources and were reluctant to get deeply involved. This attitude on the part of counsellors is perfectly legitimate and in line with their terms of reference but appeared to lead to dissatisfaction and resentment on the part of quite a number of clients.

One aspect which many counsellors appeared to cover well was that of helping the client to prepare a case for presentation to the bank. Quite a number of counsellors accompanied their clients on such occasions.

Analysis of the random sample of 62 single interview clients demonstrated that 27 of these or 43 per cent were actively seeking finance of one sort or another. Of the financial problems which proceeded to further counselling, less than one third involved serious problems of raising capital. It seems reasonable to deduce that clients only proceed to further counselling in cases where the counsellor can hold out some promise of tangible help. Thus the majority of finance raising problems are being filtered out before the stage of follow-up counselling is reached.

The fact that many clients were interested in obtaining funds raises the issue of whether or not the Counselling Service should have any direct powers to assist in the provision of capital. Many clients believe that the Counselling Service certainly should possess such access to funds.

The point was repeatedly made that without access to funds "the

Counselling Service has no teeth". However good a counsellor believes a project or business to be is immaterial to the client if no suitable finance can be found. One of the difficulties in assessing the need for funds is in trying to define exactly what sort of capital is required by small firms. Of the 27 firms seeking funds, only three or four were seeking in excess of £25,000.

One of the difficulties experienced by the interviewer was that many clients were not at all clear about the type of finance which they were looking for. A significant proportion complained that their expansion was being hampered by lack of funds which were not forthcoming for two reasons:

      (a) No remaining collateral.
      (b) Insufficient or poor track record.

Several firms claimed that given the additional funds they could have employed more people. There was a fairly all pervading attitude that lack of capital was holding back expansion. This was associated with a second view that the clearing banks were not interested in lending money unless it was very well secured. Paradoxically a number of clients pointed out that they could borrow short term funds to buy themselves a luxurious new car but could not raise addition-al finance to assist in running their businesses.

Access to funds would probably increase the credibility of the Counselling Service a great deal. It might also prove helpful in attracting more small firms and a greater cross-section to make contact with the Counselling Service. It is possible that funds could provide a useful lever for gaining access to more small firms, thereby providing opportunities for effective counselling help. Until the Counselling Service is able to provide access to its own source of funds, it will continue to lack credibility in the eyes of many potential users.

The Concept of Counselling

One potent measure of the success of the Counselling Service should be the client's willingness to use the service on successive occasions. 89.3 per cent of clients in the sample of follow-up cases stated their willingness to use the Counselling Service again, should a suitable occasion arise. This high figure lends support to the view that the great majority of follow-up clients are convinced that the basic concept of counselling is good. It also suggests that clients are sufficiently open-minded to recognise that even if the Counselling Service cannot help much in one specific situation, it may well be able to assist in other different situations.

The evidence available with respect to the sample of single inter-views, also supports the view that the concept of counselling is widely accepted by those firms which have been exposed to it: (77.4 per cent of single interview clients would use the Counselling Service again).

During the course of the survey, many suggestions were made by clients of how to improve the Counselling Service. Aspects which received repeated and sometimes vociferous mention included the need for:

(a)   More widespread publicity.
(b)   Realistic funding back-up.
(c)   "More top-line marketing expertise".
(d)   More notice of counsellors by other government agencies.
(e)   Greater involvement in implementation.

CONCLUSIONS

This paper has focussed on three main themes, the nature of counselling, the impact of counselling and the scope for improvement of the Counselling Service. In pursuing these themes reference has been made, at one point or another, to many of the conclusions which were reached and the recommendations that were made in the complete report. The strengths of the Counselling Service in the South West emerged fairly clearly from the survey findings. Over 60 per cent of clients who received further counselling were able to identify tangible benefits which had resulted from counselling. Approximately 50 per cent of clients receiving further counselling described their experience as "very useful"; a further 17 per cent decribed it as "useful". A majority of the businessmen who were interviewed expressed positive reactions to the Counselling Service.

Many clients stressed the great value of an informed discussion with a sympathetic counsellor. The opportunity to discuss a complex issue with an impartial adviser is highly valued. Whilst most respondents were well disposed towards the Counselling Service there are clearly aspects which attracted criticism.

The Counselling Service was considered to lack the appropriate level of marketing expertise. Many respondents were critical of the absence of any form of funding back-up to the Counselling Service. This factor is believed to inhibit many clients from pursuing further counselling.

There is scope to increase the flexibility of the service in terms of the willingness to transfer cases. At times it is apparent that more effective counselling could be achieved if cases were referred to counsellors with specialist skills. There is a need for more careful matching of clients and counsellors. This process already occurs on a limited scale, and deserves expansion. Matching could often be achieved on a regional basis and on occasions may deserve consideration at a national level.

Counselling is most effective when the counsellor has direct experi-ence of the client's industry and the type of problem involved. The Counselling Service is used predomin-antly by very small firms: (87.5 per cent of all users employed less than ten people). Follow-up counselling attracts more firms in the larger employment categories, but the shift up the size range is only small. The problems encountered by larger firms require more specialist function-al and environmental know-ledge than those encountered by smaller firms.

The Counselling Service is widely believed, by clients, to be under-sold and underpublicised. Publicity is a major difficulty for the Counselling Service. Small businessmen are notoriously difficult to reach and there do not appear to be any easy solutions here. Local newspapers are probably the best vehicle for promotion because small

businessmen use local newspapers and are, therefore, obliged to read
them.

   It is important to point out that this paper is based on a report
which was completed in February, 1979. Since that time the Counselling
Service has continued to assist small firms and many of the suggestions
made in the Report have been implemented.

NOTES

(1) For a further account of the services offered in the United States
see the papers in this book contributed by Allan Gibb, Director of Small
Business Centre at Durham University Business School.

(2) Area Counselling Offices are operational one or two days per week
and are based in locations associated with the library service, the
local Council or other suitable rooms. e.g. Dorset Chamber of Commerce
and Trade.

(3) A pilot scheme to provide funds for the Counselling Service is
currently being undertaken in the Eastern Region.

13 Management development and the owner manager

DAVID WATKINS
Manchester Business School

INTRODUCTION

The research reported in this paper was undertaken as part of a study commissioned by the Department of Industry Small Firms Division into the Management and Business Education Needs of Small Firms and the extent to which these are being met. (Hansard, 1977).

This study had its origins in informal discussions between senior officials of the Department of Industry and a number of academics concerned with the preservation and development of the UK small firm sector and improvements in the performance of individual firms therein. These discussions led to a number of institutions being invited to tender for a contract to study the Management and Business Education Needs of Small Firms. With the express consent of the Department, several of the people thus invited agreed to tender jointly for this study in order to bring the widest possible degree of expertise and experience to bear across the geographically disaggregated small firm sector in the shortest possible time. This led to the Department placing a contract with the Manchester Business School on the understanding that a wide range of other individuals and institutions would co-operate in the conduct of the study. These included John Collins of the South West Regional Management Centre. Michael Cromey Hawke at Gwent College of Further Education, Allan Gibb at Durham University Business School and John Stanworth of the Polytechnic of Central London.

The fieldwork for the study was carried out in the Spring and Summer of 1978 and the Report submitted to the Department of Industry in November of that year.

The more alert reader will have noticed the subtle shift in terminology between the title of this paper and that originally agreed with the Department of Industry in that the focus of this paper is the scope for management development in small, owner managed firms. By management development we mean structured learning activities through which managers seek to become more resourceful and thus enhance their ability to solve problems and sieze opportunities themselves. (Morrison Burgoyne 1973). This concept is rather broader than the common usage of 'education' or 'training' it will include counselling, but clearly excludes the kind of consulting in which an outsider may solve an individual or firm's problem without that individual or client firm developing the capacity to solve similar problems unaided in the future. For owner managers do not themselves see 'management training needs' as such (least of all for themselves); this is an analytical framework imposed on the manager and his firm by well-intentioned outsiders. Owner-managers see not 'training needs' but problems and opportunities for which they seek out solutions and feasible attainment strategies respectively.

A major aim in undertaking the study was therefore to form a view of the extent to which real developmental needs/opportunities existed in small owner managed firms, in particular, for the owner-manager himself. It is results which shed light on this question which form the body of this paper.

PREVIOUS RESEARCH

In contrast to the situation which exists in some other countries, in particular the USA and German-speaking Europe, relatively little empirical research on the management development needs of small firms has been undertaken in the UK. Of these, two studies in particular should be mentioned.

The Committee of Inquiry on Small Firms (Bolton 1971) (the Bolton Committee), which reported in 1971, contained two chapters of particular relevance to this topic; Chapter 10 on 'Management Skills and Advisory Services' and chapter 14 on 'Industrial Training'. This interesting topic division was perhaps in itself an unconscious acceptance of a widespread view that 'training' has little to do with management needs.

Chapter 10 of the Committee's Report, summarising a great deal of written evidence and specially commissioned research, concluded that:

> '...the main areas in which small businessmen
> could improve their performance are ...
> finance ... costing and control information
> ... organisation ... marketing ... information
> use and retrieval ... personnel management ...
> technological change ... production scheduling
> and purchasing control ...'

and that:

> 'the problems are mostly interrelated, and the
> individual manager will generally worry about
> the development of the business as a whole
> rather than about discrete functional
> difficulties.'

The Committee had:

> ' ... no doubt that the overall standard of
> management in small firms is low because the
> routine administration side of management
> which consumes so much of the small
> businessman's time is not properly
> systematised and delegated.' (Merrett Cyriax,
> 1971a)

In other words, there were likely to be managerial deficiencies across a

194

broad spectrum of activity.

The Committee of Inquiry also commissioned a number of Research Reports which remain useful data in their own right. Research Report 4 which sought to explain differences in the growth, stabilisation and decay profiles of small firms, is particularly noteworthy, since it concluded that:

> '... in general the factor most closely associated with differences in growth of turnover and profitability was management as it was reflected in entry into new markets, development of new products and improvement in market share.'

This study demonstrated major differences in overall company performance associated with different managerial characteristics. These are summarised in Table One.

Of the high performing 'Category A Management', only 60 percent had direct previous experience of the business which they subsequently founded. There was also a 'complete absence' of any formal qualifications.

In an empirical study conducted independently of the Bolton Committee's Inquiry but parallel to it, Boswell researched the circumstances, including qualities of management, leading to 'The Rise and Decline of Small Firms (Boswell, 1972). Inter alia, this argued that the problems of small firm management, as seen by the chief executive, were essentially those of self-management. Speaking of the young firm owner-managers in his sample, Boswell argued that:

> 'the scope for collective advice may be greater than at first sight appears. Patterns of work and leisure, health problems and the conservation of energy generally, the psychology of delegation, the logistics, indeed the ergonomics of the boss' job, these form a constellation of problems which are familiar and widely shared. Unfortunately neglected in the conventional training media, these problems are particularly critical for a more efficient use of the young firm's scarcest and more precious input; its resources of managerial talent and skill.'

> 'Thus there is a body of accumulated literature which has argued that management development is important in small firms - perhaps more so that in large - but likely to be different in kind from that practised in large corporations.'

METHODOLOGY

In the light of experience and following wide-ranging discussions with owner-managers, representative bodies, Industrial Training Boards,

195

Table 1

Association of management characteristics and growth rates

	Number in sample	Mean Turnover 1963 (x £1000)	% Growth 1963–1970	% showing decay in turnover
A. Founded by present management	18 (13%)	210	118	14
B. Managed by second or successive generations of family management	61 (44%)	150	45	16
C. Firms having one or more outside director besides present family management *	35 (25%)	216	61	6
D. Firms managed by individual purchasers of controlling interest	9 (7%)	55	56	36
E. Firms taken over during study period (1963–1970)	15 (11%)	179	97	7

* Firms managed by their founders but also with outside management excluded; included under category A.

SOURCE: Adapted from Merrett-Cyriax Table 5.5

fellow academics and others it was decided that in order to make a balanced judgement of both perceived and actual management development needs of current small business managers, it would be necessary to personally interview the chief executives of a randomly drawn sample of firms.

This approach was selected for two reasons. First, response rates to requests for personal interviews tend to be very much higher than questionnaire return rates. Thus the extent to which one can express confidence in the generalisability of conclusions based on analysis of data obtained from responding firms to sampled firms is commensurately higher. Second, the quality and quantity of data obtained is higher - interviewers can prompt with pre-determined probes in a way inert questionnaires cannot, can resolve problems of interpretation on a uniform basis, can deal more adequately with open-ended questions, etc.

The location of the study team members suggested that no attempt at full geographical coverage be attempted. Thus the study was restricted to firms in London, South East, South West, Wales, West Midlands, West Yorkshire, North Region and the North West. It was felt that this spread would give a realistic national picture.

After discussion with the Department of Industry it was agreed to concentrate (a) on manufacturing firms, and (b) within manufacturing on a few industries only. These industries met the criteria that:

(i) small firms (i.e. those employing not more than 200 people) accounted for a minimum of 33 percent of total net output within that industry and

(ii) that this sub-sector output accounted for greater than 0.5 percent of total manufacturing output.

Accordingly, a list of industries showing Net Output by Standard Industrial Classification was drawn up, as an aid to the selection of appropriate industries and on the basis of this list a judgemental sample of industries was draw, intended to reflect different kinds of small firm problems, industries on disaggregated industries, etc. On this basis Miscellaneous metal Manufacture, General Printing and Publishing, Timber, Furniture, Plastic Products and Textile Finishing were selected. These industries were believed likely to be representative of small firms in general.

A comprehensive list of independent small firms within each selected industry was then drawn up from which to sample. Unfortunately, there exists in the UK no data-base on small firms as such so that the actual procedure of constructing a sample frame was quite lengthy and time consuming (in order to avoid conducting interviews only in highly 'visible' small firms which were likely to be atypical of small firms generally). Thus a network activation approach was adopted in which small firm representative bodies, relevant Trade Associations, Chambers of Commerce, certain Industry Training Boards, etc. were asked to supply the names of any small firms in the chosen industries known to them. These names were added to those from published sources such as the BSO Classified List, Yellow Pages in each region, trade and commercial directories, etc.

This list was then screened, using the best available published sources in order to eliminate companies employing over 200 people, subsidiaries and companies not in the pre-designated geographical areas.

Randomly drawn lists were then centrally prepared for each interviewer/region structured to give a good overall balance between firms in different industries (this was not possible within a region since different industries have different spatial distributions, in particular, the North West/West Yorkshire sample was heavily biased in favour of textile finishing firms, which hardly exist in some of the other regions surveyed).

The interview acceptance rate for eligible firms was above 80 per cent. 231 usable sets of interview data were obtained.

The interview schedule drawn up was aimed at gathering information about:

1. the firm;
2. the owner-manager and his team;
3. current training provision;
4. perceived management development needs;
5. the extent to which real and perceived needs diverged.

The latter objective was one which particularly concerned us, since we hoped to be able to make a professional judgement of the scope for owner-manager development over and above the individual's current perception of his development needs and those of his managers.

In order to form this judgement, each interview concluded with open-ended questions about particular crises and opportunities which had faced the management of the firm in the recent past and firm's responses thereto. The interview schedule was piloted on a small sample basis by each member of the study team, then modified in the light of feedback.

STUDY SAMPLE CHARACTERISTICS

In addition to an analysis of the whole sample, sub-sample analyses were run by region/interviewer and by industry. In some cases significant industry differences emerged but with very few exceptions, the overall results were extremely consistent from region to region, thus reinforcing our belief that:

(i)   the approach adopted had accommodated and eliminated interviewer biases, and

(ii) the results do fairly reflect the national picture, as intended.

The majority of firms were well-established, with less than 10 per cent being 10 years old. However, as one might expect, there were significant differences between industries. Printing and publishing firms had a bimodal distribution with a significant number of very long-established businesses. The textile finishers were generally older than average and the plastics firms, as expected, much younger. The complete age spectrum by industry is given in Table 2.

Table 2
Distribution of surveyed firms by industry and by age

(N = 231)	Metal Manufacture	Printing & Publishing	Furniture & Timber	Textile Finishing	Plastics	All Firms	All Firms (%)
Years since establishment							
Less than 9	4	1	6	0	10	21	9.1
10 - 19	15	11	8	1	12	47	20.3
20 - 29	11	11	5	0	5	32	13.9
30 - 39	13	5	7	3	5	33	14.3
40 - 49	4	3	3	3	4	17	7.4
50 - 59	6	3	3	4	2	18	7.8
60 - 69	2	1	0	4	0	7	3.0
70 - 79	2	6	0	3	0	11	4.8
80 - 89	1	5	0	2	0	8	3.5
90 or more	16	16	8	7	0	37	16.0

This difference in age structure - among industries where small firms remain economically significant - confirms the belief expressed previously that the industries chosen are likely to exhibit the range of problems and circumstances faced by small firms generally.

Although no attempt was made to influence the size distribution of the sample, the firms we were most interested in were those in which non-proprietorial first-line supervision had begun to develop, but where functional specialisation was still incomplete, thus maintaining pressure on the owner-manager (or other executive) to be both a functional and a general manager. Very roughly, in terms of employment this might correspond to the range 20-120 employees. As can be seen from Table 3, the firms surveyed fell predominantly into this size range.

Here the overall picture was one of relative health, with half the firms having stabilised at their present size, and further third continuing to grow.

The firms showed wide variations in the number of people who, it was claimed, carried managerial/supervisory responsibility. One hundred and twenty-two firms (48.5%) said that less then five were involved, whereas in nineteen cases (8.3%), more than fifteen people were considered 'managers'. One hundred and twenty eight of the 231 interviewees could readily produce or sketch out an organisation chart of their firm. Great diversity was apparent, even in the number of levels in the hierarchy. Three firms - all in general printing or publishing - could identify six or more distinct levels (this in firms employing less the 200 people). In general this industry appeared most hierarchical, but the overall impression given by these Tables gives the lie to one stereotype of the small firm, that of the informally managed, unbureaucratic organisation.

Set against this is the possibility that the remaining 103 interviewees did not display an organisation chart because they managed informally and/or autocratically and there was no 'organisation' as such (this could, of course, also be true of those drawing up a chart; in organisations of all sizes it is widely recognised that formal and informal patterns of authority and control can differ substantially).

These issues can also be approached by another route, since the chief executives were also asked to quote the size of their 'top management team', responses to which are given in Table 4. These responses (N=230) are broadly consistent with span of control data derived from those organisation charts available (N=128), also given in Table 4.

These Tables would seem to suggest a situation in which managerial responsibility is quite widely diffused among small firm employee-managers, but this may be no more than lip-service. Thus in 94 cases (40.7%) the managing director alone makes 'the major decisions'. This rises to 67.5 percent of major decisions if one includes those made by the managing director and one other, whereas inclusion of triumvirates accounts for more than 80 percent.

In this context the most interesting finding is possibly the relationship of these other key decision-makers to the chief executive.

Table 3
Number of full-time employees – breakdown by industry

	NUMBER						% OF VALID RESPONSES					
	Metals Manufacture	Printing and Publishing	Furniture & Timber	Textile Finishing	Plastics	All Firms	Metals Manufacture	Printing & Publishing	Furniture & Timber	Textile Finishing	Plastics	All Firms
Less than 9 employees	1	3	6	1	2	13	1.6	4.8	15.0	3.7	5.3	5.6
Between 10 and 19 employees	10	6	3	1	4	24	15.6	9.7	7.5	3.7	10.5	10.4
Between 20 and 29 employees	9	12	9	5	6	41	14.1	19.4	22.5	18.5	15.8	17.7
Between 30 and 39 employees	9	11	5	5	5	35	14.1	17.7	12.5	18.5	13.2	15.2
Between 40 and 49 employees	7	6	0	5	6	24	10.9	9.7	10.0	18.5	15.8	10.4
Between 50 and 75 employees	16	9	6	4	2	37	25.0	14.5	15.0	14.8	5.3	16.0
Between 76 and 100 employees	8	4	3	2	5	22	12.5	6.5	17.5	7.4	13.2	9.5
Between 101 and 125 employees	1	4	6	3	3	17	1.6	6.5	15.0	11.1	7.9	7.4
Between 126 and 175 employees	1	3	2	0	3	9	1.6	4.8	5.0	0.	7.9	3.9
175 employees or more	2	4	0	1	2	9	3.1	6.5	0.	3.7	5.3	3.9

*Note: These figures have been prepared on the basis of 2 part-time employees are equivalent to one full-time.

Table 4

Size of 'top management team'

	From direct response data		From chart analysis of span of control	
	N	%	%	
One	29	12.6	19.4	
2 or 3	122	52.8	49.5	
4 or 5	56	24.2	25.2	
6 to 10	23	10.0	5.8	
11 or more	0	0		

Professional relationships outweigh family ones by a ratio of more than 4 to 1. This result runs somewhat counter to the traditional view of the typical established small business as a family firm. If this is a change, then it is arguably a change for the better since the evidence suggests that professionally-determined relationships lead to more stable and economically effective business units.

THE MANAGEMENT - BACKGROUND, SKILLS AND TRAINING

Of the sample firms, 83.5 per cent of chief-executives were also sole or joint owners of the business. Of those participating in both the ownership and management of the business, a majority were first generation, but a significant minority (6.9% of all firms) were fourth or subsequent generation inheritors. As expected, there was considerable variation across industries; no plastics firms were more then one generation removed from foundation, whereas a third of printing, publishing and textile finishing firms were best discribed as dynastic.

In many of those cases where control was divorced from direct ownership, prior personal knowledge of the manager had clearly played a part in his appointment. Twelve non-participating chief-executives were related to the owners of the firm, and a further twelve were described as 'friends'. Only in 29 (12.6%) of the cases studied was the relationship a purely professional one.

While the overall impression is of businesses controlled and owned by one individual and his family, the evidence discussed before in Table 5 indicates a genuine attempt to involve a wider range of professional expertise at the second tier.

The extent to which the quality of professional management at this level is dictated by perceptions of restricted career progression is obviously an important question. Although second tier managers were not interviewed during this study, the frustrations produced by the roles they are called upon to play suggest they are among the most likely founders of the next generation of small businesses. This appears to be a geniune fear among current owner-managers, many of whom are therefore reluctant to encourage their staffs to develop as managers. Just on a fifth of interviewees stressed that there was 'no way' in which they wished/were prepared to develop the technical and managerial competence of their managers (see Table 6). Indeed, this proportion will severely understate the fear of developing potential competitors since a significant percentage of those whom owner-managers do wish to develop will be tied to the firm by filial or familial loyalties.

Some other comments on Table 6 seem appropriate. The desire to develop managers as managers by far outweighs that of developing their technical competence; moreover, this desire is generalised rather than specific to particular functional areas. This is consonant with the view of the second tier manager (who may well be the son and heir who has 'learned the business the way I did, from the bottom' or a talented promotee from the shop floor) as looking after 'the works' while the owner looks after 'the business', i.e. the sales contacts, financial aspects and general administration.

Table 5

Ownership and control analysis of survey firms

N = 231

	NUMBER						% OF VALID RESPONSES					
	Metals Manufacture	Printing & Publishing	Furniture & Timber	Textile Finishing	Plastics	All Firms	Metals Manufacture	Printing & Publishing	Furniture & Timber	Textile Finishing	Plastics	All Firms
C-E owner of whole business	15	16	8	2	8	49	23.4	25.8	20.0	7.4	21.1	21.2
C-E a part-owner of business	7	8	10	6	6	37	10.9	12.9	25.0	22.2	15.8	16.0
C-E a salaried manager only	42	38	22	18	24	144	65.6	61.3	55.0	66.7	63.2	62.3
No response				1		1				3.7		0.4

Table 6

Areas of perceived development needs for key management staff　　(N = 231)*

	NUMBER						% OF VALID RESPONSES					
	Metals Manufacture	Printing & Publishing	Furniture & Timber	Textile Finishing	Plastics	All Firms	Metals Manufacture	Printing & Publishing	Furniture & Timber	Textile Finishing	Plastics	All Firms
As Managers/supervisors	32	29	21	11	15	108	43.2	38.7	42.9	36.7	34.1	39.7
Improvement of technical competence	6	8	5	8	10	37	8.1	10.7	10.2	26.7	22.7	13.6
Sales/Marketing	7	8	4	4	2	25	9.5	10.7	8.2	13.3	4.5	9.2
Personnel Management/I.R.	3	1	1	2	1	8	4.1	1.3	2.0	6.7	2.3	2.9
Finance/Accounting	5	10	4	0	6	25	6.8	13.3	8.2	0.	13.6	9.2
Training as successor	4	1	3	0	2	10	5.4	1.3	6.1	0.	4.5	3.7
Other	0	1	1	0	1	3	0.	1.3	2.0	0.	2.3	1.1
No way!	17	17	10	5	7	56	23.0	22.7	20.4	16.7	15.9	20.6
No Response	2	2	0	2	1	7						

* NOTE:　Up to three responses were permitted.

205

Table 7

Areas of perceived need for self-development (N = 231)*

	NUMBER						% OF VALID RESPONSES					
	Metals Manufacture	Printing & Publishing	Furniture & Timber	Textile Finishing	Plastics	All Firms	Metals Manufacture	Printing & Publishing	Furniture & Timber	Textile Finishing	Plastics	All Firms
No response	1	0	0	1	0	2						
None! (and no action planned)	29	51	19	15	17	111	41.4	45.6	44.2	51.7	39.5	44.4
To improve technical competence	5	4	2	3	4	18	7.1	5.9	4.7	11.5	9.3	7.3
'Yes'/other unspecific answer	0	0	1	2	1	4	0.	0.	2.3	7.7	2.3	1.6
Business Administration & Finance	8	12	7	1	7	35	11.4	17.6	16.3	3.8	16.3	14.0
Management skill/delegation	13	12	6	4	7	42	18.6	17.6	14.0	15.4	16.3	16.8
Personnel Management/I.R.	3	3	0	0	4	10	4.3	4.4	0.	0.	9.3	4.0
Don't know	2	0	0	0	0	2	2.9	0.	0.	0.	0.	0.8
Marketing	7	4	8	1	3	23	10.0	5.9	18.6	3.8	7.0	9.2
Computing/Languages	3	2	0	0	0	5	4.3	2.9	0.	0.	0.	2.0

*NOTE: Up to two responses were permitted

206

The subjective immortality of the owner-manager is readily apparent. Although historically his successor would come from within the business management development for succession was contemplated by only 3.7 percent of interviewees.

This complacency over development extended to a very significant number of owner-managers where self development was concerned, with nearly half making it quite apparent that there was no way in which they wished to develop their own managerial competence. A further, smaller group was interested only in developing their technical expertise further. Those who were development-oriented were in the main preoccupied with general management issues - with the way in which the different areas of the business interacted and, in particular, with the question of effective delegation. Financial management and administration of the business with respect to financial and legal/accounting issues were also perceived as developmental needs (see Table 7).

Of course, among those whom we have described as 'complacent' there may well be a number of highly experienced and qualified individuals whose analysis of their own situations - i.e., no scope for management development - is well founded. Some light on this may be shed by discussion of the educational and prior work experience of current small businessmen.

14.4 per cent had received a first degree level (or equivalent) education a further 30.6 per cent had had substantial further education. This indicates a very similar educational level to that found in those small manufacturing firms surveyed by the Bolton Report. (Merrett Cyriax, 1974) (Main Report, paras 2.6-2.8).

The educational level of the key managers in each business was similarly examined. Although the data were not always to hand during the interview (indicating perhaps that formal qualifications are not a major influence on personnel decisions at this firm size level) the data in Table 8 are believed to represent a balanced picture. From this it can be seen that there is a tendency for the owner-manager to be better educated than his key managers.

Table 8

Educational level of chief executives and other key small firm managers

	Chief Executives	Others
	(%)	(%)
School level only	55.0	63.2
Some further education	30.6	26.0
Degree level or equivalent	14.4	6.0
	(N = 229)	(N = 220)

Relatively few of the interviewees had any kind of formal professional

qualification (64.9% did not). Of those who did, the formal professional competence was technical rather than managerial. 23.4 per cent had
some kind of technical qualification (including 17 (7.4%) with professional recognition within a branch of engineering). However, only 4.8
per cent were qualified in accountancy, while a further 4.8 per cent had
professional recognition as managers per se (e.g. Institute of Marketing). Interestingly, more than twice as many chief-executives had
qualified as a result of part-time study as had taken full-time courses.
This tends to lend weight to the view that at least a significant number
of owner-managers experience strong feelings of social marginality
(Stanworth and Curran, 1973). However, the impression is that the range
of educational experience and professional expertise to which these
firms had access was somewhat limited.

It was in the field of work experience that this was most clearly
demonstrated. Overall, a quarter of chief-executives had never worked
outside their present business.

Here there were major industrial variations, however, with only 53.8
per cent of textile finishers having outside employment experiences on
which to draw, whereas only 5.3 per cent lacked this managerial resource
in the plastics firms.

However, the extent to which direct experience of other firms might
assist managerial performance in the present business was much more
restricted than the basic data in Table 9 may suggest. Firstly, this
experience tended to be quite old - more than 10 years in well over half
the cases and in some instances, dating back before World War 2.
Secondly, many of those who had had previous industrial experience
before joining or establishing their firm - 41.3 per cent - had gained
their prior experience in firms exploying 100 or less.

Trying to identify what kinds of prior experience had been most
helpful in managing the present business proved inconclusive. Contrary
to what one might expect - and what interviewers encouraged by seeking
multiple responses - managers were reluctant to specify functional areas
(even those in which they had worked) but rather stressed the benefits
from the general management aspects of their experience (including that
gained in the Armed Forces), along with the techincal aspects of the
business. These responses were poorly related to the jobs occupied when
previously employed, since in very few cases had specific employment
opportunities been sought out as a conscious learning experience in
preparation for running one's own business.

The inescapable conclusion is that in general none of the factors in
the owner-managers' prior experience - not education, nor professional
studies, nor work experience - had been an appropriate or adequate
preparation for the stewardship of one's own business.

So far we have assumed that specifically identifiable skills would be
called for in running the businesses visited. To what extent did
interviewees share this view? And what interpretation did they place on
the word skill?

Respondents were asked the related questions, 'Are there any
particular technical skills you need to exercise in running this
company?' and 'Are there any particular managerial skills you need to

Table 9

Experience of chief executives

(N = 230)

	NUMBER						% OF VALID RESPONSES					
	Metals Manufacture	Printing & Publishing	Furniture & Timber	Textile Furnishing	Plastics	All Firms	Metals Manufacture	Printing & Publishing	Furniture & Timber	Textile Finishing	Plastics	All Firms
Never worked outside present business	12	25	7	12	2	58	18.8	40.3	17.5	46.2	5.3	25.2
Other employment experience	52	37	33	14	36	172	81.3	59.7	82.5	53.8	94.7	74.8

exercise in running this company?' Interestingly, many owner-managers found it difficult to differentiate these two general areas. Thus finance, accounting and marketing skills were discussed as 'technical' skills rather than as aspects of the 'managerial' skills cited (which seemed very often to be vague generalisations like 'common sense', 'patience' or 'logic').

From an academic perspective, this division seems somewhat eccentric, but many owner-managers seem to reserve the term 'management' for those aspects of running a successful business which are inate, unlikely to be learned and cannot be taught. This apparent rejection of management as a concept is supported by the fact that 109 respondents could not, or would not, cite any specific management skill required in running their company. At the very least this surprising result has obvious implications for the semantics of any programmes designed to upgrade the managerial performance of small businessmen.

PERCEPTIONS OF MANAGEMENT DEVELOPMENT NEEDS

This section discusses responses to that part of each interview which explicitly examined chief-executive's perceptions of management development needs in their firms and their general feelings about the value of management training. Thus, we are here dealing more with values and beliefs than with matters of fact.

About half those interviewed felt they did not have any problems with training/developing their managers. Of those that did, the main perceived problems were those of finding and developing a successor, and encouraging the right management style in him and others (76 firms). Personnel management and the recent associated legislation was regarded as a problem which training could help solve in 13 firms. The extent to which problems in finance and administration or marketing were ammenable to solution through training was regarded as minimal (2.8%).

Seventy-nine firms (34.2% of the total) described these problems as either 'serious' or 'very serious'.

The impact of these problems was likely to be higher in the firms interviewed than in larger firms better able to attract trained managers on the open market. Here the management team was twice as likely to have been developed up through the firm as it was to have been bought in.

Even in the case of established managers, interviewees were prepared to accept that training had an important part to play in developing competence; 94 firms (40.7%) felt its effect on management competence could be 'significant' and only 10.9 per cent were either unsure or felt that training made no impact (see Table 10).

Probing the basis of these beliefs again emphasised the importance laid on experience and practicality. Among textile finishers particularly there was wide agreement that training was important and a desire to undertake more management development activities, but those programmes which had been suggested as available to them in the past had been too far divorced from practice and application. The furniture and timber companies on the other had had no complaints of this nature, and

Table 10

Effect of training on managerial competence: Interviewee's perceptions

	NUMBER						% OF VALID RESPONSES					
	Metals Manufacture	Printing & Publishing	Furniture & Timber	Textile Finishing	Plastics	All Firms	Metals Manufacture	Printing & Publishing	Furniture & Timber	Textile Finishing	Plastics	All Firms
Significant effect	13	26	19	17	19	94	20.3	41.9	47.5	63.0	50.0	40.7
Moderate effect	28	21	12	4	8	73	43.8	33.9	30.0	14.8	21.1	31.6
Marginal effect	15	11	3	5	5	39	23.4	17.7	7.5	18.5	13.2	16.9
No effect	4	2	3	1	4	14	6.3	3.2	7.5	3.7	10.5	6.1
Don't know	4	2	3	0	2	11	6.3	3.2	7.5	0	5.3	48

Table 11

Interview perceptions: Areas where training would improve managerial competence of firm*

	NUMBER						% OF VALID RESPONSES					
	Metals Manufacture	Printing & Publishing	Furniture & Timber	Textile Finishing	Plastics	All Firms	Metals Manufacture	Printing & Publishing	Furniture & Timber	Textile Finishing	Plastics	All Firms
All or many	2	6	3	1	2	14	2.7	7.9	6.0	3.7	5.0	5.2
Management/Supervision	5	5	5	0	3	18	6.8	6.6	10.0	0.	7.5	6.7
Personnel/I.R./Legislation	10	7	8	8	5	38	13.5	9.2	16.0	29.6	12.5	14.2
Technical Skills/Production	14	15	9	2	8	48	18.9	19.7	18.0	7.4	20.0	18.0
Finance/Accounting	18	13	13	3	9	56	24.3	17.1	26.0	11.1	22.5	21.0
Marketing	9	15	8	3	8	43	12.2	19.7	16.0	11.1	20.0	16.1
None	16	15	4	10	5	50	21.6	19.7	8.0	37.0	12.5	18.7
(No Response	6	4	5	5	7	27)						

* NOTE: Up to 2 responses per interviewee were allowed.

were generally enthusiastic about the relevance of past programmes to their own problems and situations.

As regards which functional areas in their own firm might most benefit, the response was unexpected. The finance/accounting area was most often specified (in about a quarter of all firms) and marketing also figured strongly (about a fifth of all firms). In both cases, between two and three times as many firms felt they would benefit from undertaking management training in these functions as had actively done so in the recent past.

The mechanism whereby management developmental/training needs were assessed, varied substantially from firm to firm. In about a quarter of cases there was some degree of internal formality, but most firms either claimed never to make such decisions, could not articulate how they came to be made, or said it was a question on which the managing director himself would decide. In only 37 cases (14.1%) was the advice of an ITB sought. In only one case had independent consultants been sought and no firm had sought assistance of this nature from an educational institution.

On the fundamental question of perceived overall benefit from management training, the information collected proved ambivalent. 35 interviewees declined to answer the question (usually on the grounds that none had ever been undertaken by them/their firm); 97 felt it had been of no value and 25 that it had been of only limited value. On the other hand, 54 firms described the benefits as 'immense'. It therefore seems likely that some firms had been luckier than others in matching appropriate provision to defined needs. In these cases the use of external advice appeared to have been beneficial.

PERCEIVED VERSUS REAL NEEDS OF SAMPLE FIRMS

The last phase of each interview was considerably less structured than those parts on which the preceding discussion has been based and involved wide-ranging discussion of crises and missed opportunities, which have been faced by the firm. It was stressed previously that a major element of management development in the small firm is the encouragement of resourcefulness and we hoped to find indications of this by discussing situations of potential or actual change.

In this we were not disappointed. A majority of firms could identify events which had threatened the survival of the business; a substantial minority could identify major opportunities on which they had not been able to capitalise. (2)

The crises experienced by our sample firms would fill several books of case studies. They include the three-day week, war, fraud, flood and fire; declining total markets, the unexpected loss of a major customer, the emergence of an aggressive competitor; exporting disasters and the removal of tariffs; chronic shortage of capital, sudden dramatic cost increases and unpredicted cashflow crises; the failure of new technologies; strikes, unionisation disputes and legal actions for unfair dismissal; the defection or sudden death of a partner, key manager or skilled, personality conflicts and unwelcome take-over bids. However, it is possible to classify these occurences under a number of more general headings corresponding roughly to recognised functional areas. 'Crisis in' does not equate totally with 'weakness in'; nor would anyone suggest that management development could have mitigated all the weakness of managerial analysis and behaviour which even our brief interviews revealed. Nevertheless, there is a striking correlation between the areas where 'catastrophies' had occurred and those perceived areas of weakness, discussed in the preceding section, in which owner-managers tacitly accepted training would improve their firm's managerial competence - marketing and finance - but where actual training experiences had not been focussed. Disasters of a technical nature, where training was also perceived as improving competence and where training was more actively pursued, were far less frequent. (of Table 12).

Over and above these crises, firms were also questioned about other major changes in recent years. Again, changes in markets were the largest single factor and were reported by 121 further firms. Predictably, the major missed opportunities also related to markets, resulting from inadequate marketing information, difficulties or perceived difficulties in raising finance and problems connected with proprietorial motivation.

What, perhaps, a majority of the sampled firms lacked was anything approaching a clear business strategy - a view of what the business is now, might become, and of the way to get there. Weaknesses in marketing information, research and policy emerged on many occasions, but even if a marketing orientation had been more apparent (and recall that a majority of firms believed competition was increasing in their markets), a lack of information about financial markets, about how to approach external sources of finance and a general disinterest and lack of sophistication in the finance/accounting area would have prevented many firms from successfully exploiting the market opportunities open to them.

SUMMARY

Summarising this argument (which was reinforced by analysis of the data collected concerning major current problems and opportunities), the firms surveyed were generally inward looking and had a rather limited time-horizon.

The owner-managers (and many other managers) were too close to the day-to-day problems of running an independent business to look positively outward into the environment in order to secure a more prosperous future. Given this, coupled with the narrow educational and experiential base on which most of the firms have been built, and the short term, inward looking, information-oriented training subsequently undertaken, the most pressing developmental needs are arguably the cultivation of a better general environmental sensitivity, the skills to then construct a sound and coherent policy for the firm, and the ability to communicate this fully within the organisation.

Table 12

Areas in which 'crises' had occurred within firm

	Number of Crises	% of firms reporting such crises
None	43	18.6
'Acts of God'	24	10.4
Market crises	88	38.1
Financial crises	72	31.2
Technological Crises	12	5.2
Personnel/I.R. Crises	30	13.0
Managerial Crises	33	14.3
Geographical/Other	11	4.8
Total	313	

* Note: A maximum of three responses per firm was permitted.

NOTES

(1) These figures include the advice given by ITB supported training groups.
(2) It is important not to lay too much stress on the actual figures. That these firms had survived and grown at all clearly differentiates them from the typical independent business venture; that some of them could not identify crises or, particularly, missed opportunities, does not mean they have not existed. More important are the areas of weakness which discussion of these issues revealed and their relative incidence.

REFERENCES

'The Rise and Decline of Small Firms', J. Boswell, George Allen and Unwin, London, 1972, p.70.
Hansard 25-5-77 508.
Report of the Committee of Inquiry on Small Firms, Cmnd 4811 London, HMSO, 1971.
'Dynamics of Small Firms', Merrett Cyriax Associates, Committee Inquiry on Small Firms, Research Report No.12 London HMSO 1971.
'Developing Resourceful Managers', J.F. Morris, J.G. Burgoyne, Institute of Personnel Management, 1973.
'Management Motivation in the Smaller Business', M.J.K. Stanworth, J. Curran, Gower Press, 1973.

Index